T0064936

Advance Praise for *Coquilles, Calva & Crème*

"French food and travel with a dash of history—what a treat it is to sit at the table with this smart, engaging writer. A delicious read from start to finish."

—Barbara Fairchild, bestselling food author,
longtime editor-in-chief of *Bon Appétit,*
winner of the James Beard Award.

"Has France lost its culinary edge? After decades living and chronicling the good life in Paris and overseas, Gerry and Joanne Dryansky lead us to unsung chefs still championing the country's gourmand heritage."

—Gael Greene, bestselling author of *Insatiable: Tales from
a Life of Delicious Excess* and InsatiableCritic.com,
winner of the James Beard Award.

"Gerry and Joanne Dryansky's book is a lovely ramble through a lifetime of experiences in France's high spots and some low ones too. Reading it brings as many delights as a marvelous long meal."

—Patricia Wells, celebrated food author,
winner of the James Beard Award.

"I had the incredible good luck to have dozens and dozens of French meals with Gerry and Joanne Dryansky, and he was never wrong. I mean, never. We would travel down some little street, some little restaurant, and then, delight, pure pleasure. I was back years and years to a far more delicious France. And now, he tells all. There's nobody I know, in Paris or in New York, who understands French food the way Gerry does. And surely nobody who writes about it as well as he does."

—Alan Furst, bestselling author and
author of the forthcoming *Mission to Paris.*

"Tuck this delicious tome in your hamper between Proust's madeleines and the champagne—then feast your soul. The Dryanskys remind us that in France—at least sometimes and in some places—authenticity still rhymes with simplicity, and great writing makes a fine relish."

—David Downie, author of *Paris, Paris: Journey
to the City of Lights* and the *Terroir* food series.

"GYD is the greatest gourmand in American letters today, the most gourmet of inquisitive journalists, the most French of foreign correspondents in Paris. When he recounts his exciting adventures in the Hexagon, we're amused as much as we salivate. Delicious and savory!"

—Gilles Pudlowski, France's foremost food critic,
founder of the *Pudlo Guides.*

"Congratulations to Dryansky. It was a great pleasure to read his text, both so well documented and free of polemics."

—Christian Millau, co-founder of *Le Guide GaultMillau*,
herald and godfather of "La Nouvelle Cuisine" in France.

"*Coquilles, Calva, and Crème* vividly brings back my years of working in Paris in the 1950s. When I contemplate my cooking journey of the last half century, from classic to nouvelle, from fusion to modern American to molecular, the only reminiscences I have is of food that touches my soul or makes me salivate. Gerry Dryansky writes honestly and eloquently about these simple, honest, essential dishes in his engaging, compelling, and delicious memoir."

—Jacques Pépin, celebrity TV chef,
James Beard Award winner.

"Part memoir, part travelogue, *Coquilles, Calva & Crème* is a hymn to French food and wine and the joy of wining and dining in France with "convivialité" - which for the French is key. Dryansky has many a story to tell about the past (lunching with the likes of Coco and Yves) but in this present *tour de France* he greets each dining experience, each new chef, each new winemaker, and each new region, from Alsace to Le Massif Central, with genuine curiosity, an open mind, and a discerning first rate palate. This entertaining, erudite, and elegant book is a must for Francophiles and food lovers everywhere."

—Harriet Welty Rochefort, bestselling author of
French Toast, French Fried and author of the
forthcoming *Joie de Vivre*.

"Reading this book is like lunching with Gerry Dryansky: from coquilles to Calva, with crème in between, it is seasoned with wit and charm. Rich with food-lover wisdom, it captures what France does best."

—Mort Rosenblum, Editor of *Dispatches*, author,
foreign correspondent, winner of the Overseas Press Club,
Mencken, Harry Chapin and James Beard awards.

"A delicious and delightful read, especially for those who think they might know this country. When you sit down to a meal with Dryansky, you taste the very soul of France."

—Eleanor Beardsley, France Correspondent,
National Public Radio.

COQUILLES, CALVA, & CRÈME

Exploring France's Culinary Heritage

A LOVE AFFAIR WITH REAL FRENCH FOOD

G. Y. DRYANSKY
WITH JOANNE DRYANSKY

PEGASUS BOOKS

NEW YORK

COQUILLES, CALVA, & CRÈME

Pegasus Books LLC
80 Broad Street, 5th Floor
New York, NY 10004

Library of Congress Cataloging-in-Publication Data is available.

ISBN: 978-1-60598-329-5

10 9 8 7 6 5 4 3 2 1

Printed in the United States of America
Distributed by W. W. Norton & Company

For my grandmother Tamara

BY THE SAME AUTHOR

Other People

The Heirs

Chant d'Adieu

BY JOANNE AND GERRY DRYANSKY:

Fatima's Good Fortune

Fortune's Second Wink

Satan Lake

ABOUT THE AUTHOR

G. Y. DRYANSKY has been living and writing about the good life in Europe for most of his life. His innumerable stories appeared in major American publications before he became the senior European correspondent for *Condé Nast Traveler*. Along the way he has met and written about Nobel Prize winners, heads of state, and cultural heroes of literature, cinema, and fashion. His fascination with food is a story of personal pleasure and also part of an interest in what we create and perpetuate to define our world, beyond the current superficial star wars of exalted chefs.

Gerry and his wife Joanne moved to Paris not long after he'd earned degrees from Princeton and Harvard, and have made it their home ever since. They write screenplays and fiction together. Their recent novel, *Fatima's Good Fortune*, after being published in the United States and worldwide, is going to the screen.

ACKNOWLEDGMENTS

My great thanks go to the people who took time to talk to me, despite the hassle of running restaurants with devotion and earnestness—an exhausting and precarious obsession in our times. Thanks go again to those who parted with the recipes they cherished. I think that it is worth adding that the sincerity of my gratitude is informed by the fact that Joanne and I paid for our meals wherever we went.

Writers frequently thank the friends who read and advised them, and it used to be that you wound up thanking your typist. I had no friends or advisers reading me as I went along. My typist named Samsung is insensitive to gratitude. Truth to tell, in a way, *I* was the typist, moving my fingers in sync with the constant insights and advice of Joanne. And all that adds up to this being her book as well as mine. She has been in so many ways my guiding star since we were adolescents, and if I were properly to thank her for that, well, that would be a bigger book of its own.

"Butter, butter, butter, and more butter."
—Fernand Point, godfather of *la cuisine* lite

COQUILLES,
CALVA,
& CRÈME

FOREWORD

I n what is left of old French etiquette, it is actually impolite to use the word *manger*, to eat. One lunches, one dines, one sups, and takes the little breakfast. If you were "well reared," you eschewed making reference to a bodily function. In a larger sense, what seems so quaintly punctilious is very wise. Eating, with profound associations, is more than stimulating or titillating the taste buds and sating hunger. I like the expression "soul food." Its textured meaning conveys all that I have to say in this book. A fully satisfying repast is one evanescent, evocative touchstone to a time and a place . . . and to a civilization, of which France, all things told, is an admirable example.

Soul food: that expression that Americans of African descent gave us is of two words profoundly mated. Eating, among our most fundamental physical acts, is bound firmly into the warp and weave of our lives, which we call our culture. We are what we eat, yes, but more than that, our rituals of eating are ways of communing with the culture that defines who we are.

Hitler called us Americans mongrels. Ask most Americans where their families are from and you can get a roll call of geography. But it has been this mixture that has made us such a vibrant, open, and creative society. A mixture that is at the same time more of an emulsion of things that don't dissolve. So many of us are bound, indelibly, to the someplace else that brought a bounty of its presence here. And part of that bounty we sometimes identify as soul food.

I grew up without religion, which is not to say without being taught morals, and with no real ethnic allegiances. But my mother was a Litvak, an Ashkenazi whose mother came from Lithuania, a lovely country my grandmother left to meet the man she loved who was in America, and who never showed up at the New York pier to greet her. Marriage to a scoundrel afterward left her a single mother with three children. I can remember my mother telling me how poor they were, about their sharing a pear for dinner.

Somehow, though, my grandmother passed on a wonderful way with cooking that brought her back to the land of woods and fields covered with sun-bleached linen that was her true home. My mother inherited her hearty but fine way with food. I remember her krep lach, those Ashkenazi ravioli or wontons. I remember her hand with blintzes, twice fried, and rolled, not folded, the ends tucked in, remotely like *a mille-feuille*.

All that reverence, if you will, about what food meant was part of my baggage when I moved to France and had the luck of getting to know intimately the food of that culture, not as a critic of someone's imagination, but by making contact with a way of life that was varied, complex, and devoted to refined pleasure.

Some time after I began writing this, the newspaper *Le Monde* was at my doorstep with the news that UNESCO had inscribed "the French gastronomical meal" into the annals of the "immaterial culture of humanity." UNESCO calls the French gastronomical meal a "social practice" by which the French celebrate important moments of their lives.

Some of those terms do resonate ponderously. And many French themselves contest the accolade. Writing in *Le Monde Diplomatique*, Sébastien Lepaque, the journalist and literary critic, lashed out against it.

"Putting French cuisine on a pedestal is grotesque," he wrote, "even indecent. . . . French cuisine is under threat despite the elaborate meals consumed in luxury Parisian restaurants and hotels by the super-rich with a taste for the flashy, who order the most expensive dishes rather than the best. It is threatened despite multi-starred chefs appearing on TV."

He adds: "The excellence of sophisticated 'trophy' cuisine cannot make amends for the slow disappearance of popular cuisine."

Strong words yet clear observations. Competition for the trophies bestowed by critics—with the stars, the scores, and celebrity interviews—has indeed turned dining in the most noted restaurants into something like shopping in an art gallery. A narrow reduction of what *la cuisine* has meant to a people's way of life. A privilege for diners who seem not to get indigestion from paying—check the guidebook menus—more than a thousand dollars for two for a single esoteric experience. I said just a thousand dollars, wine included, unless, of course, you've set your heart on a trophy wine.

Yet, talking to many people, traveling and sampling exceptional food, I was encouraged to learn that there's a groundswell now in France for keeping cultural roots alive, and with that comes appreciation of a meal as an event with ripples of important associations. People are also talking more about *convivialité* in restaurants than *créativité*. The outdoor markets where food arrives directly from the farms are more heavily crowded than they've been, and more and more restaurants are boasting of *la cuisine traditionelle*. *Terroir*, the term that defines the formative presence of a particular, geographical place in a food, is being rehabilitated by a group of chefs, revolting against globalized "fusion food." They coyly call themselves the *terroiristes*.

Creative cuisine has become a worldwide phenomenon, and the critics, ever keen to reveal what's new, have reached beyond France, the matriarch of gastronomy, to proclaim as superior talents chefs elsewhere, be it Spain or, say, Denmark. In reaction, the leading stars of French cuisine have banded together in an effort to reclaim their turf. The Collège Culinaire de France's fifteen members are calling on the government to help bolster their image—to promote what, in the group's inaugural meeting with the international press, Guy Savoy modestly called "the gastronomic pedestal of cuisine on this planet." They received the journalists at a restaurant on the iconic Eiffel Tower. Beyond the subjectivity of their talents, their proclaimed allies are incomparable French products—the bounty of France's particular soils and of devoted artisans. *"La cuisine française,"* Michel Guérard insisted, "is a cuisine of *terroir*."

I remember what Curnonsky, the best-known critic and gourmet in the annals of early twentieth-century French gastronomy, said, when he was interviewed about his love for simplicity—while he admired the "clever dishes" of *la haute cuisine*:

"Perfection in cuisine, it's . . . when things have the taste of what they are."

Ever careful of being out of fashion, the most media savvy of all the famous chefs, Alain Ducasse, has, as we'll see, proclaimed—at least proclaimed—an era of "simplicity."

Meanwhile the *confréries* that celebrate and promote the unique, gastronomical presences of a region continue to flourish throughout the nation. Those "brotherhoods" that include women, with their robes and ceremonies for the sake, say, of a variety of tripes, a distinct sausage, or a special garlic may seem silly, until you understand that they perpetuate rituals of attachment that go back to the Middle Ages.

France is a country where places and folkways come together and assert unique and cherished presences in a globalizing world. Would it be pretentious to suppose that our forays ahead in gastronomy were also anthropological?

I think again of what Guy Savoy, perhaps the most down-to-earth of the French stars of the kitchen, repeats whenever he's interviewed:

"Cuisine is the art of tranforming instantly into joy products carrying the presence of history." Art? Let's not go there. But there is soundness to his motto. In any case, I hope that, like a basketful of Proust's *madeleines*, the savors evoked in our journeys in this book will be endearing touchstones: to knowing the people, to their ways of life, to the several cultures that make France such an enviable place to live, as it has been for Joanne and me over a long time.

NB: In France, chefs invariably cook without measuring—*au pif*, by instinct regarding proportions. Those who have given me their recipes have had to scratch their heads to come up with the measures, which I've translated into American standards. If the proportions don't seem to suit your taste, the essential methods are correct. Up to you to procede *au pif* to your personal accomplishments.

1

SÉBASTIEN'S FEAST

Joanne and I were heading to a village called Orvilliers to begin this book with the accomplishments of a twenty-six-year-old chef, who was cooking and catering out of a tiny country restaurant. Not long ago, he had revived, with both admiration and inspiration, his mother's cooking, which had become legendary in the region, the acme of exceptional *cuisine bourgeoise*.

We took the train, careful not to drive, after what we suspected would be a well-irrigated lunch, but we'd motored this way many times before. Less than an hour southwest of Paris, after the highway climbs out of the bowl in which the bright city lies, and quickly past the edges of suburbia, you're in another, green country. The meadows roll, dotted by little forests.

You pass the discreet roads that lead to the secondary homes of what, in the pecking order of French class identification, are still sometimes called *la grande bourgeoisie* and the second-tier *bonne bourgeoisie*. In the first tier, for example, a gaggle of Guerlain perfume heirs have houses here. The designer Philippe Starck, as attached as he is to the cutting edge of present mores, had an old house in Montfort l'Amaury that belonged to his father, a noted airplane manufacturer. Celebrities have also lived here. Montfort is where the composer Maurice Ravel had his retreat. Edith Piaf, who was once a street waif in the slums of Paris, realized a dream manor nearby, and Colette, who lived in a cozy little apartment overlooking the Place du Palais Royal, aired out her life retreating to the green, in the regional village of Méré, which may have recalled her country childhood. . . .

The structure of French society, happily, is much more permeable these days, the rungs on the ladder not so perilously distant between the *grande*, the *bonne,* and the *petite bourgeoisie,* and all others who are simply the people or *la noblesse,* with those names as long as dresser drawers, as the French like to say. I'm in no way nostalgic about the meticulously divisive system that prevailed, in the French Republic, well into the twentieth century and that still hangs on here and there. It was never my realm. But this privileged and lovely little pastoral region near Paris still exists, and travelers who are drawn to get in touch with the particularity of places, in a physical world getting more and more homogenized, could do worse than take a leisurely drive through Montfort l'Amaury, Les Mesnuls, on to Orvilliers . . . and on the back roads toward Houdan.

My own memories here bring to mind an unpretentious older couple, good friends to Joanne and me; we lived near each other in Paris. Pierre Schildge was the heir to a company renowned for making luxurious silk fabric. His wife, Liliane, was from a banking family, and they had a house in Les Mesnuls, near Orvilliers, forty minutes during off-hours from Paris, with a tenant farmer on the property and a couple of saddle horses. Pierre was mayor of Les Mesnuls, an honorary position, which required him to wear a red, white, and blue sash when he married people in the town hall before the many elegantly catered, country-estate wedding parties. When the champagne flowed and the cuisine was elegant too.

Like its class system, French cuisine has had its divisions, sharper, as I say, than they are now. The regional differences are obvious; the social differences were equally marked off: *la grande cuisine, la cuisine bourgeoise,* and the no less delicious, when deft, economical dishes of the most humble, that are still unabashedly called—with the ingrained class snobbery that has also been a characteristic of France—*les plats canailles.* Food for the rogues, with a great presence of cheap cuts and entrails that become, with canny treatment, memorably good.

La grande cuisine was once the purview of a handful of master *cuisiniers* who turned banquets into dramatic experiences for the summit of society. *La cuisine bourgeoise* has been the traditional fare of the well-off. It's the food that used to be prepared by the cooks who were part of every prosperous household.

The savory, full effluvia coming out of a concierge's Parisian lodgings that you passed at mealtimes announced the presence of *les plats canailles.* . . .

In Orvilliers, near Liliane and Pierre's house in Les Mesnuls, there was a place we loved to go to with them. The luxury or perhaps the perceived ostentation of having resident cooks was already gone from even the grandest households among those country houses. Liliane cooked herself, quite simply, with the exception of an occasional imaginative dish out of *Elle* magazine. *La cuisine bourgeoise* at its high end of finesse was all the same kept alive locally for those for whom it was a fading heritage, by a corpulent couple in a tiny place on the road to Houdan. They were surrogate cooks to all the great houses, through a bustling catering business. They also had a restaurant called La Table d'Hôte with a few tables. The wife did most of the cooking. The husband, who'd been successful in an antiburglary equipment business, and who had turned exclusively to his interest in food usually did the serving. Their *cuisine bourgeoise* was at its most refined level and of the highest quality we've known.

Their son is at it again.

Pierre Petit has retired, but his wife, Christine, still keeps a hand in the place, where Sébastien, their son, reigns over the stove with a sure and resourceful hand.

A chauffeur-driven Mercedes had come and gone, Sébastien said, before we arrived. Out of it had stepped four bejeweled, leggy, blonde Russian women, who'd also come to eat. They wanted breaded shrimp with French fries, and Sébastien gently told them they'd come to the wrong spot. No doubt their directions, if not their taste, were right. Sébastien's place, now known as Le Relais Gourmand, was probably recommended to them by someone with the right Parisian friends, also staying at the Ritz. The guidebooks haven't shown attention to this place, but the wealthy are a kind of cosmopolitan fraternity, and members have houses out here. Nothing, however, about Sébastien's Relais Gourmand—with its two gazebos sheltering tables and chairs on the lawn, a dining room with white and floral fabric and prints on the walls—speaks of opulence or ostentation.

Serendipity brought the Petits to this spot in 1987, after the police had called Pierre to repair an ATM machine that had been burglarized in nearby Houdan. On his way, he saw the house at the end of the lawn here for sale, a stone house with a roof of ancient tiles, built by hand by the owner selling it. Pierre was fifty years old, and when Christine jumped at the idea, he decided to give up his anti-burglary business to begin a new life here in the country, centered around their former avocation: cooking pedigreed French cuisine in its most delectable state of refinement.

At the end of the lawn near the road, there was an outbuilding in disrepair and covered with bramble. They restored it and made it into their kitchen and restaurant. Once it had been the servant quarters of the man whose ancient house was across the narrow road. He lived there in the early sixties with his Croatian mistress, far from the excited life he'd led elsewhere in the world. His name was Orson Welles.

When Joanne and I first came here with Liliane and Pierre, anxious to taste, in particular, Christine Petit's incomparable hollandaise sauce, Welles's former house had been squatted in and vandalized. Not long before Sébastien took over, a similar fate had struck the restaurant. Tired after a few years, the Petits had sold the place to someone who ran it into the ground and ran up bills. With the help of local artisans and some of the guys he'd grown up with, Sébastien restored the restaurant. They worked on Sundays when everyone was off work elsewhere, and his friends' reward at the end of the day was whatever was in the larder. It was, as our lunch would confirm, no small reward.

Sébastien had promised his grandmother he'd follow in his parents' footsteps in their devotion to their consummate *cuisine bourgeoise* that had been renowned throughout the region. He'd been cooking in hotels and restaurants since the age of sixteen, had cooked his first omelet at home at the age of six, and reproduced Christine's extraordinary hollandaise at fourteen.

He had been up since five in the morning the day we arrived, so as to prepare a seven-hour leg of lamb for people coming to taste it that evening for a party he was to cater. A seven-hour leg of lamb is a classic of French *cuisine bourgeoise*. The lamb, which Sébastien first marinates, is roasted at the low temperature of 185 degrees Fahrenheit for seven hours. It remains pink inside, with no flavor lost.

Sébastien explained that he was accustomed to fifteen-hour workdays, since there is no one else with him in the kitchen. After nights when diners linger until one in the morning, he is up a few hours later to select his ingredients for the day. He drives to Metro, located in a suburb of Paris quite different from Rungis, where the Les Halles market has relocated.

I raised an eyebrow. All I knew about Metro was that it was a professionals-only supermarket where today's run-of-the mill bistros and cafés get industrial food to reheat in their micro-ovens and serve as *plats maisons*. Ever smell cooking in these places these days?

No, Sébastien assured me. Metro is a huge place whose wares cover the whole range of restaurant food, from the most luxurious, with its freshest produce, fish, and meat stands, to its rows of packaged food. (His take on the place was confirmed to me some time later, when the newspaper *Le Monde* pointed out that Metro, part of a German-owned conglomerate, had four hundred Michelin-starred restaurants among its customers.) "The advantage of Metro over Rungis," he said, "is that you can get there at 6:00 A.M. and everything has arrived. At Rungis, the things come in one truck at a time, different things at different times, and you have to hang out all morning to fill your needs."

Because his staff is composed of only himself and his mother, with only him in the kitchen, compared to the squad of twenty-odd in a restaurant such as, say, Joël Robuchon's, he can afford to fill his larder at the sections in Metro where the luxurious restaurant people shop.

"I would rather be unemployed," he said, "than make my living by opening cans and packages."

With that Sébastien brought the *apéritif maison*, the beginning of what would be our exceptionally irrigated, exceptional lunch. We rarely drink anything alcoholic at lunchtime, and we didn't need an *apéritif* to make us hungry, but the very look of that drink was alluring. Rich ruby red, I said to Joanne, who recognized the color of the velvet in Napoléon Trois décor. The association was not off the mark. The *apéritif*, an accoutrement of fine dining for centuries, was becoming an antique.

For a long time, the *apéritif* was an alibi in an alcohol-bibbing culture that had ravaged many a French liver. The big distilleries in the nineteenth century even used to advertise it shamelessly as an aid to your health, enabling your digestive juices to get going, aided, after the meal, by another of their nostrums, the *digéstif.* Amer Picon, Suze, several vermouths, various versions of *pastis*, the folkloric beverage of the languorous south, which had replaced absinthe. . . . There was an *apéritif* that boasted of the digestive virtues of artichoke present in it, and another that even claimed to be full of oxygen. Nowadays, the French are less alcohol oriented. In an everyday restaurant you'll see more Coca-Cola bottles on the tables of young people than bottles of wine. Just as you see young and old sucking plastic bottles of Coke, once commonly reviled as *"le Beaujolais de* Texas," in the *métro* or on the bus. The change has helped out the health insurance system, which was much devoted to dealing with cirrhosis, and also put an important part of the traditional economy, winemaking, in a state of worry. The *apéritif* makers spend a lot of money on advertising these days, proclaiming ways that their potions, mixed with other beverages, are the new chic. Nobody seems convinced.

For French ceremonial meals, however, beginning with an *apéritif* lives on. We were going to take the train back to Paris rather than driving with a buzz. It was a lovely summer afternoon under a gazebo. What the heck. . . . Joanne and I clicked our glasses of the house *apéritif* in a toast—another antique habit.

Apéritifs are generally distillations of various things, or combine wine with herbs and other flavors. They tend to be at the same time sweet, acid, and bitter. Often they are served mixed with a cold white wine. Think of the *kir*, a drink of white wine flavored with black currant liqueur, *crème de cassis,* which I first tasted at a dinner given by Canon Kir, the priest and mayor of Dijon, who invented that *apéritif.* (He was a great gourmet who ended the speech making at that formal event by shouting, "My pots are burning!")

The most upscale version of a white wine–based *apéritif* calls for champagne, but in point of fact champagne loses its personality to the strong flavor of the *apéritif* base, and it's a flashy waste served that way. Honest restaurateurs will give the drink the added pleasure of a fizz using any of a number of effervescent whites.

Sébastien's *apéritif* contained a *crêmant*, or bubbly, from Alsace, his mother's native home. The other ingredient was a *ratafia*.

Ask most Frenchmen today to define a *ratafia* and you'll draw a blank. This ancient beverage has become far more obscure in French fare than the *apéritif* in general. A *ratafia* is fermented rather than distilled, using mashed fruit or dried fruit pits. The *ratafia* glowing in our glasses, Sébastien explained, was created from the pits and pulp of cherries from the region; they were *griottes*, of the same bitter-sweet variety that made the cherries of Montmorency, forty-odd miles away, famous, when orchards stood where suburban houses do now. Sébastien adds barley grains to increase the fermentation.

Our long afternoon of gastronomy had begun. These drinks were quite delightful overtures, flashes of fanfare, and our *apéritifs* went down in time for the first course we'd ordered to arrive: for Joanne, *pétoncles*, which are tiny relatives of scallops, with *sautéed* large shrimp, in a sauce of cream and garlic, very slowly thickened. Sébastien would not dream, he said, of thickening his sauces with feculants. *Foie gras* was my starter, which Sébastien had made from scratch. For the traditional alcoholic maceration of the liver, he had done a mixture of white port, Armagnac, and Madeira, imparting a complex fruitiness that goes well with the taste of the *foie,* which includes an unctuous, faint bitterness.

Two pink slabs came out with a pear that had been poached in spicy syrup and a *brioche* with a bit of pistachio in it, a local baker's specialty. With it came a little glass of sweet white wine, naturally sweet, like Sauternes, from having its grapes harvested late, when the "noble rot" that colors them brownish gold imparts its complex sweetness. It was another Alsatian wine, a Gewürztraminer 2007, *vendage tardive*, from a little vintner named Pierre Sparr in the village of Sigolsheim. The sweet wine and sweet fruit are classic accompaniments to a *foie gras* appetizer, but I've never drunk a Gewürztraminer that way. This was a contribution of Christine Petit, née Kopp's heritage, a substitute for the Sauternes or say, the Jurançon or Barzac restaurateurs usually serve. This Alsatian wine had the quality of being especially fruity and flowery; it formed a clean fugue with the sweetness, a bright taste like rose petals and citrus.

We didn't regret not having to drive home, when the *trou normand* arrived shortly afterward. A *trou normand* is an alcohol-flavored ice that separates courses in a traditional French feast. The *trou* refers to the clearing of more room in your stomach brought on by the ice's cooling effect on the digestion. *Normand* speaks of the usual alcohol used, calvados from Normandy.

Sébastien challenged us to identify the flavoring of his ice. It had a nutty taste. Joanne, knowing his attachment to things of the region and having read about some recently, spoke up and hit the bull's eye, sounding like a prodigious food connoisseur. (Which I believe, actually, she is.) "Noyau de Poissy," she said. Normandy was close by, and Sébastien might have got away doing a *trou normand* with calvados, but Poissy, a village on the Seine, and Orvilliers, twenty-six miles away, are both in the *Île-de-France,* sharing its particular history and geography, and the ability to give distinctive definitions to a dish of food.

Christine, who was hovering over our table as we were asked to make the guess, spoke up. "Monsieur Duval, who did the Noyau de Poissy came here one day years ago for lunch and thanked us, having heard that we were using his *noyau.* He signed the *livre d'or.*" The Duval family, we learned, had a little shop in Poissy, where they sold a beverage that had once been widely celebrated and was first served in the local inns in the seventeenth century. It is still produced, by the current owners, as always, using apricot pits, in a little distillery near the shop.

Pits? What could be more in the French tradition of being close to one's *sous* and letting nothing that could be useful go to waste? Some of the best French sausage is made of tripes—the *andouillettes* of which the city of Troyes is famous. Exhibitionism, on the other hand, came late to being common in France. It had been the domain of royalty and high nobility, and even they had to avoid too much show. Nicolas Fouquet, Louis Quatorze's finance minister, went to prison for life after he gave a feast more splendid than any his king ever had. Marcel Boussac, who was, when I met him, the richest man in France, owner of Dior, received me in his office in a humble Parisian neighborhood, sitting in a chair with stuffing sticking out. When I took Tom Murphy, the brilliant man running Capital Cities, back to meet him, Murphy left feeling like Christopher Columbus among the natives.

Exhibitionism, in any case, was not on our menu for this lunch. Joanne's second course was scallops with spinach, green asparagus in a hollandaise sauce, with a bit of puff paste. The hollandaise was the sauce that had been a lodestone to food lovers in the area. Smooth and thick, with no thickening agent added, the rich emulsion of Norman butter, from the town of Isigny, and egg yolk mellows in your mouth in the wake of a dab of lemon juice. Christine gave me some to taste on country bread. "It's just a mayonnaise using butter instead of oil," she said modestly, leaving out the patience that it takes to add the butter to the yolk in a double boiler, a tiny amount at a time, keeping the emulsion from coming apart and the eggs from cooking too much. A variety of this sauce was already in the celebrated chef François Pierre de la Varenne's cookbook, *Le Cuisiner François,* first printed in 1651.

My main course was half a lobster under a puff paste cap, in a *sauce amoricaine.*

Sauce amoricaine or *sauce américaine?* The annals of French cuisine use both terms. Curnonsky, that celebrated food critic of the first

half of the twentieth century, has it that a French chef named Pierre
Fraysse, who opened a restaurant in Chicago, was pestered before his
opening day by a group of diners insisting on a lobster meal. Fraysse,
the story goes, had nowhere open to buy ingredients and he put
together what he had, made a sauce of tomato, spices, cognac, and
white wine. The dish became celebrated and crossed back to France
with him. The simpler story says the sauce refers to the ancient name
for Brittany, where French lobsters are caught. The going recipe,
in any case, is more complicated than the Fraysse potluck version:
There's tomato, shallots, garlic, Basque Espelette pepper, and a reduction of lobster shells simmered in white wine, with creamed lobster
roe, and a dash of cognac.

Whatever you rightly called it, it was what it was in my plate, and
it was delicious. I looked over at Joanne's scallops, and I chastised
Sébastien. "Where's the coral?" I asked. He had apparently bought
his fresh scallops out of their shells, with the little hooks of orange
roe, the *corail* cut away. I was going to give him a demerit in my
notebook. Christine came to his defense:

"We used to buy scallops in the shells and serve them with the
corail," she said, "and people left them in their plates. They looked at
them funny. The frozen scallops they put in their shopping carts these
days come without the roe, and some people have never even seen it."

I conceded that nobody I knew in America ever served scallops
with the roe attached, although the roe, with its own fuller taste,
is as delicious as the scallops themselves. Joanne passed me a scallop
to assuage my dismay. It was unctuous, firm, and delicately sweet,
very, very faintly tasting of the sea. The dollop of hollandaise I put
on it made it as good as it could get.

Christine came back with a dish of hot *pommes dauphines,* such as
she was serving with *filet de boeuf au poivre,* to the only other diners
at lunch, farther down on the lawn. *Pommes dauphines* are crisp
potato puffs made of mashed potatoes covered with *choux* pastry.

Influenced by his mother's Alsatian origins, Sébastien added cumin to the classic dish.

"There are people," she said, "who come to eat here and ask me what these are. All they know of *pommes dauphines* are the marbles they get in packages in the supermarket."

I ate all the temptations on the little plate, an act that confirmed our decision to skip the alluring cheeses on a wicker tray that would be our next course. It would have also meant a change in wine, from the dry white Gewürztraminer we were drinking with the seafood to a sturdy red with the cheese. The white was a wine called l'Auxerois, from a vineyard owned by a man named Paul Anselm who lived in Christine's village of Bernardswiller. Auxerre is a town in Burgundy, but what we were drinking had nothing to do with Burgundy. A man whose surname was Auxerre had planted a vineyard in Bernardswiller, in Alsace, in the nineteenth century, and had done a good enough job of it to have his wine perpetuated and, as we judged, rightfully revered. A mellow, well-balanced, fruity white.

Cheese does not make red wine taste better; it is rather the other way round, and the combination calls for a red with great body to keep its head up with the cheese. We passed on the cheese. Not that we would have passed out with more wine, but we had just enough room for dessert: We had been lunching for about three hours.

Joanne managed a little *génoise*, a classic cake in the sponge family, which had absorbed Cointreau and was topped by a dark chocolate mousse with bits of filbert, and over it a white chocolate mousse with bits of pistachio. I tasted an array of little pots of custard— flavored alternatively with Bénédictine, rum and pistachio, Brazilian coffee, and caramel with Malibu, a cordial made of Caribbean rum and coconut. With them came a scoop of black currant sorbet and strawberries in peach liqueur.

"A *digéstif*? " Sébastien asked. Dear God. But could we slight Christine by not at least sipping the wild raspberry *eau de vie* that a cousin distilled in Alsace? Making *eau de vie* properly is a very inefficient exercise. It takes a lot of fruit to end up with a little bit of nectar coming out of a still. In the case of the Nusbauer *eau de vie* that we sipped—from a distillery that Christine's great-grandfather had once partly owned—those wild berries had not given up their essence in vain.

The bill for our memorable afternoon came to 105 euro, much less than half of what we would have had to pay to experience the prowess of a rising star among the media-celebrated chefs of France. Christine had added felicities from her Alsace to an essentially classic *cuisine bourgeoise*. Sébastien had brought his vision to the genre.

On the train, we deconstructed, to borrow the buzzword, Sébastien's feast. It was far from simple, but it was in no way gratuitously bizarre. If our young man were famous, he might have been adding his recipes to the annals of French cuisine, contributing his individual talent to enriching the tradition. Everything we ate had a pedigree in that tradition, a story to tell, evoking a local place and a past, while being a fresh presence. No shot glasses of foam or baby food to start us off, no combinations shrilly baroque. If he were famous, which perhaps someday he might become, Sébastien's disciplined inventiveness might take its place among the recipes of culture heroes of French cuisine: say Escoffier, whose achievements are often maligned by the *sans culottes* of today's kitchens, or Louis Diat, who created *vichyssoise*, out of memories of *la France profonde*, while cooking in the United States.

Our meal had been our moment of sensuous contact with presences passed on, at a there, as Gertrude Stein doubtless would have put it, that *was* there.

Was there anyone else in the region, we asked Sébastien, doing interesting cooking with a pedigree? Joanne had read somewhere that Maurice Ravel, the composer, who had lived in Montfort l'Amaury, was fond of the special local breed of chicken, *la Poule de*

Houdan. Was anyone still cooking Houdan chickens? The chickens of Houdan were said to have been the most favored by European gourmets, up until the Great Depression, when the cost of raising them made them exotic.

"There's this fellow in Houdan with a restaurant called La Poularde," Sébastien said. "He raises them not for *poules,* but for roasters."

Poules are hens that go into the pot after a career of laying eggs. A *poulet* is a chicken; a *poularde* is a neutered, young hen, rendered fatter and more tender. On our way back to Paris, we called Sylvain Vandenameele, longtime owner of La Poularde in Houdan, on my cell phone. Could we reserve a date to eat a *poularde de Houdan, chez lui?*

"I stopped raising them for food two and a half years ago," he said, "and nobody does anymore. They were too expensive to raise."

A Houdan chicken, he explained, is fed until the right age for roasting, five months. "That's a month longer than for a *poulet de Bresse,*" he said. I recalled that the free-range chickens now commonly sold all over France come guaranteed to be ninety days old. The *poulet de Bresse* has a world reputation and is the most expensive chicken in France, probably in the world.

"Actually," Vandenameele said, "the Houdan chicken is far better, but who knows that nowadays?"

We mentioned a club near him in Mantes, originally founded in Houdan in 1905, that was dedicated to the perpetuation of the breed and to its nearly extinct close relation, also from the Houdan region, the *Faverolles.*

"Yes, but they don't raise them for eating," he said. "I still raise some in my yard, just to keep the breed alive."

We asked him what was special about both Houdan fowls.

"The *poulet de Bresse* is soft and fat," Vandenameele replied. "The Houdan chickens are tender but also lean. Their flavor is incomparable. Rich. Resembling partridge or pheasant."

I said that we had indeed usually found *poulet de Bresse* rather short on taste, although long on tenderness, a combination that often corresponded to the palates of our times.

Have tough times, by the way, increased the allure of tender food in France? Perhaps that is something for a scholar of the communal mind-set to ponder. For example, true chocolate cake is hard to find in a bakery, where, just as on restaurant menus, it has been replaced by a pudding-ish *fondant*. The traditional crisp almond-flavored French *macaron* has become Paris's latest trendy *Nasch*, transformed into softened crusts with a variety of colored goos between them. Everybody seems to need a little tenderness, like the women you sometimes see slipping coins to the butcher's assistant, to be sure of a soft steak.

"If you let me know in advance, I could roast a Houdan for you," Vandenameele said.

Joanne wrote "roast chicken" in her notebook, with a question mark for the date. And underlined the notation.

Sébastien Petit's Lobster à l'Amoricaine "Montgolfière"

Sébastien calls his version of this classic dish "*montgolfière*, the French word for a hot-air balloon, because the cap of puff paste swells in baking. It looks appealing, but the cap also holds in all the savor of the dish, and its buttery crust is great for sopping up the sauce when you're eating it.

For four people
   a little less than 1 cup of cognac
   2 medium-size live lobsters
   12 scallops
   6 big tomatoes seeded and peeled

1 finely chopped onion

a pinch of sugar

4 cloves of garlic

1 sprig of thyme

1 bay leaf

a sprinkle of olive oil

a little more than a ½ qt. of white wine

3 scant tsp. of paprika (*piment d'Espelette* if you can get it)

3 scant tsp. of curry powder

3 scant tsp. of *herbes de Provence* (an equal mixture of

oregano, marjoram, and thyme would be a substitute)

a few strands of saffron

freshly ground pepper and salt

Prepare a standard butter-based puff paste large enough to cover the four individual porcelain *pots* in which the dish will be served.

Make a tomato sauce by cutting the tomatoes into small cubes; heat the onion with the olive oil. Add the tomatoes, thyme, laurel, sugar, salt, and pepper. Let it simmer, then add the garlic finely chopped. Separately, boil the wine with the spices. Cut the lobsters in half, the long way, and cut the tails in half again. The French chop live lobsters, but you can kill them in a quick boil. Break the shells of the claws with a hammer. Cut open the heads, and carefully remove the stomachs. Sauté the tails and claws in olive oil at a very hot fire, flame them with cognac.

Sauté the heads in the same way, separately. Divide the boiled wine in half and pour a half on each of the flamed preparations. Reduce the sauce for 5 minutes. Add the tomato sauce and let it all simmer for 10 minutes. Remove the lobster from the shells once cooled. Sauté the scallops in a little olive oil. In

4 individual porcelain *pots*, put 3 scallops, the meat of a lobster claw, a half of a tail, and a bit of a joint, then fill the little pots with the sauce including the sauce from the heads.

Brush the puff paste with a beaten egg; cover the *pots* with it. Put it all in the refrigerator for 10 minutes, then in a 350 degree Fahrenheit oven for 20 minutes. Serve hot. If you don't have the little porcelain *pots*, it all can be baked in one porcelain bowl, and divided out.

After our afternoon at Orvilliers, while our train neared the Montparnasse station, our thoughts turned to comparing our lunch with another repast. The New Year's Eve dinner we'd last had, deep in the country. There was, as the idiom goes, no comparison.

2

J'ACCUSE

Call him Monsieur X. I'll make him a gift of anonymity. You can say that it's a pardon in exchange for inspiring Joanne to push me to do this book. He nearly ruined our New Year's Eve, but we're not pinpointing him to avenge that. He's a little guy who rose high in his profession—to a high reputation. We won't begrudge him his ascent. It's what has happened to his profession that got him there that dismays us. We're talking about a venerated craft that has turned too often into a shaky claim to art.

Monsieur X is a cook and innkeeper. Michelin honors him with a star, and his place is full of signed photographs of himself with all the celebrity chefs in France who have become his friends. Monsieur X's story takes place in Auvergne, where, when we first knew him, he had a little hotel with a restaurant that relied on vegetables from local gardens, the butter and cream from local dairies, veal and beef from the neighboring herds. It was straightforward food, yet more subtle than some of the food of the region that can be heavy, to fortify hardworking peasants. It was an innovation, as such, in the neighborhood.

We're fond of Auvergne, having spent a lot of time in this mountainous heartland of France on vacation, and later as the producers of our son André's documentary about the threat to the local agrarian way of life called *A Family in France*. In our role as producers, Gerry drove the van and Joanne held the sound boom. Larisa, our daughter, made sandwiches of local sausage and *pâtés*, and the regional Cantal cheese. Our headquarters was a centuries-old farmhouse that Monsieur X's cousin rented us—Monsieur X comes from generations of farmers—and we took our dinners at his little hotel.

That wasn't the most memorable culinary experience we'd had in Auvergne. Before then, on vacation, we'd stayed at a hotel not far away, higher up in the partly once-volcanic Massif Central. The food was similarly local, although not country cooking. Catering to city people, the owners were, like Monsieur X, shy of seeming primitive. The larder of the hotel La Sapinière nonetheless relied on the red-hided Salers cattle, a lean breed native to Auvergne, which gives less milk than those of industrial dairies and less meat. But the milk-fed veal and the beef had a sui generis delicious quality, the veal very faintly nutty, and the beef slightly resembling game in strength of flavor. But the cream was what was most exceptional. Our innkeeper explained that the steep mountains above the hotel were covered with lush grass as well as with wildflowers. In the past, men would climb up there with hand scythes and cut this rich fodder to store as a winter provision for the cattle. That was some time ago, he said, since which no one has been willing to climb the mountains and spend their days getting blisters scything. People drive tractors now, but no one would be foolish enough to risk accidents driving a tractor on those steep slopes. Yet the villagers, being frugal as Auvergnats are wont to be, wouldn't say no thank you to an asset nature bestowed on them. All summer, they would drive their cattle up there to gorge themselves on the grass and flowers as long as they could. And that was how the cream served with local strawberries at La Sapinière was a suave mouthful of flowers. We'd known a spectacular example of an element that in French culinary annals goes by the name of *terroir*—the unique contribution of the qualities of a place discernable in food from that place.

Although throughout the world many foods that originated somewhere are copied elsewhere—Danish "camembert," California "champagne"—the French defend, with the law, the uniqueness of presences in gastronomy that come from one place and one place only. Just as wines, cheeses, and other foods are granted "appellations of origin," different soil, different grass, tied to local, traditional techniques give something its pedigree, discernable to the palate.

I remember a farmer near the town of Vimoutiers in Normandy who explained that the local breed of cattle eating the local grass gave a subtlety to Camembert inimitable elsewhere. And the French government agrees. Monsieur Daniel Courtonne was a devotee of detail. I asked him why he hand milked his cows, when the other cheese makers in town used machines. "With machines, you have two choices," he said. "If you don't clean them with detergents, they ruin the milk. If you use detergents, the inevitable traces of detergents ruin the milk." His Camembert merited the grandiose name it had: "Le Royal Montgomery." It related to the hamlet near Camembert where Courtonne had his farm, Saint-Germain-le-Montgomery.

By the time we went back to Auvergne, on a recent New Year's holiday, La Sapinière, in Thiésac, had burnt down. And the nearby Monsieur X had moved upward in his career. To match his ascension as a chef, he'd *"relooké"* his hotel, as they say in contemporary French, into a strange personality, a mixture of pastiche styles. We recalled how often the famous chefs' places that we'd visited in France had risible taste in furnishing. There seemed to be a correlation between pretentious furnishing and striving gastronomy.

Then came our New Year's Eve dinner.

There arrived, as we sipped champagne with the wind whistling outside our lobby window, something that has become a cliché in contemporary French restaurants: our *amuse-gueule*. It is a curtain-opener to a meal with which, in tiny portions that used to be called *hors d'oeuvres*, our maestro does a flourish of his creative talent. It translates literally as a "mouth amuser." The word for mouth here, the one you use for an animal, is sassily used rather than *la bouche*. *Ferme ta gueule,* for example, means, "Shut your face!" We were in any case not amused, as we opened and shut our mouths, faced with this opus, served—as is the cliché for *amuse-gueules*, when they don't come as just foam or baby food in a shot glass—on a thin, rectangular glass plate. We were a long way from the ocean, and the warm oyster on the plate had the taste of having made a trying journey. Elsewhere in the lineup were a cherry tomato glazed like a candy apple, a coinlike cheese biscuit recalling a Ritz cracker, and, not to be left out, a shot glass full of foam—of beets and cream—along with a dab of *pâté de fois gras*, poorer cousin, containing pig's liver, to whole *foie gras*.

The language on the menu of what followed was a dithyramb to the creativity involved. The food was far less inspiring: soggy langoustines lying on mashed potatoes rebaptized as an emulsion, then slices of turbot crowned with orange juice–flavored fennel. The turbot came in such precisely similar slices that we were led to believe that our chef had bought such slices frozen—rather than whole fish. When we turned ours back—it tasted unpleasantly fishy—we were served insipid slices of sea bass instead. Was it a coincidence that sea bass and turbot are two fish that are farmed in France, in contrast with wild fish?

The *plat de résistance* was a slice of veal resembling a strip of bacon wrapped around lettuce. The sweets that followed were a strangely salty *crème brulée*, served in a little mason jar, another cliché among today's trendy restaurants, and mango and banana cannelloni. We'll give Monsieur X his due, which earned him his star: He had done dishes that no one else had likely done before.

Why are we going out of our way to bad-mouth this benighted fellow? It's not his folly that matters; it's the seismic shift of which he is a telling caricature. His dinner shook us up. What has happened is that French cuisine, as part of a phenomenon that has spread worldwide, has become a matter of performance, in which creativity is the predominant criterion of success. This with the aid of critics who react like those who go to art galleries, and of eaters who leave behind their daily diets of industrial food, for the titillation of a fashionable meal.

A publication rivaling Robert Parker's numerical grades for the wines of this world is called *Wine Spectator*. Perhaps we should call the restaurant critics with their numbers and stars "food spectators."

Do I sound like some kind of unenlightened reactionary?

Looking into our plates, in this little place surrounded by mountains, where changes used to make their way in slowly—it took long hours on winding roads to get here, before the *autoroute* passed nearby—we realized that our meal was a paradigm of the wider world. How had Andy Warhol put it about everyone's forthcoming celebrity? "In the future, everyone will be world-famous for fifteen minutes." We were in an age of ultracommunication, when everybody had a story to upload and many were fabrications. What was phony cooking compared to the scams that rocked the economies of the planet?

As for *la cuisine*, listen to Christian Millau, the man who, with his late partner, Henri Gault, first encouraged and spread the news of the big culinary change in our time: "We are now in a ridiculous period, ridiculous, pretentious and stupid."

With their magazines and guides, Millau and Gault did more than anyone else to foster and publicize a new movement in cuisine as it spread from France to the world. They shook up Michelin with their personalized, detailed reviews. More than groupies in this new movement, they became its gurus, while still sticking to the objectivity of the journalists whom they were from the start.

Christian Millau is in his eighties now, and has quietly turned his back on being arguably the world's most noted food critic. He has detached himself from ownership in the Gault Millau guides and turned to writing books, without any public pronouncements about the world he'd abandoned. I went out to see him for the timeline of his influential career and I got a revelation of the disenchantment that accompanied the career change.

We spoke for my recorder in his spacious apartment in a leafy suburb of Paris, while he was about to receive the galleys for his novel based on the young Hitler. I'll have more to recount about that conversation later, but his epithets ring in my ears: "ridiculous, pretentious, and stupid." Before I left him, the man who did the most to put the searchlight of media attention on the culture of restaurant cooking expressed a note of sorrow about what, in general, has affected our society since:

"In the end, it all comes down to two things, the media and the money."

Is Millau out of it? Among France's food writers, no one could be called more *in* these days than Gilles Pudlowski, who has a long raft of books and guidebooks to his credit, along with medals from the government and a pulpit at the important news weekly *Le Point*. Without telling him what Millau or I thought, I asked Pudlowski to sum up his own take on today's restaurant scene.

"Christian Millau," he volunteered, "was in a sense the sorcerer's apprentice for what happened to cooking. We've seen a lot of stupidity since, but I think that we're returning to the triumph of reason. I see everything bizarrely complicated becoming *démodé*. It's time for the more serious, more traditional, more *raffiné*. And classicism."

Listening to Pudlowski and Millau as well as to a lot of Parisians who eat out, I have been hearing, to stretch the metaphor, the earth shaking again on the cuisine scene, with baroque constructions tumbling. Ferran Adrià, the Spaniard, who one-upped the French celebrity chefs with his celebrated but increasingly controversial *tecno-emocional* molecular cuisine, decided to close his restaurant for two years, while teaching "culinary physics" at Harvard, no less. Adrià's next ambition was to open a foundation for research and creativity in cooking, with his restaurant as a museum. His lofty decision to bow out at what might be a prudent time gave the roll call of famous chefs of France more room to capture again the gold ring *pour la patrie*. These French virtuosos who, as I wrote earlier, have banded together to shore up their prestige in the world have formed a code of ethics. Their Collège Culinaire de France pledges to use only food cooked on the premises from fresh prod-ucts with the pedigrees of their regions. We're hearing *terroir* again, the unique savor of things that are what they are because of where they are.

The foam of molecular cooking has gone flat in the media, while *"terroiristes"* have stepped into the spotlight, granting nature a big role in their striving for personal culinary fame. Even though the vanguard of the *"terroiristes,"* emulating the celebrated chef Michel Bras, is trying to shine doing dishes made of wild plants that no locals considered eating before.

Nature, Simple, sain et bon is the title Alain Ducasse, the dominant worldwide entrepreneur among celebrity chefs, has given to a recent book. On that wavelength, on the tenth anniversary of his flagship restaurant in Paris's Hôtel Plaza Athénée, Ducasse proclaimed a new "simplicity" in cuisine, to match the minimalist *relooking*, as the French call redecorating, of his dining room.

Among his novelties was toast simply garnished with precious, matured, Colonnata lard. With this gesture Ducasse's simplicity approached that of the most humble Berlin *Kneipe*, where you get *Schmalz* instead of butter with your black bread.

What defines Ducasse, perhaps, is that he has the surest business head and the most impressively comprehensive objective of all the creative chefs. With his bistros as well as his luxurious restaurants, his globalized touches as well as regional cooking such as in his 1998 cookbook, *Flavors of France*, Ducasse puts a stamp of Ducasse originality, like a branding, wherever there's food to be cooked and served to the public. His aspirations are more ambitious and more securely grounded than novelty. Their motto might be: *"La cuisine, c'est moi."*

Perhaps, all things said, we are indeed in for a big correction, to borrow a term from the financial world, where conceit, deceit, and cynical innovation caused disasters far more consequential than disappointing meals. But, like creative derivatives in the financial world, the hype still goes on, at famous or would-be famous kitchens included.

In a sense, the Modern Age came late to cuisine, and with it the age of "communication" and its sibling, hype. The modernism that arrived in the twentieth century turned its back on tradition, as if it were recreating the world from scratch in its time. We saw an upheaval in art and in architecture, much of which was a breath of fresh air and much of which was impoverished. Of all the modern and contemporary paintings and sculpture and installations in museums, how much is profoundly moving, which is what art is all about, and how much a succession of trivia whose virtue is its insignificant uniqueness? In all that has been built in the last century, how much has the lyric quality of late Gehry, the finesse of a handful of other architects, and how much became soulless ghettos? The Modern Age was also the era of new and more powerful authoritarianism: Fascism and Communism. In all areas of human activity, he who screamed the loudest, who took the most extreme, intolerant positions, got the most attention.

I wrote about fashion in my early years in France, and the change in French cuisine—from a careful tradition to a shrill competition for the critics' attention, through conspicuousness—tellingly matches what happened to fashion. I remember the brilliant originality of great designers who created a custom of dressing that had allure and subtlety, and which, in that context, could also be wisely provocative. I've known what Chanel, Saint Laurent, Balenciaga, and Givenchy achieved. I witnessed, too, the time when they were replaced by a crowd of newcomers to aesthetic values, who competed in outlandishness because the critics were looking at the clothing as if from the point of view of art critics, for whom, again, newness was all they could understand. And with the cynicism that has characterized the economics of our age, *les créateurs* would gain big reputations, on which they could cash in, by putting their names on T-shirts.

With cuisine we see the *créateurs* doing restaurants with their names on them all over the world, with someone else in the kitchen.

Truly talented chefs have indeed come on the scene inventing exciting new taste combinations, admonishing the flaws in the building blocks of traditional cooking (although often falling back on them), and opening their search for ingredients to what is available in the whole world (although sometimes drawing on it for new clichés). Let us praise them and grant them their talent, and their ambition to do something new and alluring. Georges Blanc, for example, has created delicious new harmonies, inspired by a taste for natural quality that goes back to two generations of country cooks in his family. Alain Ducasse, when he's working in that same register and is less of a dandy, comes up with delicious dishes. But in France and elsewhere in the world, the greats of the kitchen are not numerous enough to keep food critics busy. Yet their celebrity has inspired their whole corporation, and their criterion of originality has become the benchmark for quality.

As Guy Savoy, whose well-earned three Michelin stars no one would dispute, told an interviewer: The ersatz heirs of *la nouvelle cuisine* would "do any old thing" to shine.

So a generation of "creators" has turned eating out into a would-be appreciation as if of art. The worst this has meant is that restaurateur after restaurateur who didn't lock step, who didn't adhere to the monopolistic criterion of conspicuous inventiveness, came upon hard times, neglected by critics and subsequently by a trend-following public. Meanwhile, the chefs paradoxically strived to keep up: Creativity became modified by the desire to be "me too" with the latest touted trends. From the days when kiwis were the accolade garnish for almost everything, we've moved on to more elaborate clichés, the most daring of which was Ferran Adrià's invention, "molecular cooking," a kind of alchemy that turns everything into the new experience of eating foam. It has become an ephemeral fad that crossed the pyramids from Spain. Never mind that diners at the restaurant of a chef famous for his foam in England complained of being poisoned by dubious, chemically dependent mixtures. Millau disdainfully called doing the foam of molecular cuisine "cooking with a bicycle pump."

As for the public these days, the French far less often have a mother or wife at home cooking, or a skilled domestic at the stove. You can't regret the liberation of women that implies. Nonetheless, gone are the days when French people went home to eat lunch, on a two-hour break. At midday now, the cafés in Paris are full of those who come to wolf sandwiches and Coke, or a processed *plat du jour* from that supermarket called Metro, where café and restaurant owners can stock up on wholesale industrial dishes. There are now more McDonald's per square foot in Paris than in New York. As for what gets eaten after work, spend a moment on a supermarket line in Paris and see what is in the shopping baskets: industrial food, which inures the palate to the coarse. A public reared on such food, eaten daily, has—allow the conceit—a callused palate, although one still able to perceive newness.

You still see fresh, long *baguettes* sticking out of the briefcases of people coming home from work toward dinner, but Harry's American-style white bread, i.e., a clone of Wonder bread, smeared with nut paste, often makes up the *goûter,* the traditional snack that mothers give their children after school. For how long will we still get the rich smell of the four o'clock *pains au chocolat* coming from the bakeries, where men who work before dawn go back to their ovens before *goûter* time?

French dinner parties among the well-off in our era still provide a break from the routine of convenience food at home. They've become less ritual, and that's not a bad thing: Gone, pretty well, are the days of not so long ago when the hostess presided with a little bell at hand to call her servant to change courses, when she gave the cue for when you stopped talking to the person seated to your right and turned to your neighbor to the left, when she'd have called the foreign ministry to be confirmed in the pecking order about who was seated where, and when guests who were offended by their place at table could turn their dishes upside down and not eat. And, with the serving of orange juice after the *digéstifs,* our hostess signaled that the evening was coming to a close.

Paris still has its resplendent outdoor markets. But what's out there has seen changes. No problem finding mangoes, passion fruit, and Chilean strawberries in winter. (To think that Faust sold his soul to eat strawberries in winter.) But the variety of French produce has shrunk. Rare are the cardoons of yesteryear and the salsifis that French tradition considers the ideal accompaniment for roast veal. What happened to the cherries shaped like hearts called *"coeurs de pigeons"*?

There's no point in romanticizing everything about the past in the culinary history of France. Many things have actually gotten better.

Time was, not long ago, when you had to shop around a lot to find a free-range chicken such as are available in supermarkets everywhere now, although those going soft under sanitizing cellophane are inferior to the ones a good butcher will have. Big flour mills have joined hands with innumerable small bakers to recreate the "traditional" *baguette*—that emblematic bread of France that had degenerated into a cottony thing. Lionel Poilâne, the late perpetuator of his father's rustic, round loaves, just like those the revolutionaries cried for—when Marie Antoinette is falsely said to have advised them to eat *brioche*—told me that he scorned the *baguette* as a nineteenth century invention, from the start a shortcut for proper bread making. But today's *baguettes de tradition* are fragrant, delightfully chewy, and tasty.

Nowadays, you don't hear much about the *court bouillon* that is a staple of the conventional poaching of fish—a mixture of wine or vinegar with aromatics and diced vegetables, designed to flavor the fish while poaching. It was, in point of fact, too often a way of dealing with fish not fresh enough to stand on its own taste. Somewhere I read how fish reached Paris until well into the nineteenth century—dragged from the coast of Normandy on sledge-like wagons, for days. Books of the Belle Époque give housewives ways of testing butter and milk for the fraudulent presence of chemical additives—chalk, animal fat—a common danger in those times. Formaldehyde was often a food preservative in France until a law of 1898 outlawed the practice. Last I heard, the Chinese are still using it.

Today, the laws for food purity are strict. But stricter still, it seems, are those that seem designed to harass the small persons in the food chain. Where the laws are laid down by the European Community in Brussels or by the French government in Paris, the industrial conglomerates have strong lobbies. The excuse of sanitation standards drives locals to spend more than they can afford to adhere to them.

I remember the day that Joanne and I hiked up to visit a farmer making Salers cheese at the top of a mountain in Auvergne, where his cows had been driven for the summer. He was milking a cow by hand in the grass when we arrived, and he went on to show us his little *buron,* or creamery, up there. True Salers cheese of the Cantal region had become rare. The Salers cow gives indeed much less milk than the Montbéliard that has greatly replaced it in the region, but the man was a stickler for the way of doing things he'd done during a long lifetime. In the *buron,* he showed us his new press. He had been forced to change the one he'd had for years, because its components were of wood, deemed not up to the sanitary standards of plastic. He spent, he said, a fortune to replace it, only to have the inspector come back and tell him to revert to the current version using wood again.

Chopping blocks in restaurant kitchens have also had to be replaced by plastic, although there is good evidence that wood is more hostile to germs. Frédéric Chaumez, the owner of the Hôtel Moderne in Barfleur, a faithful perpetuator of Norman cooking, whose delights we'll see in the pages ahead, told us his story of the rolling pin.

He had been still using the rolling pin of hard boxwood that was a memento of his apprenticeship as a pastry maker when the food inspector came and went through the kitchen, approving of everything until he saw the rolling pin. "That rolling pin is wooden," he chastised. Chaumez had to buy a plastic one, but he still uses his old friend when the inspector is not around.

Michel Dubois, the owner of the restaurant Le Languedoc in Paris, whose handmade mayonnaise we've enjoyed on *oeufs mayonnaises* over the years, as well as his own whipped cream on desserts, regrets not making his own ice cream. He doesn't have the room to do it. If you make your own ice cream in a restaurant, the law says that has to be done in a place in your kitchen remote from other food, as if mere proximity would easily contaminate the ice cream.

With all these precautions written into law, why has every breakout of salmonella or listeria that I've read about involved industrial foods under plastic in supermarkets?

As I began writing this chapter, the French newspaper of record, *Le Monde*, revealed, in a full-page story, that the president of the EU's European Authority on Safety in Food (EFSA)'s board of directors was also on the board of directors of a food industry lobby called the International Life Science Institute, including four hundred companies worldwide, prominent among them Kraft, Nestlé, and Monsanto. While ILSI's mission statement on the Web is to improve the health and well-being of the public, *Le Monde* pointed out that it defended the tobacco industry when it was under pressure from the World Health Organization in the 1980s.

Later, the watchdog of the European Union regarding safety in food, known as L'Observatoire de l'Europe Industrielle, charged four other members of EFSA's board with conflict of interest involving their ties to food industry lobbies.

Le Monde also recently reported an interesting survey. Which merchant on the Net gets the most hits? You probably guessed the answer for the United States and Great Britain: Amazon. The Chinese, whose access to reading and entertainment is what it is, favor Adidas, the sporting goods and sportswear manufacturer. The French? Findus, the nation's leading producer of frozen food.

When Joanne and I settled into Paris, we learned some things French people took for granted. That milk in coffee, for example, was a frightful challenge to the liver, moonlight faded the furniture, and that it was improper to drive the wrong way on a one-way street, except in reverse. We also became acquainted with the cornucopia of delights there for anyone who walked through a French outdoor market.

Joanne and I moved into an apartment facing the ancient Château de Vincennes, where Henry V of England, victorious against the French, died of dysentery in 1422, and where Mata Hari, wrongly accused as a spy, fell before a firing squad. In that traditional *petit-bourgeois* neighborhood with excellent food stores, Joanne would shop for meat *chez le boucher,* for fowl at the shop of the *volailler,* and for *foie de veau* from someone with the calling of *tripier,* an innards authority. Each specialist was proud of his finite expertise. Today generalized butcher shops are going out of business competing with supermarkets that sell cellophane-wrapped cuts.

We remember when Paris's first supermarket opened in a big basement in the rue de Passy. Hard to believe? Those were the days when people competed to buy someone's phone line, rather than be on a waiting list for two years to be attributed their own.

The glut of industrial food in a French *supermarché* today matches that of any supermarket in America. Drs. Jean-Michel Cohen and Patrick Serog have written several successful books that point to how that has deteriorated French eating habits. Their last book, *Savoir manger, la vérité sur nos aliments,* examines seventeen thousand products, including "ham" that is sixty-five percent ham, packaged sushi that is twelve percent fish, and a roll call of additives ever present. The gondolas from which our good doctors filled their shopping carts were loaded with junk food.

When Joanne and I first came to France, if you saw vastly obese persons in the street, odds were that they were American tourists, who had been on the supermarket diet for their entire lives. Nowadays, you hear them speaking French.

So there, I accuse, is where we have been with *la cuisine.* Who can hold back change? Yet regarding recognizing excellence, newness has often become almost all.

Almost.

As our travels ahead will demonstrate, all things said, the appreciation of what is real and of intrinsic quality hasn't been totally lost in France's renowned culinary heritage, and the trend to perpetuate it is definitely growing. That heritage is long and deep in France and like a natural function, it's stubborn; it prevails in a windstorm of commercial pressures.

What should one expect? If I haven't sounded like some Rip van Winkle, please read on.

3

WHERE WE'RE COMING FROM

At a pier at the Red Hook waterfront of Brooklyn, the Black
Hawk lifted anchor. Aboard the little freighter were twelve pas-
sengers, who, for $175 each, were going to be coddled on a ten-day
voyage to Antwerp. It was September 13 of the year 1963.

The Black Diamond Line offered the cheapest way to get to
Europe, and Joanne and I have never since seen such value for
our money as our mahogany-lined mini-suite and four meals a
day, not even when we'd come to travel frequently, taking other
people's vacations for them as journalists. This trip, for us, was no
vacation. Having abandoned what I foresaw as a less-than-exciting
career as a scholar, after degrees at Princeton and Harvard, I had
become a reporter for *The Philadelphia Inquirer*. Joanne had fool-
ishly abandoned her own studies, to follow me wherever I went.
Philadelphia was a lovely, civilized, and calm city, which did
not, we believed, merit the old saw: "First prize, one week in
Philadelphia, second prize, two weeks in Philadelphia." I came
to know the violent underside, covering robberies and murders

from 5:00 P.M. to 2:00 A.M.—as a "cub," which rookie journalists were then called.

Philadelphia, in any case, was not Europe, a place that we felt—although we could only long to be there—very much on our wavelength of sensibility. As high school kids, we'd dreamed of escaping the boredom of Queens for a place of fabled loveliness, more attuned in a civilized way to the senses. Part of the way there, for a couple of teenagers, was Manhattan, which in Queens you called "the city." A white city on the hill for the nascent aesthetes we were. In the city there were museums full of the splendors of European civilization, there were little movie houses that showed films in French that would never make it to the Valencia in Jamaica, a Hollywoodian fantasy of the Moor era in Spain, which has since become an African American church. There were these movie theaters where they gave you coffee as well as the film, coffee in little cups called demitasses. And there was Larré. There were great French restaurants in New York. The names of those who've disappeared come back with a vicariously inspired *frisson*. Café Chambord, Le Pavillon, Lafayette, La Caravelle. . . . They were havens of soon-to-be-dated elegance—the widow Jackie Kennedy would be turned away from Lafayette for wearing trousers—and, in a sense, they were museums of the *haute cuisine* that their chefs remembered from the last time they'd seen Paris, often before the war. Duck *à l'orange, crêpes suzettes, sole bonne femme*—Kennedys, Cabots, Vanderbilts, and their like had the best tables at these places. We could only read about them and salivate. Even if we had the $50 for two that a meal could cost—multiply by ten today?—it would not have been sure that we would even be given a table in the back room.

Larré was someplace else. It looked like what we'd later know French bistros to look like. Informal but comfortable, with woodwork that spoke of a past. If the grandees reproduced the hallowed repertoire of *haute cuisine*, Larré served dishes that were part of an ordinary Frenchman's heritage: garlicky snails, frog's legs, *steak au poivre, boeuf bourguignon, cervelle au beurre noir.* Could all that really have been on a $2.50 fixed dinner menu? I can't precisely remember the low prices, but someone on the Web recently said that was so. The mood in that welcoming, unpretentious room, the crowd of people who were savvy but not flush, the redolent food—not always successful—formed our first contact with the pleasurable cultural phenomenon that was eating out in the French tradition.

In Philadelphia, we saved our money to go to Europe. Philadelphia had not yet awakened to high gastronomy. There was Bookbinder's for crab cakes. We favored ethnic places. A Lebanese joint with a belly dancer on Saturday night, an Italian place where they watered the open wine, but did great spaghetti *alle vongole.* And once we went to a place high up in the Germantown neighborhood that served American food from a menu whose graphics dated to the thirties. We started with something called mashed potato salad, while in another room a group began their meal singing, "Thank you, Jesus, for saving my soul." I don't remember the rest of the repast. It might have been chicken à la king. There was a *Bräuhaus* attached to the Schmidt brewery, in North Philadelphia, where we enjoyed a *Kalbshaxe,* a roasted shank of veal. Many years later, I would remember that meal, when I ate the dish again in Trieste, where, thanks to the city's Austrian history, it was a local specialty.

We didn't have enough money to go to Europe after our first year in Philadelphia. So we headed on a vacation to someplace almost there. Montreal. I know Montreal now as a place very profoundly New World, with French folklore for tourists. It seemed exotic then. The language and of course the food. We ate in places that recalled Larré. One memory stands in my mind from this trip distant in time: the herbal and unctuous, first-time taste of *sauce béarnaise* on a great steak with *frites.*

That trip and our evenings at Larré amounted to our ingenuous introduction to the joy of French eating. . . .

We left Philadelphia the next year. I had been promoted from cub reporter covering police to labor editor. I'd been following Jimmy Hoffa around. He was in town to suppress a revolt in the Teamsters Union and forge the last links in his nationwide contract with the trucking companies. Jimmy liked to let me sit in while he bullied the truckers in their negotiation meetings. Jimmy called me "country cousin," since his forefathers were from Poland. I didn't tell him that my father's country, when he left it, was called White Russia, and the Poles were the unfriendly neighbors nearby.

I was enjoying myself, even if my preoccupations seemed less noble than doing New Criticism about Jacobean plays that no one performed any longer. But something unexpected happened. Joanne was going to have a baby. Someone less insouciant than we two would have said, "That's it, now we don't know when we'll ever get to France." Instead we agreed: "It's now or never." And so I quit *The Inquirer* with the blithe belief that when we came back I could walk into another reporter's job. In those days, that was a safe assumption. We'd stay in Europe until our resources reached the point of return. Our resources came to six thousand dollars. And we booked passage. . . .

The *Black Hawk* sailed gently out of the harbor of New York. We passed where a great bridge was going up, to tie Staten Island to Manhattan at last. The sun shone. "You'll be back in a month," Joanne's father predicted. As it turned out, once we made our way to Paris, it would be our home for nearly half a century.

It was smooth sailing all the way. Despite its ominous name, the *Black Hawk* was an appealing place to spend ten days crossing the Atlantic. We had our outside cabin paneled in mahogany with adjoining toilet and shower. We ate a few times at the captain's table. We had four good meals a day, including open sandwiches at four o'clock. Somehow those are all I remember of Norwegian food. Delicious herring, in several varieties, and hard cheese you sliced with a special utensil.

We landed at a cobbled pier upriver in Antwerp. People were riding on bicycles rather than in cars. Braving the raw cold that had set in, teenage boys were wearing short pants. That was how they flaunted their virility in those days. It all partook, in any case, of the exoticism of our new world.

A train bore us to Frankfurt, where, putting my school German to use, we bought a secondhand VW from a private party who had put a classified ad in the *Frankfurter Allgemeine*. We'd owned a secondhand Volkswagen in Philadelphia. At the time VW's had an aura of being indestructible. As it turned out, the one we bought in Frankfurt would last us for years, and it got us to France.

The war in Europe was fewer than two decades ago, and still very much on people's minds both in Germany and France. As we got off at night at the Frankfurt station, a guy who resembled the weasel-like fellow with the ratty fur collar in *The Third Man* whispered conspiratorially to me: "*Sind sie aus Argentinien gekommen?*" Did I arrive from Argentina? At a bar nearby, where we lunched next day, a more pleasant man ran out and bought a red rose for Joanne when he learned that we were Americans. "Hitler," he volunteered, "had two pistols, and all *we* had were handkerchiefs. So we waved our handkerchiefs." It was a novel interpretation of history, but we accepted the flower and the subtext of apology graciously. In the streets of Frankfurt, there were mutilated men wearing yellow armbands with black dots on them, which, we learned, were the badges of soldiers mutilated during the war. We stayed a day more, ate dumplings with sauerkraut and corned pigs' knuckles, drank good beer, and headed toward Burgundy. The Germans have an expression for bliss: "to live like God himself in France." Collectively, they've aspired to that more than once. Individually, it was going to be our turn to discover elements of truth in that adage.

After we crossed into France through the region known as the Franche-Comté, we got a French side of the story. Driving slowly through the town of Dôle, our Volkswagen bearing German export plates was surrounded by a mob of schoolboys, who began to rock it shouting, "*Boches, bouchers!*" German butchers! It wouldn't be the first time we'd innocently be subjected to scorn in France while driving with our German plates. Hard to believe now. Time heals.

We drove on. We'd decided to come into France passing through Burgundy almost as a whim. We were avid readers of *Gourmet* magazine, rest in peace, and someone had written a story praising the wine of Fixin, a community not far south below Dijon, which he contended was extraordinary, despite its little mention in the litany of great Burgundies. He was particularly taken by the Clos du Chapitre. We drove to Fixin, through a few villages known for the wine that they bottled, but Burgundy was not overwhelmingly attractive. Vineyards are boring to look at, and in winter, as we'd know later, the rows of pruned, barren vines resemble nothing more than a military cemetery. The Clos du Chapitre was closed, and on second thought, the idea of our visiting vineyards in our little old VW on our even more modest budget didn't seem a sensible thing to do. The time would come when, as a journalist again, I would sample several vintages of the breathtakingly wonderful Romanée Conti, at the property, as well as Richebourg, Chambertin, Montrachet, and many other great Burgundy wines, and when Joanne and I would attend, several times, the noted auctions of the year's best crops, at the Hospices de Beaune, with their memorable accompanying banquets.

We settled for a delicious lunch in Fixin, at a restaurant called Chez Jeannette, which announced a twelve-franc *prix fixe* meal on a board outside. Twelve francs each came to $4.80 for the two of us, a sizeable portion of our daily budget, which we had fixed at $10. We had brought along a guidebook by a man who became very rich inspiring a generation of young travelers with a passion for discovery beyond their very modest means. It was called *Europe on $5 a Day*, and we had pledged to keep to that figure.

It was our first real lunch in France, after a pasty *blanquette de veau* in the town of Dôle—a place worth forgetting—having crossed into France from Switzerland. It was delicious. A hare *pâté*, an unctuous *coq au vin*, a very assertive cheese called *époisses*, which contrasted well with the crisp salad, a slice of decent apple pie, the way the French like to do it, with a thin crust and a bit of applesauce under the apples. We drank an open red wine that the *patron* said came from the village. It was faint and undistinguished, but it added a positive touch to the food in any case. We would come to learn that our host couldn't be much blamed for the wine. Many of the wines in Burgundy are undistinguished, but a handful are heavenly. Thus the town of Gévry-Chambertin, which was once called just Gévry, with a few fine vineyards, including the excellent Clos de Bèze, gets a bigger rub-off in reputation from the extraordinary Le Chambertin, a wine that Napoléon Bonaparte loved, even though he added water when he drank it. There is a great distance in quality between most wine from Gévry-Chambertin, good but not wonderful, and Le Chambertin, compared to the proximity of their vineyards. Proper red Burgundy comes from a single grape, the *pinot noir*. It is a very delicate grape, with a pale juice, vulnerable to disturbances in climate, and because it is not blended with other grapes as the varietals of Bordeaux are blended, its flaws are hard to correct. You can understand why the region long suffered a reputation for wines adulterated with sugar and heady Algerian wine, a reputation that kept the region under a cloud for much of the twentieth century, until a wine and travel writer born in Spearfish, South Dakota, named

Frank Schoonmaker came to Burgundy and applauded the owners of parcels of great vineyards, who carefully bottled their own wines rather than giving them to merchant/shippers. I'd come to know descendants of those devoted souls.

We were in a hurry to get to Paris. We had a good friend there, Paul Schwartz, who was writing about art for the Paris edition of *The New York Times*. Paul had been spending time in France since he was a teenager. His father, Manfred Schwartz, had once lived as a painter there, in the circle of artists that included Matisse and Picasso. Paul would be a help in our finding our place in what, with all its qualities, was surely an intimidating city, with denizens impatient toward halting French. We settled into the little Hôtel Saint Sulpice, a clean and comfortable place on the Left Bank in the rue Casimir Delavigne, a few steps away from the ancient Odéon theater: 22 francs ($4.40) per night including two breakfasts.

If that seems a figure hard to believe, believe that the dollar was regal in those days, when the rate was a steady five francs to one. Beyond the exchange rates, the cost of living was far cheaper in Europe than the United States, a fact that encouraged many creative and intelligent people to cross the ocean, until the matter went into reverse.

We two were in Paris at last, but a big thought had been weighing on our minds. Insouciance had its limits. What would happen when we'd be three? I was going to be a father and I had no work. I told Joanne I should go to the Paris *Herald Tribune* and ask for a job. The day before I walked in, the economic editor had been fired in a row with Bernie Cutler, the editor in chief, a person not fond of harsh disagreements. The man, whose beat was the economic scene in Europe, was infuriated that his day-to-day accounts about an organization few readers connected with, the European Economic Community, were being spiked. Without him, the show had to go on for the businessmen readers. I had been labor editor for a major

American paper. As Karl Marx had emphasized, labor was inseparably tied to business. Bernie hired me on the spot. I had to break the news gently to Joanne—we'd thought that, with the winter settling in, we could head south and squeeze in a stay someplace warm on the continent.

There would begin, in Paris, a fresh, long story in our lives. For me, it would partly be the tale of the surrogate trencherman.

4

PARIS ON AN EXPENSE ACCOUNT

I did not tarry long at the Paris *Herald Tribune*. It was a place you could be proud to be, for the many interesting people who'd preceded you there, people who were often less devoted to journalism and more attached to a meal ticket allowing them to pursue creative lives in the City of Light. I don't have at hand the roll call of noted Paris *Herald* alumni. Everyone remembers Art Buchwald. I remember that the poet John Ashbery was a proofreader when I was there. An air of bohemianism rather than hard-nosed news hounding characterized the environment. A veteran at the copy desk told me that, in the old days, not long after the war, whenever there wasn't much news, the boys made up stories to fill the paper. I didn't mind the environment at all, but there was a problem: father-to-be was earning $90 a week and Joanne and I were spending more. When a guy I met told me he was leaving

the Paris bureau of Fairchild Publications to be its man in Milan,
I went to see Fairchild's headman in Paris, James Brady.

Jim, rest his soul, was an extraordinary person. John Fairchild
had hired Jim to work for *Women's Wear Daily* shortly after Jim
came home a combat hero from the Korean War. He had written
advertising copy for Macy's before he left for the Marines—a faint
connection to the world of fashion over which John, equally young,
plotted to reign as its ultimate arbiter. But their eyebeams crossed.
John had a basically mischievous, iconoclastic nature that was one
side of him, which was all the same in conflict with his admiration of the mores of the blue bloods, among whose number, despite
the wealth of his family's publishing group, he didn't quite figure.
The Kent School and Princeton brought him close to New York's
upmost, while his sensibility kept alive his detachment. I think of
F. Scott Fitzgerald, the Catholic boy from a modest background in
the Midwest, forever marked by his experience among the WASPs
of his Princeton era, as much in awe of them as critical.

John, who would contribute with his writing to the renown of
the New York restaurant La Grenouille, was not the sort to eat hash,
among the socially registered at 21, with its reverse snobbism of
uninspired food. John is an aesthete, who, at the time I met him, had
his Brooks Brothers suits custom-made without rear trouser pockets
and his shoes shaped to his feet by Lobb. He was discerning about
wine, and during the many times that I would dine with him, I was
impressed by a palate that could perceive the virtues and flaws of a
given lamb chop like no one else. He had unwavering admiration
for the sensuous world of Europe, compared with America, while
he wasn't free of the American remove of relative prudishness. Paris
would be a glorious, notorious, and victorious moment in his life,
and he would retire to live in London.

Jim came from a modest family in Sheepshead Bay, the brother of
a priest. What did they see when their eyebeams crossed? John saw

the Marine, someone with guts who could be his trusted second in his ambition to change the flagship of his family group of industrial papers, *Women's Wear Daily*, informant to the world of corsets, bras, and the Garment (a word that he scorned) District. He aimed to make what he'd rename *WWD* nothing less than the revered and feared Vatican of fashion that it would indeed, in the hands of John and Jim, become.

The family sent John, its heir to hegemony, to Paris. And the world of French Couture sat him in the last rows of its collections. This until sketches he was having sent back to New York—flaunting the talented pen of Kenneth Paul Block—plus the reviews—raves or scathes—of the fashions, began to grab the attention of the American luxury stores and upscale manufacturers, on whom the couturiers depended for selling patterns of their clothes. That was a part of the couture's business as important as its rich private clientele. We're talking about a time before ready-made-clothing designers had made a dent on influencing fashion, when fashion came down into the streets of the world's major cities in the form of reproductions or reflections of the likes of Dior, Chanel, Givenchy, and Balenciaga creations. John courted the talents of the time, wined and dined them, gave them a window on the world with pages of sketches and long articles. Or gossiped against them. When, in his eyes, they flopped, he wrote about it mercilessly. From the young man in the back of the room, he willed himself to be the most important person in the Paris fashion world, someone on whom it would be best to confer special treatment. Soon the designers would give him the privilege of publishing sketches of their new clothes before they were revealed in their collections. The time came for John to return in triumph to New York, take over the company, and do the same thing, and, with his many bureaus, see to it that his power would carry over to the fashion world everywhere. After sending Jim to the Fairchild London bureau, he installed him in Paris.

What did Jim make of John? I never asked him for a serious answer to that. When Capital Cities bought Fairchild and John endorsed someone other than Jim to run the company, Jim broke away and briefly ran *Harper's Bazaar*, before becoming a very successful novelist and columnist. In the end it was Jim's bent as a keen observer that made him interested in the world of fashion and high society. A world of glamour and vanity. Fascinating for an observer who didn't get sucked into it. Truth to tell, though John was more impressed by it than Jim, both were brilliant satirists of their subjects, neither tried to become part of the Tout Paris or the Tout New York while they admired talent. There was a telling paradigm in what Julie Baumgold, writing in *New York* magazine, once depicted: John and Jim taking a plebeian ride through the bowels of the subway to that flower-laden *bonbonnière* of Fashionables who lunch, La Grenouille.

John unfairly considered Jim's departure after decades of collaboration as a betrayal, and the two never spoke again.

Where did I fit in? Jim hired me to replace his second-in-the-bureau who was headed for Milan. He thought that with my background as a journalist for *The Inquirer* and the *Trib*, I could handle that role with competence. The role was reporting for all the other trade papers on the Fairchild roster. To wit, *Electronic News*, *Drug News Weekly*, *Supermarket News*, *Footwear News*, *Home Furnishings Daily*, and *Daily News Record*, as exciting a journal of the men's clothing industry as *WWD* had been for women's clothing, before the big change wrought by John. It meant for me a twenty-dollar-a-week raise, and I'd see what would come next.

I wrote, sometimes not understanding what I was writing, about things I knew nothing about, in particular electronics, and, once in a while, I stumbled on a scoop in its domain. For *Footwear News*, I remember meeting a man in the shoe business whose ambition was to corner the market in South American leather.

"The standard of living in the Soviet Union has gone up," he confided to me, as we enjoyed Argentinian steaks, "and it will get better in all those third world countries where people go around barefoot. I promise you, there is going to be a big shortage of leather."

A promise unfilled, although it made a good story. I don't know whether he lived to see all those canvas and plastic contraptions on people's feet wherever on the globe, but it might be fair to say that there are generations alive now who've never worn leather shoes.

Jim was leaving Paris to join the company in New York, and fate had it that the person from New York whom John and Jim had chosen to be the next Paris bureau chief quickly turned out to be a fish out of water in the City of Light, more at home with the nerds on the *Electronic News* scene than keeping close to the designers of fashion.

Joanne and I spent an evening with John at Régine's insiders' discotheque in Montparnasse, then called New Jimmy's, where we'd become part of the crowd that danced and migrated, late into the night, between Régine's and the other Right Place, Castel's, in Saint-Germain-des-Prés. There was never a line of hopefuls outside either. Nor bouncers. You couldn't hope to enter unless the woman watching the door knew you. At Régine's, where those who couldn't sleep would be treated to spaghetti breakfasts around dawn, you'd find Françoise Sagan alone with a scotch at her table in the entry, while deep inside, Catherine Deneuve, sitting with David Bailey, would be playing with her long blonde hair. A group of *Nouvelle Vague* filmmakers, among them Claude Chabrol and Jane Fonda's onetime husband Roger Vadim, would hang out at the bar chez Castel, making wry comments about the young people passing them on their way downstairs to dance. King Hassan of Morocco's brother, Moulay Abdallah, spent a lot of time at Castel's when he was in Paris, but Jean Castel refused to let the king in. His Royal

Highness arrived at the door with his bodyguards and wanted them to enter with him. Jean refused, unless they left their guns in the car. The king was not amused, and left.

Castel's had a restaurant upstairs, decorated in a swooningly kitsch red Belle Époque style that served classic food, but the young crowd favored a little room on the ground floor called *la loge du concierge,* whose walls were covered with a needlepoint landscape and the sundry tchotchkes of a typical concierge's abode. Here, on the other side of a counter in a tiny open kitchen, a guy prepared food before your eyes, such as *steak au poivre,* or served a *plat du jour,* say, *hachis parmentier,* which Americans call shepherd's pie, but which, like a *boeuf mironton,* you could inhale from concierges' kitchens in Paris. A favorite was *rognons flambés:* The kidneys came in a natural envelope of suet. Our man cut them open, put a bit of the fat in a pan, and hastily sautéed them, before finishing it all off with flaming cognac. Served with freshly peeled shoestring potatoes and a bottle of unadulterated Beaujolais. No concierge in town would have been displeased by it, and for not much more than a concierge could afford. Jean Castel, a former rugby man, was not a natural businessperson; he lived for the prestige, the pleasure, and the inside knowledge that were the rewards of his avuncular role in a rare world. You could keep a bottle of scotch with your name on it chez Castel, for less than it would cost to frequent a nightclub for tourists. Jean died in retirement, having survived night after night of convivial drinking with his people, ever lucid and sharp.

Joanne and I passed some kind of test with John Fairchild that evening when we introduced him to Régine, an ebullient woman, but a discreet person, who knew a lot about her people and never gossiped. People unravel their lives in the wee hours. Régine, who had a humble and war-ravished childhood, became, beyond a *confidante,* a friend to the notables who swept past inspection at the door to New Jimmy's. She was among the invited to one of the historically lavish balls of the century, the Bal à l'orientale given by the Baron de Rédé, Marie-Hélène de Rothschild's boarder at her extraordinary town house, l'Hôtel Lambert. Régine never made it to the ball, because the elephant she'd hired on which to arrive got her lost in the Bois de Boulogne.

Not long after our evening at New Jimmy's, Jim's successor was sent back home, and, with whatever intuition, Jim—who would become a lifelong friend—agreed with John that I could carry the flag for *Women's Wear Daily*. I was anointed the title of European Director of Fairchild Publications, although, truth to tell, no one at Fairchild other than John and Jim directed anything. I was soon making more money than I was spending. Plus an expense account.

Like Jim's, my background was far from the scintillating world I was entering. I could be awed by it and absorb its values, or my distance could be a privilege for seeing it in greater focus. It was unquestionably fascinating. My nature as a writer led me on the latter path.

Where did my education in eating come into all this? Think about what it was like to have an expense account that *required* me to keep in good contact, across the best tables in Paris, with the fashion makers and their business partners—and added to that, to be able to discover the newest, the best restaurants in town, as part of reporting about the city to guide the New York fashion world.

We were at a time when the high and mighty couturiers would begin to see their influence challenged by ready-to-wear designs inspired, in turn, by the fads of the street. And just then, too, the establishment of French cuisine was also on the cusp of a big change. Until all that happened, I not only got to know how excellent in every way Balenciaga, Chanel, and some of their colleagues— learned artisans as well as artists—could be, turning luxurious fabrics into clothing that exalted the body, I also experienced that other phenomenon of high culture, inspired French cuisine, as it had carefully evolved in the history of the nation.

It became obvious to me that the memorable experience of a meal, like the vision of an alluring and elegant woman, reached out beyond the finite experience. Awareness of place and of how what was there got there, counted greatly.

Eating out is a form of communion with a culture.

Great culinary experiences, as I would come to know them, are more than the activity of a critical taster.

I had leave to eat in any restaurant in town on John Fairchild's family money, but not all my meals with the people with whom I was obliged to keep in contact were on the town. Two key persons on my beat rarely ate in public: Coco Chanel and Yves Saint Laurent.

Coco had an apartment above her couture house next to the building that housed my office, with several rooms except a bedroom. She slept across the street at the Ritz. I was told that living in the hotel, she avoided having a French residence and French taxes, preferring a more lenient arrangement with the Swiss. She had a house in Lausanne. In any case, dinner or lunch with Coco was always in the flat above the store. Vodka to start with and Krug champagne throughout the meal were the two constants of those dinners. The food was unelaborated and of first quality. The leg of lamb was unsurpassed. François, her maître d'hôtel, before eventually becoming Coco's bridge partner and jewelry designer, whispered to me once that it was a joint of hard-to-find *agneau de pré salé,* with flesh reminiscent of the salt flats on which the lambs grazed near Mont Saint Michel. Coco would talk nearly nonstop through the dinner, usually belittling the other couturiers for their vulgarity. She would pause to remove a necklace of costume jewelry or a scarf from her neck and bestow it on another woman at the table. Joanne was among the recipients of those gestures. After dinner we would walk with her across the street to the Ritz, and she would hold our hands and, no matter how inclement the weather, chatter for an hour more. We understood that Coco was pitifully lonely. The woman who had been much more intimate than we with Grand Duke Dmitri, the Duke of Westminster, Boy Capel, and other glamorous figures of high European society was holding our hands, rather than going off to her lonely bed. . . .

A handful of the press was admitted, in those days, to the couture shows for private clients and for buyers from New York stores or factories who came to follow the dictates of Paris fashion. The skill the latter had at their craft came home to me during my first season of collections, with John and Jim in town. *Women's Wear* was barred from attending the collection of Cristóbal Balenciaga. It wasn't that John had panned Balenciaga's monumental talent. A personal matter had caused the rift. Although John never printed what he was supposed to have said, word had got back to the dignified Spanish designer that John had told a story about him and his beloved dog. To wit, that when walking his dog, Balenciaga always finished why they were there by wiping the canine's rear with his silken handkerchief. As we learned from our own sources in the Tout Paris grapevine, the story, true or false, was perhaps spread by Marie-Louise Bousquet, a fashion critic and also someone who held court in one of the important salons of the city. There were still salons in those days. She was an eccentric woman who liked to wear an alarm clock around her neck as a memento of her young years as a mascot of the Dada movement. Things got more complicated when somehow Balenciaga was given to believe that Coco Chanel, his good friend, who admired him—a rarity in her opinion of her colleagues—had spread the story too.

"If he believes that I would be capable of saying that about him, I never want to see him again," Coco told Jim. She never did. As for Marie-Louise Bousquet, Coco's description was: "Mouth like a sewer, talks like a sewing machine."

John was not too panicked by being barred from the Balenciaga collection. He knew that Balenciaga's salon would be full of buyers with photographic memories, even though sketching was not allowed during a couture collection and it would be years before I would negotiate with the couturiers' association for the presence of a single photographer at the collections, on the strength of *Women's Wear's* influence among the buyers. (There are hundreds of photographers at the collections these days.) The buyers were admitted for a fee of about $2,000 for a right to see the collection, or bought patterns to do line-for-line reproductions of the models. That was how fashion for the many took its cues from what the high designers created for the privileged few in those days.

Right after Balenciaga showed, we hurried with Kenneth Paul Block to the room at the Ritz of a man from Bergdorf Goodman. He sat on his bed and from memory sketched the entire collection for Kenneth, who'd redo the sketches that John felt belonged in several pages of the paper. Next day, we wrote about and illustrated the collection as if we'd been there. The buyer had been sent to Paris and put up at the Ritz, with the others from Bergdorf, just to purchase hats, but he knew fashion. His name was Halston Frowick, and before he died a premature death, Halston would rise to be a major figure on the New York fashion scene.

I never got to see a live Balenciaga collection, although I'd seen a lot of ladies in his restrained but sensuous clothes. *WWD* never got a pardon from the master, but in my role as the good cop in the trio we represented, I often smoothed the ruffled feathers of those John did not flatter. Hubert de Givenchy, a close friend of Balenciaga, had showed his loyalty by barring *Women's Wear* as well. Over lunch at the Relais Plaza, I made peace with Hubert. I met several times with André Courrèges and got *WWD* back into his collections, where we were not the only ones who had been barred. Revolted that his hard-edge white designs were a huge success all over the Western world, in the form of copies, Courrèges decided to ban all press from his collections, buyers as well, and admit only the private customers that he was sure were legit. He was driven with bitterness even to ask Baroness Marie-Hélène de Rothschild—who would get gifts of clothes just for her presence at other collections—to show her identity papers at the door. Courrèges did not lack self-esteem, although he was, perhaps, short on understanding ridiculousness.

When Courrèges's colleague Pierre Balmain, who shared the same building with him, was asked on TV if they'd ever crossed paths, Balmain replied that he'd seen a guy in a pink jumpsuit (one of Courrèges's futurist designs), but "I thought he worked at the filling station out front."

Courrèges defied French legislature, which then required children to be given saints' names, when he named his daughter Clafoutis, a country dish like a fruit pudding and a cake.

John Fairchild had once, incidentally, printed something about Baroness Marie-Hélène de Rothschild that was displeasing, and it became my mission to assuage her over tea and sympathy in her splendid town house. She was a woman with great charm despite her looks and an illness that deformed her hands, swelling her knuckles. She wore, nonetheless, many precious rings. Unrelated to my mission, someone nasty in the Tout Paris would say that she had "burglar-proof fingers." La Baronne Guy was a smart and perceptive woman whose intelligence might have been numbed among the oxygen-scarce heights of the Paris social scene, where the word in French for its socialites is *mondain*, worldly, and where they don't get the irony of the term.

The buyers themselves were not shy to opine about collections that displeased them. I was sitting beside Jack Lazar during one of Emanuel Ungaro's collections in his couture house, where the models paraded through two rooms. In the first, there were all of Emanuel's friends, including Lauren Bacall; in the second, there were the press and the buyers. Jack owned a knitwear company called Originala, which reproduced the originals of the couture, and he'd hope to find part of his line at Ungaro. The models passed first through the room full of friends, where there would be huge applause, but when they entered the room with the press and buyers, there was leaden silence. It was a dismal collection of ill-matched, droopy prints. As a model passed near us while the applause in the next room still went on, Jack leaned over to me and said, "I wonder what he's showing them in the next room."

Yves Saint Laurent was almost pathologically shy, although he knew his own worth, and, as I said, only seldom was seen on the town. You would sometimes find him late at night at Le Club 7, a restaurant that served excellent and simple food to a trendy, restricted clientele.

Once Joanne and I were lunching at the table next to Yves and his partner, Pierre Bergé, in a restaurant of fleeting in-ness called L'Assomoir, in Montmartre. Aside from movie-world people who have a community up there, fashionable Parisians didn't brush with the tourists on Montmartre, but because someone in the fashion world had, I think, a crush on the owner, L'Assomoir was the restaurant of the moment, serving, again, plain, old-fashioned food, such as *poulet au vinaigre*, a classic dish tastier than it sounds. Pierre and Yves had stirred out on a quiet Sunday. After we'd exchanged greetings, our son, André, who was very young, went up to Yves. "Are you Coco Chanel?" he asked. Yves blushed, I think with pleasure. Of all his predecessors, Coco was the one Yves most admired for her devotion to making women look good in their clothes.

John Fairchild was always in and out of good terms with the couturiers, and barred often from attending a designer's collection if he'd panned the previous one. Yet *Women's Wear* stood by Coco and her repetitive landmark style when the rest of the press was looking for more titillation in fashion. The paper also had close relations with certain buyers, whose opinions John respected greatly, enabling us accurately to predict what new fashions would be successful with American women. Among John's favorites was a woman with a sure eye for what women want in dresses. John and Jim wanted to show their esteem for her, and so I arranged to make her a gift of something she'd often mentioned as her dream: dinner with Coco Chanel. She was in from New York for the collections as was Jim, when Joanne and I arranged a dinner with them chez Coco.

Our friend was so awed by the event that she was nearly shaking, steadying herself with Coco's Stolichnaya as the evening began. From there to many glasses of Krug. In the middle of dinner, she had what the French call a *malaise*. No one saw fit to take notice of how often her glass was filled by François. A woman can have a *malaise* for many reasons. Joanne helped her up from the table and escorted her to the bathroom, where her condition got worse as she breathed the effluvia of Chanel No. 5 that the bathroom ventilator was designed to waft. Miraculously, she made it back to the table and her condition improved. Coco was very solicitous and you would not have thought that Mademoiselle Chanel was at all surprised that a woman could get into that state of nervousness over being in her fabled presence.

Next afternoon I went round to see Coco. Serge Lifar, the veteran brilliant dancer of the prewar Ballets Russes, which she'd subsidized and for which she'd done costumes, was sitting on her lap, as I'd seen him do before. He'd come to borrow money, as he'd done before. After he left, I wasn't able to open, gingerly, the matter of last evening, before she said:

"I had one fear about all that. I was afraid that woman would throw up on my carpet, and I'd never be able to use that room again."

Big disappointments in her *vie sentimentale* had hardened Mademoiselle's manners. Privileged to watch her work, I'd known her to drive her assistants to tears with her aggressive perfectionism. But she also had a generous side to her nature. When in 1968, people were saying that the street turmoil was heading for "a revolution," she told me over lunch: "The Cadillac will be downstairs." (I don't know of anyone else who had a Cadillac in Paris in those days.) "You'll bring your wife and son, and we'll drive to Switzerland."

My lunches with Yves Saint Laurent and Pierre Bergé, about the time we became acquainted, would habitually take place in their apartment in the Place Vauban, across the square from where Napoléon Bonaparte lay in state in the church of the Invalides. The flat was full of paintings by Bernard Buffet, who had been Bergé's protégé and lover before Buffet ran off with a woman named Annabelle. Bergé rose far above his chagrin when he and Yves fell in love. He would be the tough, shrewd force behind the ascension of Yves's talent.

Not long after we met, they would get rid of the Buffets or hide them and move on to a more sumptuous flat in the nearby rue de Babylone, and their taste would go beyond Buffet's brittle images to a collection of works of art that Bergé would auction off after Yves's death for about a half billion dollars.

When I met them, Yves and Pierre were the employees of Dick Salomon, heir to the Charles of the Ritz cosmetic fortune, philanthropist and overall mensch as the word is philosophically defined. When Saint Laurent had been fired from designing for Dior, friends found an Atlanta, Georgia, banker to create a house in his name. It was common practice in those days for couturiers to have backers who owned the house. Chanel never owned hers. The banker, J. Mack Robinson, sold the house of Saint Laurent to Salomon, who finally facilitated Yves' and Pierre's owning it themselves, after he sold his own business to Squibb. Dick went on to dabble with design by putting money behind a guy in New York creating armchairs out of old cardboard boxes. They quarreled and went separate ways. The man's name was Frank Gehry.

It is easy to remember what I ate with Yves and Pierre. Over and over, roast veal. Yves would order that to be his lunch day after day. It wasn't that he had an obsessive love of roast veal; he rather had little interest in what he ate. But his devotion to quality that would be a trademark of his creativity was not lost with that monotonous choice. Veal, like lamb, is a dish with a range of subtle differences in quality. The best, which we always had, comes from little beasts raised on the milk from their mother's teats. Their flesh is pink, not white like the anemic flesh the Italians fancy. Its subtle yet pronounced flavor is incomparable.

Pierre had none of Yves's reluctance to eat in public, and he and I would often lunch tête-à-tête, discussing literature and politics— a break from fashion. Pierre believed in a longtime hopeful in the Socialist party named François Mitterrand. I was nostalgic over Charles de Gaulle, who had despised Mitterrand. When Mitterrand at last made it to the top, Pierre had become a close friend of his. They would dine often at Le Pichet de Paris, an obscure, old-fashioned restaurant off the Champs-Élysées, not far from the presidential palace. They would chow down on raw seafood and a rare rib steak for two. I won't reveal my source, but I understand that President Mitterrand never picked up the check.

Pierre is brilliant and once envisioned a literary career before succeeding, with his unconventional prowess, in asserting his will in business, first for Buffet and then for Yves. He was among the few people who, as a very young man, would go out to the suburb of Meudon, to pay homage to Céline, an immortal figure of French writing, despite a reputation badly stained by his delirious anti-Semitism and collaboration with the Nazis. Pierre and I would meet regularly at the right restaurants for fashionable Paris: Maxim's and the Relais Plaza. We were also curious about exploring the restaurant scene elsewhere.

There was Jamin, a few steps from where I lived on avenue Kléber in the Sixteenth Arrondissement. Jamin was not the owner's name;

it was the name of a horse. The owner, whose own name I forget, won a big long bet on a trotter named Jamin—enough money for him to open the restaurant. He was a man from Bordeaux, whose menu made that clear, and whose manners had the conservatism of the Bordeaux upper crust, who speak French with English accents.

By then, my own French had improved greatly, greatly enough for him unsuspectingly to slur the palates of Americans in chatting with Pierre and me. "Everything the Americans eat comes out of a can," he said. "Monsieur," I replied, "I am American, and indeed I go nowhere without my can opener."

The *lamproie à la bordelaise* the man served me, the first dish of potted lampreys I'd ever eaten, came out of a can. You need live lampreys to make your own *lamproie à la bordelaise*, and where are you going to get live lampreys in Paris? Years later, as we'll see, I'd learn that lamprey aficionados in the Bordeaux region greatly preferred canned or jarred lampreys to a fresh dish, with the belief that the the flavor of the wine and blood sauce improved over a few years, like Bordeaux wine.

One of Jamin's cooks was a man named Joël Robuchon, who would, of course, later rise to fame among the torchbearers of *la nouvelle cuisine*. More fondly than the lampreys, I remember Jamin's truffle omelets. After you were served your omelet starter speckled with black truffles, the owner would come round with a whole truffle and shave much of it onto your dish. Nowadays, the cost of the favored variety of black truffles in a dish like that would strain a platinum bank card. You see preserved truffle garnishing and truffle sauces on trendy menus, but I'm willing to declare by experience that only fresh truffles have any culinary value. Truffles give off their essence into the air like an open bottle of perfume. Henry James knew that when he wrote about eating eggs flavored with truffles: You put the raw eggs, shell and all, into a basket with fresh truffles, and you cover them. After a while you can do what you want with the truffles—throw them away—their entire flavor has gone through the eggshells into the eggs, and you can do what you want with the eggs; they'll be delicious.

In those days, I would go to Milan for the fashions and always bring home a good handful of white truffles without spending a huge sum of money. They've become much more expensive now, and still compete well with the black for flavor for the buck. I remember a batch of them going rotten when Joanne and I put off deciding what to prepare them with. It wasn't as if we'd thrown a fortune out the window while not having even enjoyed those luscious parasites of the vegetable world, whose taste would come back into your mouth, long after you'd eaten them.

There were other restaurants the Good Crowd of Paris attended. I was the first English-language journalist to my knowledge to write about L'Ami Louis, which would become a superexpensive Mecca for rich gluttons, as often American as French. I first went there introduced by Jacques Rouët, president of Dior and one of the most knowledgeable gourmets in town, with two huge and extraordinary personal wine cellars. Rouët was a member of Le Club des Cent, a club of high-powered people who shared an interest in high eating, limited to one hundred members.

Rouët's travels for Dior brought him often to New York, where he would buy cases of great French Bordeaux at Sherry Wine and Spirits, for less money, shipping included, than they'd cost in Paris. Rouët inevitably came out ahead because of the difference in taxes and the fact that Sherry catered to knowledgeable wine drinkers who were nevertheless not yet succeeded by those who were happy to pay high prices to consume conspicuously. With Rouët, on an afternoon in his Paris cellar, I sampled two bottles of '59 Branaire Ducru, one that had been bottled at the château in Saint Julien, Bordeaux, and the other that had been bought in the barrel, or *barrique,* by the London merchants Justerini and Brooks, who do J&B scotch.

As late as that year, some of the fine châteaux were still selling their wine to the British before bottling. J&B, perhaps less bothered by cash flow, had held off bottling much longer. Rouët was the first to pronounce that the wine that had aged longer in the wood in London was subtler and rounder than its French twin. The British, whose ties to Aquitaine go back to the Hundred Years' War, in the fourteenth and fifteenth centuries, know their claret perhaps better than anyone, and probably the only place you might have found a better cellar than those of Rouët would have been at a London club. The names of some of the noted Bordeaux vineyards recall anglo-saxon owners, names such as Lurton, Smith, and Brown. And among the *chartrons*, the tradition-imbued wine merchants in the city of Bordeaux, it is indeed *bon ton* to speak French with a clipped British intonation. . . .

Joanne and I, shortly after we met Monsieur Rouët—I don't know who called him Jacques, except, perhaps, for his lovely Swedish wife—went with him on a tour of drinking wine and eating at the best châteaux in Bordeaux, where his good friends received us, with, alas for our own livers, *foie gras* as a starter at almost every meal.

Driving down with Rouët's chauffeur, we stopped at a café in the Loire valley, to snack on an extraordinary cinder-coated goat's cheese. I don't know when Rouët, the consummate gourmet, had filed away that address. We spent the night at the château of the Comte de Billy, where the family had hidden treasures of the Louvre during the war. The count and countess, from that family of American lovers, were very warm hosts. I remember the *truite au bleu* that was part of our dinner, a rare wild trout from the neighboring stream. Farmed trout are insipid in comparison. Joanne and I slept in a four-poster, where figures in history had slept before.

Some time later, Monsieur Rouët and I went down to Château Ausone, so that he could have the corks replaced on the bottles of Ausone '29 from his cellar, a process that perforce included topping up the bottles with newer wine from Ausone, pace purists. We left the bottles, and after sharing a bottle of '59 with the cellar master, in the deep limestone *caves* of the château, the only deep cellars in the region, we were off to a lot of less celebrated vineyards that Rouët thought were underrated. At Château Olivier, the owner, at lunch, gave us a bottle from a vineyard that his family once owned. It was an esteemed Château Gruaud Larose. Its year was 1864, harvested from vines before they had to be grafted with American shoots, to rescue them from phylloxera. It was the oldest wine I've ever drunk, and just a pink and watery ghost of itself.

The next oldest, a Mouton Rothschild 1874, which I once drank with Baron Philippe de Rothschild at Mouton, was, on the contrary, still vivid.

Wines have lives, like people, and are perhaps as equally complex.

5

A DETOUR AMONG THE VINES

The memory of that bottle of 1874 Mouton brings back a flood of others about food, precious wine, and exceptional people, all of it centered around Château Mouton Rothschild, that Shangri-la of suave elegance that belonged to Baron Philippe and his American wife, Pauline. At Mouton, Pauline and Philippe had shunned his inherited little hussy of a Napoléon III manor, and instead they'd transformed a vast wine shed into a beautiful home and haven for exquisite hospitality. They would not only invite persons they liked or admired to stay at Mouton, the invitation sometimes came, for those in other countries and less financially privileged, accompanied by plane tickets. I remember being there when Stephen Spender and his wife were in from England, and on another occasion when David Hockney was there to grace a label of Mouton with his talent. Raymond Mortimer, the noted British critic and writer, was a favorite guest. Philippe, with his love of English literature, was an unconditional Anglophile. For those ensconced at Mouton, eating off *famille rose* precious antique china, or having the Lapsong

Souchong tea with your breakfast in bed come in an eighteenth-century English silver pot, were part of the ultrarefined routine. The croissants came open and toasted, soaked in butter, and with them there was jam from black currants grown on the estate, which also provided an extraordinary *crème de cassis* liqueur, made for private consumption. Philippe would have his breakfast in bed last until late morning, while he translated Elizabethan poetry into French. Four soft-boiled eggs would arrive on his tray, and he would open each of them and eat the one that was cooked the closest to his liking.

The daily eating and drinking at Mouton would be lifetime experiences.

I had become acquainted with Pauline and Philippe through John Fairchild, and I had spent time with them on several occasions at Mouton, as well as at the castle that they rented for the summer on an island in Denmark. Their fare was the repertoire of a gentleman named Mesmin, who had begun his service to Pauline as a general handyman. Pauline somehow saw a great chef in him, and that he did become, after Pauline, an obsessive perfectionist, taught him what she knew, having lived with a grandmother in Baltimore for whom cuisine mattered greatly. In Paris, she was known to have had Mesmin prepare rice seven days in a row, so that it would be perfect on the eighth try for her dinner party.

At Mouton, the bass from the nearby Atlantic would come with black peppercorns and a *sauce mousseline*—hollandaise rendered more delicate by folded-in, unsweetened whipped cream. There was often lamb from the neighboring Pauillac salt flats, and the leftover roast of the evening would become *hachis parmentier*, savory shepherd's pie, at lunch the next day.

Philippe was more lavish than that in the wine he served—although, having created an oversized decanter of his own design he would often re-serve wine that had been opened at lunch with dinner, its personality preserved intact thanks somehow to his invention. Such, though, was not the practice when he treated his guests to the rarest wines from his heterogeneous cellar of Bordeaux, which had been built up over the generations when the great château owners of the region would exchange cases every year. I remember the 1911 Haut Brion, venerable Moutons after Moutons—among them a '43 that the wine world had given up on as a badly harvested wartime vintage, but which had survived to a distinguished old age. Once, egged on by his fellow diners, Philippe served a Lafite Rothschild, despite his quarrels with his cousins who owned that vineyard across a dirt path from his. Philippe had been trying for years to change the prevailing 1855 Classification of Bordeaux wines so as to have Mouton elevated from a second growth to a first growth, such as Lafite. He eventually achieved his goal, although his jealous cousins had used all their influence to block him. Philippe had retaliated by trying to have a refinery owned by Shell, in which they were major shareholders, moved from where it stood on the Gironde River and where, Philippe maintained, its fumes were pol- luting the vines of the region.

The rift between the Rothschilds was repaired by Philippe's daughter, the sometime actress Philippine, after his death. Philippine, the plain daughter of an earlier marriage to the only Rothschild who died in a concentration camp (and who wasn't Jewish), had her own antipathy to her stepmother Pauline's exquisite and expensive elegance. Philippe had changed the name of an adjacent vintage that he owned from Château d'Armailhacq to Château Baronne Philippe in Pauline's honor. With Philippe and Pauline gone, Philippine changed the name back again, and moved her family into the manor on which Pauline had looked down, for its heavy fussiness. The wine, in any case, was not close to a first growth.

The Lafite to which Philippe treated us, provoked into that moment of truce with the neighbors, was a 1914, quite healthy still, and even he admitted its clean while complex merits. Like Philippe with his soft-boiled eggs, Raoul, his cellar master, would often open four ancient bottles to be able to bring to table the one whose contents were still alive.

After dinner at Mouton, desserts—do I remember a perfect *tarte tatin?*—came with Château d'Yquem from the 1920s, served so cold it was well on its way to sherbet. I was told that Pauline had taught Philippe that imaginative way of serving Yquem. But the then owner of that grandest of all sweet white wines had been lobbying against allowing Mouton to join the club of first-growth Bordeaux. Philippe the poet might have been treating Yquem that way as a metaphor for humbling its grandeur. It was all the same delicious.

Oh yes, the 1874. I was staying at Mouton a while after Pauline had passed away, going over her papers for a biography I never completed. She had nothing in her life about which to be ashamed, but she'd left behind years of anguish and disappointments when she met Philippe at a party in New York and stole his heart by saying, "Ah, the poet among the Rothschilds." I was inhabited by a strong intuition that Pauline, one of the most discreet women you could meet, would not have wanted her whole life reeled out in a story told by someone else, and I dropped the project, not without having been fascinated by some of her intimate correspondence with such people as Isak Dinesen and Somerset Maugham. She had been an old chum of Louie, wife of Harry Hopkins, who was so close to FDR that the Hopkinses lived with him and Eleanor in the White House. I remember reading Louie's frustration over Eleanor's fondness for hot dog dinners, an expression, perhaps, of her ideological modesty.

Joan Littlewood, the great British theater director, was living at Mouton after Pauline had died. She had been traveling in France with the man of her life, Gerry Raffles, and had stopped in Vienne in the south, to enjoy a great meal at Fernand Point's noted restaurant. Raffles died of a heart attack soon afterward, and Joan was so grieved that she was pining away, unable to move, at a hotel in Vienne when

Philippe, who had just lost Pauline, was told about her distress. He drove his Mercedes from Pauillac to Vienne, picked her up, and took her to live at Mouton. The trip no doubt shook her out of her torpor, since Philippe, who had raced competively in his youth, still drove everywhere as if he were on the track at Le Mans.

If that gesture was a stellar example of Philippe's astute hospitality, he was at the same time resistant to the many blandishments of people hopeful to know Mouton. However, the day came, while I was down there, when the Japanese ambassador called up and announced that he was coming to lunch. He was touring the Bordeaux region with the head of the Japanese Diet, its parliament, anxious, it seemed, to show off his intimacy with the best of French mores. Joan, feisty and frank as she was, told Philippe to tell him to bugger off. But Philippe decided that he would belittle the ambassador's peremptory gesture with his own magnanimity: He would do a memorable lunch. Memorable it turned out to be, although, alas, I forget the menu, as well as three of the four wines served. I gave the printed menu card to my daughter, Larisa, whose passion in life is fine art, and, impressed by neither grand wines nor barons, she misplaced it. But I have not forgotten the 1874. Perhaps, alas, again, because the guests' appreciation of it that day was marred.

At table with us was the curator of the Bordeaux Museum of Fine Arts, who, despite her local upbringing, was not used to drinking much wine, and certainly not four fine ones at lunch. She fell into a swoon, and had to be laid out to rest on the Queen Anne couch near our table. Fortunately, the president of the Diet had been a medical doctor. It sufficed to wake him up, since, unused, as well, to wine, he was snoring at the table. It all ended with his massaging the lady's wrists until she reached consciousness, and in a few minutes, we were all down on the lawn below, where the ambassador took the baron's picture and drove off.

While I was writing this, Simon Davies, the distinguished marketing director of Fine and Rare Wines, London, told me that he knew of one bottle still around of the 1874 Mouton, which, although he could give no guarantee, might yet be eminently drinkable. You could try it by buying it at his website, at the pound equivalent of $10,941.05.

The 1874 at that lunch? Delicious, bright, complex. A miraculous survivor. But Mouton was a magical place where miracles could seem natural.

Philippe took a constitutional walk with his Labradors every day, and I would accompany him beside the bordering vineyards, some of whose names meant nothing among noted Bordeaux wines. Once we paused where depressions in the soil among the vines looked as if a mass grave had been dug and had sunken afterward. The baron explained that those scars were witnesses of the Great Depression. "Things were so bad for some people here," he said, "they couldn't sell their wine. They were so desperate that they sold their soil for gravel."

The soil of the vineyards of Pauillac, renowned for producing a few of Bordeaux's greatest wines, appears to be more gravel than dirt. And it's largely this, the winemakers believe, that gives their grapes unequalled quality, although there are a number of Pauillac vineyards that are, all things taken into account, unequal to the grandees such as Mouton and Lafite. These modest neighbors had been most hit by the Great Depression.

The gravel's minerals impart their share of benefit to the wines of Pauillac and to fine wines in general. Even more generally, superior wine is paradoxically born of austerity and many forms of hardship. Gravel instead of fertilizer. Vines crowded in close rows to limit their growth and their productivity, and trimmed sharply. Hot, parched summers that stunt the grapes, and make them dense in sugar. These make up earth's nursery of great wine. They say of dry, hot summers in Bordeaux that "the vines suffer" and, sadists if you will, they're delighted by that.

After the sixties, when the social structure of the developed countries was shaken up by new ways to wealth, the world of wine, Bordeaux included, changed drastically. For some, the era that brought a host of new people to drinking wine for pleasure and prestige—the nabobs of China and Japan among them—can be called a renaissance. But that's far from a term used unanimously in the wine world of France.

Years after my days at Mouton, I met the man most praised and also most blamed for the change, Emile Peynaud. We met during his retirement at his home in a surburb of the city of Bordeaux. Peynaud was a professor of enology at Bordeaux University, who, in the 1950s, together with his mentor, Jean-Ribéreau Gayon, discovered maleolactic fermentation. Peynaud, a sturdy man who lived to the age of ninety-two, was born and reared in the Madiran region, where they make a frank, solid wine, which nicely cuts the fat in peasant food. Scientific studies have found it richest of all wines in antioxidants, thanks to the tannat grape; those studies add to explaining why people down there stay healthy for a long time, eating heavy food, while leading relatively unstressful lives.

At the age of fifteen, Peynaud began working for the Bordeaux merchants Calvet, but he went on to earn his doctorate at Bordeaux University's Institut d'Oenology, where he studied under Gayon, with whom he had judged wines at Calvet.

"For years," Peynaud explained to me, "the wine would start fermenting again after it was assumed to repose in the barrels or a second vat. No one had explained why. We revealed that it was special bacteria, not anything else, that caused that, and we demonstrated how, under good hygienic conditions, this was a highly positive thing in the vinification process, softening the wine."

If you want to know what softening of wine can mean, drink the Beaujolais nouveau that traditionally gets drunk ceremoniously in the cafés of France the third Thursday in November, before any maleolactic fermentation can take place. Your palate and perhaps your stomach will know what rough means.

Peynaud went on to be the major figure in promoting wine-making as a careful application of chemistry beyond tradition and lore. I met him to do a profile that Tom Hoving, the controversial, ebullient former director of the Metropolitan Museum of Art, had asked me to do for *Connoisseur*, the magazine that he'd taken over. By then winemakers in various parts of the world growing merlot and cabernet sauvignon grapes were claiming to equal or surpass the wines from the gravely vineyards of Bordeaux. Peynaud himself had become a successful consultant, offering something like key-in-hand to vineyards. In my travels I'd visited Château Carras, in the north of Greece, created from scratch by a shipping magnate with that surname whom I'd met, and designed by Peynaud. He had also been the prime mover in a major change among the Rioja wines of Spain. Peynaud's alchemy reached a height with his collaboration on creating Sassicaia in Tuscany, with French cabernet sauvignon and cabernet franc varietals. Joanne and I drank Sassicaia only once, after it became a star in grand Italian restaurants. It was delicious, but for us it lacked the depth of fine Bordeaux whose flavors extend like the wake of a perfume. In a way it was the lively ghost of a Bordeaux, as close to the real thing in many ways as a knock-off can get. In a way it was eerie.

Post-Peynaud enologists from all over, in particular the graduates of Davis in California, were soon into the development of a new version of wine applicable to all varietals. It was wine for the changed, newcomers' market, a wine quickly understandable, a wine that you drank without its having been lain down for a long time, a highly expensive process for a winegrower. It was, to say it provocatively, a wine for those who previously knew and liked what juice and soda tasted like and what a jolt of alcohol felt like. They could also appreciate the easily identifiable vanilla-like taste of oak that new barrels could provide and that oak chips thrown in—as done at the lower end of this market—could do even better.

Peynaud was the authority who may have given what they asked for to some clients who knew what the market wanted, although he never stood on principle for superficial new wines. The first asset of his methodology was the quality and the cleanliness of the grapes, after which came precisely controlled vinification. I remember his having expressed regret that much wine being marketed was losing its rare presence as the subtlest of beverages in civilization. He did honor the credentials of young wine from cleanly harvested late-maturing grapes. Peynaud's Pandora's box was a vinification process that he promulgated called carbonic maceration. It involves macerating the grapes uncrushed in vats topped with carbon dioxide. The resulting wine, with the grape flavor preserved, could be a juice plus alcohol combination that pleased a lot of palates. Conservatives scorn it as "jammy."

In his book, *Knowing and Making Wine*, Peynaud goes on the record with a refrain of caution over the technique:

"The enhancement of the aroma, its originality, and the loss of specific varietal flavors may offend tasters accustomed to the classical styles in quality wine-growing areas. On the other hand the improvement is very plain for certain mediocre varieties. . . . It is beneficial for preparing semifine wines to be drunk young. Wines in this way keep their agreeable character during the first year but do not withstand aging well and lose their special fruity qualities."

I'm not qualified to say that all or most of the contemporary wines seeking to go from the minors to the majors rely on carbonic maceration. This said, in Bordeaux there are the "garage wines" that have commanded great publicity in the wine world and top prices—with the ambition of belittling the great, classified châteaux. And these are potpourris of forceful flavor and high in alcohol. Revamping obscure vineyards, the *garagistes* create what their fans call "blockbuster" wines. For other than their fans, these are caricatures, but to high rollers, say, from Silicon Valley, they may seem the height of technical achievement.

I remember Christian Millau's parting words after we talked about *la cuisine*: "In the end, it all comes down to two things, the media and the money."

Last I heard, the garage wines might be becoming a passing fad. If I correctly read the wine list of that epicures' El Dorado in California, the French Laundry, I noticed only one famous garage-type wine, a Château Valandraud, and its sibling Virginie de Valandraud, inserted in a long roll call of hallowed Bordeaux reds.

Robert Parker, the lawyer turned wine writer, who made his taste buds a fearful benchmark for quality in wine with his passion for full-mouthed, alcoholic wines, appears to show signs of turning more traditional in his predilections. But I confess not to have a constant hand on the pulse of the wine world, and I won't declare myself a wine authority. Philippe de Rothschild used to tell me that you have to have been drinking great wine all your life to understand truly the intimate revelations of great wine. He could afford to talk. Parker has been racing through vineyards since the seventies, tasting a hundred wines a day and giving each five seconds of his palate. He says that this tells him all. I know resentful winegrowers whose sales have been badly hit, or who live in dread of that happening, because of coming up short on a Parker report card. They contend that no matter whether you spit out the wine you taste or not, the alcohol absorbed through the lining of your mouth makes truly tasting a hundred wines in a day physically impossible. Don't ask me, but it seems to me that there's a difference between the quickie of five seconds in the mouth and the seductive charm of a great bottle of wine. If you allow me an instant of cattiness, I confess, too, that I've wondered whether Parker's taste for big-mouthed flavor, in particular for the licorice-y merlot grape in Bordeaux, suggests that he has drunk myriad seconds' worth of Coca-Cola for a good part of his life. Once a woman who worked for an American magazine brought me a bottle to Paris of a California wine that Parker had rated close to a hundred. It was nearly black, aggressively flavored, and had fourteen degrees of alcohol. (Traditional Bordeaux is 12.5.) I felt ready to spit it out before five seconds in the mouth, and so did the wine shop owner tasting it with me. We are living in a time when subtlety has been overpowered in many areas of life by exaggeration, except perhaps among the brainiest of theoreticians. Parker's successful stock-in-trade has not been subtlety.

Joanne and I share less than a bottle of Bordeaux every evening at dinner in Paris. The wine is simply Bordeaux, although it has an insignificant other name as well. It's a blend of various wines grown and vinified in Bordeaux. The production of a classified Bordeaux château is legally limited as an assurance of quality. Nowadays many of the grand châteaux, with too much wine on their hands and new vines giving less good grapes, bottle a second wine of their crops under another name recalling theirs, as if it were a kid brother of the grand wine. It used to be that this wine went onto the market anonymously as just Bordeaux. We regularly drink nonclassified Bordeaux assembled by its bottlers—"assembled," as the winemakers prefer to say—shy of the demeaning sound of "blended," like whisky. All Bordeaux, at whatever property, is actually assembled—from the juice of the year's best grapes including different varietals, mainly merlot and cabernet sauvignon. Since our cellar was burglarized we store no wines and buy our nonnoble Bordeaux in a supermarket. If you don't keep a wine cellar in Paris, the best place to choose a pleasant wine is at certain supermarkets. Their chains employ expert *sommeliers* who are great at choosing quality and who drive hard deals by buying in great quantity, deals they pass on to the consumer. A plain Bordeaux can be better than the wine from the grapes and soil of a minor single vineyard. The latter, bearing the name of a château, all the same can command five and more times the price, particularly in the specialized wine shops that can't compete for my money with the supermarket I frequent. I won't tell you what our daily Bordeaux costs, but if we ever draw a cork together, I'll let you guess. You'd be surprised at how little.

The trendy garages of Bordeaux are not distant cousins of the small winemakers of Burgundy, who since far back have owned parcels of great vineyards and vinify traditionally in humble surroundings. I will remember for a long time the bottle of A. Rousseau Chambertin 1990, a wine of the century, that Joanne and I and our children shared over Joanne's *boeuf à la ficelle*. I don't remember how much that bottle, which now sits empty among our souvenirs, had cost. I've blocked the figure from my memory. You live once. It would cost a sum geometrically greater today.

I couldn't afford to be a wine connoisseur these days. I came to drinking wine as an undergraduate at Princeton, when there was one wine shop in town, and where I remember buying a bottle of Château Lagrange '45, a classified third growth, for a dollar-something and a Château Suduiraut of that same hallowed year—a first-growth Sauternes a notch below the extraordinary Yquem—for about that same price. Yes. When Joanne and I were living on the Fenway in Boston, while I attended graduate school across the river, we used to eat at an Italian restaurant around the corner called Casa Amalfi. With our spaghetti, we'd drink a La Tour '45 or '49, and pay a check resembling that of a spaghetti dinner. We surmised that the owner had bought the premises along with its cellar when the former owner was in distress and he didn't know what he bought. Something like that. Those were very naïve wine times indeed in America. I'm not making this up. The wine merchant in the town of Princeton seemed unaware of his own treasure somehow, as well, or was in need of unloading it quickly. Wine, in those days, was in any case something to drink, not a token of one's ability to spend, the more lavishly the more prestigiously.

Those were the days of gastronomic naïveté in many ways, in the U.S. of A. I can remember even more recent times, when I bought a bagful of *ricci di mare* at a little Italian fish store on the West Side of Manhattan called Citerella, for next to nothing, while back home in Paris these sea urchins, known as *oursins*, would have cost me twenty times as much. Summering off the coast of Ibiza, our six-year-old son and I used to sate ourselves gathering *erizos de mar* for nothing off the rocks underwater near shore. We plucked them gingerly, to keep the spines from stabbing, poked them open with a stick, rinsed them in the sea, and ate that orange roe with a delicious flavor rounder and richer than the oysters the French prize first of all among shellfish.

As I hurried off from Citerella to introduce sea urchins to my niece and her husband at their apartment, I recalled what I'd overheard at the Italian market in Boston some time before, where there were such delicacies as razor clams, live snails, and sea urchins for sale. I overheard, "Italians will eat anything." Since my bounty of urchins at Citerella, the store has become a gourmet venue, and sea urchins called *uni,* having arrived as sushi, are very expensive. And alas, last I saw, the *erizos de mar* were gone from the shores of Ibiza. And Citerella is in the restaurant and food business for the well-heeled in New York and East Hampton.

As for what has happened in the wine world, I noted recently that the price of a bottle of Mouton Rothschild *en primeur,* that is to say, bought in advance of bottling, was fifteen-hundred euro a bottle. The wine has been six months or so in the *barriques,* with another year or so to be there; the cellar master hasn't assembled the ulti-mate combination of the different grapes, but he does a hypothetical assemblage to be tasted as a prediction of what the ultimate wine will be like. But in those barrels, the wine has a mind of its own, hard at that point to direct. Paying that kind of price is something to dine off for those who buy, conspicuously, famous wines, on the wavelength of a fame fornicator, with the alibi that they're buying something precious that may be all gone before it reaches the bottle. Once a friend told me that he knew another writer who was very successful and also a drug user. He informed my friend that he had "put a Ferrari in each arm." We were never addicted to wine, Joanne and I, but, before the painters came to our building and coyly left our burglarized cellar with one bottle of Mouton, we must have had at least one Rolls-Royce in our *cave.*

Today, there is a vast difference in price between a pleasant wine and one that has something memorable to say, whether drunk at home or in a restaurant, where prices can be even more breathtaking. In between the two levels of quality, as I'll say again, the increases in price aren't really justified by what more pleasure or knowledge you get. That's one subjective opinion from someone not involved in the wine world. But all opinions of taste even among the aficionados of that world are shaded with subjectivity, which is why you see grades differ in wine tastings.

I am reminded of a lunch I once had with Philippe de Rothschild and Alexis Lichine. In those days, in the starchy world of the great château owners of Bordeaux, Lichine, a Russian-born American who had been divorced from a glamorous movie actress, Arlene Dahl, was a bit too "people," as those magazines of today call pop celebrities, to be part of Bordeaux wine's *haut monde.* He'd nonetheless become a world-noted wine writer and wine merchant and had bought Château Prieuré in the Margaux neighborhood of Bordeaux and renamed it Prieuré Lichine. Philippe's own snobbism was based on his perception of quality in people rather than their history—he had married a remarkable woman who'd been the waif of an impoverished, wellborn, but wild American mother. And he and Lichine had something in common. They both challenged the validity of the sanctified and ossified 1855 Classification of Bordeaux wines. Lichine had done his own list, which elevated Mouton to a peer of cousin Lafite, as a top *cru hors classe*, more modestly classing his own 1855 classifed fourth-growth wine as a *grand cru*.

Lichine's dining room was in any case, *hors classe,* with its walls covered by a big collection of priceless, old Delft porcelain. Philippe, whose own abodes were full of precious things—I think of the extraordinary Chardin painting above his bed, in his avenue d'Iéna Paris apartment—must have appreciated that, while their conversation nonetheless took the form of a little fencing match over what they perceived in their glasses. Philippe was too civilized to be critical about the man's wine, although the wine we'd been drinking back at Mouton left it well behind. It was all about tannin and maturity, none of the tobacco, hay, mango, and such supposed gustatory relatives that wine authorities go on about these days. The wine match was deteriorating into a pissing contest all the same. So here were two bona fide experts, talking with different views about the same liquid that had passed through their mouths. Talking perforce subjectively.

I tuned out, thinking about Arlene Dahl, with whom I had lunched, one lovely day, on a restaurant terrace opposite the seventeenth-century Château de Dampierre, near Paris. Her charm and fresh beauty had filled that moment so much that, today, I can remember her long red hair but not why we were there or, least of all, what we ate or drank. I must have been writing a story that concerned her. I know that if she were still the *maîtresse de maison* that day at Prieuré, she'd have given the discourse a warmer, more charming turn. Lichine finally said something to Rothschild that sounded like he was mollifying him, but it was a trap.

"I drank the Mouton '68 lately," he said. "Felt enormous respect for it."

"Really?" Philippe said, raising an eyebrow. "A mediocre year to say the least. The grapes were all saturated with rain. It was a terrible August."

"I meant the 1868, Philippe," Lichine replied.

The baron, who apparently didn't remember having drunk his 1868, remained silent, and the meal proceeded to its quiet close.

So there you have it. Please believe it. Once upon a time, not that long ago, a few, very privileged people owned and occasionally sampled wines even more than a hundred years old for the rare, unique experience of their palates, putting those wines in the folder of memory of their own tastes, as they perceived them. Odds were most high that almost all that wine had turned to vinegar, and one would open several bottles of old vintages to find what might still be alive, even feebly so. Baron Philippe, singularly extravagant with his cellar, kept Raoul, his *maître de chais*, busy at that endeavor. There was a paradigm there, too, of the pathos of making contact with lost time, a solemn gesture. Perception as an appreciation of ephemeral life. Somewhere, I believe, it was an act approaching that same impetus behind art. And if our attachment to partaking of the same foods that gave pleasure to our ancestors shares something with art, it's in that shared emotional intention.

They drank, in any case, and not often, those curiosities for the rare experience, and not for self-aggrandizement, and nobody dreamed of paying the equivalent of fifteen hundred euro a bottle for an unbottled wine that was not yet sure about what it was going to be. Wine, in any case, does not get better the older it gets, past its peak of maturity. Nowadays those old bottles, with conspicuous nonconsumption, sell at auctions for tens of thousands of dollars and will never be opened. What has happened brings back to mind Christian Millau's judgment of what befell *la cuisine*: "The media and the money dictate everywhere in our times." Rothschild and Lichine believed that wine was essentially defined as something to drink, while they were also, in many ways defined, elitists. But the world of fine wine, as much elsewhere, hasn't become more democratic, although you can purchase some prestigious bottles at a local supermarket. Elitism has changed hands. And people congratulate themselves for being able to pay a fortune for a bottle of vinegar with a faded label. Alas, what has also changed, been diminished on a broader scale, in cuisine as elsewhere, is the attachment to things for what they really are. Why else does a celebrated name written large on a banal T-shirt made in a Chinese sweatshop create something to cherish and flaunt?

NB: In our travels ahead, we won't be sampling grand wines, but some that are interesting local presences. Otherwise, famous wines are what they are wherever they are drunk, whether in Bordeaux or Shanghai, while memorable and affordable, pedigreed cooking lives on, attached to where you find it.

6

SIMPLY AS GOOD AS IT GETS

In Paris, l'Ami Louis, in the rue du Vertbois, was owned by an old man with a white beard named Antoine. I don't know who Louis might have once been. Antoine worked in wooden shoes—for comfort, not for the folklore—in front of a wood-burning stove, which is said to be the very best stove for roasting.

L'Ami Louis was on a then shabby street in the Fourth Arrondissement, and it was a humble-looking place. Deliberately. During the Second World War it was a black market hangout for gourmets, and its appearance disguised the luxury of the food. The storefront outside was shabby when I knew it and the inside had not been painted since the war. All that had become Antoine's *shtick*. You had to be among the Knowing to be aware that once past the door, you would be treated to exceptional quality: just straight out stuff, *foie gras* in slabs, roast chicken, rib steaks sauced with melted butter, fried potatoes in three versions. Plain? What was at hand was simply as good as it gets—no better elsewhere. And you had the extra experience of being among the Knowing. Once, after Fairchild sold his company

to Capital Cities, Joanne and I took an executive from that conglomerate and his "bride" to L'Ami Louis to dinner. As the cab stops in
front of the place, she pokes her husband in the ribs and whispers,
"Do you see where they're taking us?"

On another evening, I crossed the Duchess of Windsor on the little
corkscrew staircase leading to the then basement WC. We brushed
past each other as she was heading back up and I was heading down.
When I got to the loo, I saw that Her Highness had pissed all over
the floor rather than sit down on that toilet.

The duchess was obviously used to better surroundings for her
repasts. She and her husband were constantly wined and dined by the
Tout Paris at their dinners "*en ville,*" as dinners at home among the
lofty were called. The lesser lofty, people with money who hoped to
entertain their way into high society, had a chance at the Windsors
too, but to be counted among their guests, the royal couple charged
a fee. A wannabe divorced from a cosmetic magnate told me that
she would pay them two thousand dollars per dinner appearance,
but the fee might have varied depending on one's degree of accept-
ability, and, in citing a low figure, she might have been vaunting
the level of her own.

There was one thing that Antoine served that you'd be hard-
pressed to find in another restaurant: *ortolans.* They were already
rare, before being declared an endangered species. An *ortolan* is
a bird not much bigger than the top joint of your thumb. They
would net them down in the grasslands of the Southwest and keep
them, darkened, in a cage, where they were not given water to
drink. Instead they got Armagnac. The birds, driven by thirst,
would drink the Armagnac, which would swell their livers. After
a while, when the Armagnac had yielded its presence to their entire
flesh, the birds were smothered. The result for the gourmet was an
incomparably flavored little fowl. Tradition had it that when you
ate *ortolans,* you put your napkin over your head, so that none of the

delicious aroma escaped. I never sacrificed my dignity on the altar of gastronomy that way, but I saw it done. I wonder whether François Mitterrand, president of France, had the strength to put a napkin over his head when he ate his notorious *ortolan*. *Monsieur le Président*, long after *ortolans* were declared endangered and forbidden to commerce, obtained an *ortolan* for his last meal, as he lay dying of cancer. Such were the last licks of a shady guy.

I ate *ortolans* for the last time in Athens. In the Plaka neighborhood full of tourists, there was a tiny place, where, with arch, reverse snobbery, the politicians and other movers and shakers of the city liked to lunch, exclusively. It was called Zephiris, after the name of the owner, an old grouch, a soul mate of Monsieur Cazes, owner and cruel arbiter of status at Paris's Brasserie Lipp.

Zephiris was a small cube of a room, whose plaster was painted, long ago, in green, and there was a balcony to accommodate the overflow, in case the five or so tables were taken. They weren't when I came there alone, on an Athens insider's tip, but I was sent upstairs to sit by myself, being nobody in the Tout Athènes. The personalities or personae of those who run restaurants that mistreat the unchosen are indeed a matter Dr. Freud might have explored, in lucubrations on sadomasochism. I was surprised to see *ortolans* on the menu, which my waiter decoded from the Greek, and I didn't hesitate to order them. They came out in a typical Greek tomato sauce. Those rare little birds that gave their lives for this fate might as well have been meatballs.

Sometime later, in Cairo, I came close to an *ortolan* experience in the restaurant of a little hotel on the island of Zamalek. I had come to Egypt to interview Anwar Sadat, who received me in one of his residences on the Nile, wearing a black silk, pajama-like suit that looked like a Saint Laurent for Men, revealing a surprising alter ego of his noted, pinstriped elegance. In the course of our conversation, I gently asked him if he ever feared being assassinated. "When I buried the Shah," he replied, "I walked from one end of Cairo to another and anyone could have killed me." His assassin was released from prison in 2005.

Zamalek was the best neighborhood in Cairo at the time, which meant that, if you navigated the protective deceptiveness of a shabby, authentically Third World hall, you could be received in an apartment done to the nines in Louis Seize furniture, like the Paris apartments of well-off French nobles. There was a little hotel on the island, where discreet, refined Egyptians stayed, rather than at the international tourist and business hotels. The basement housed a bar, whose walls were covered in Black Watch plaid. With your glass of scotch, came, as if with peanuts, a tray of tiny roasted birds to snack on. They were, my French-speaking Egyptian friend explained, *bec-figues*. For me they were clones of *ortolans*, but they are different birds. Old French books on gastronomy, including Alexandre Dumas's famous dictionary, mention them, although I have never seen them in France. These came from the grasslands of the Nile delta, noted for the excellent quail netted there. I haven't found the English for *bec-figues,* named for birds fond of eating figs off trees, with their long beaks. Figs might have accounted for their sought-after taste, resembling in faint sweetness the Armagnac in *ortolans.* The ancient Egyptians, who are said to have endowed the world with *foie gras,* force-fed their geese with figs. Legend says that the Jews who were slaves in Egypt brought the technique of making *foie gras* with them with the Exodus, and the Jews who eventually settled in Alsace introduced the practice to France. Jewish cooking since gets blamed, in many cases, for keeping Alka-Seltzer a going culinary staple, but it's credited with this contribution to *la cuisine française.* Jews who left Spain during the Inquisition also brought chocolate with them across the Pyrenees to the Basque Country of France, where chocolate is still highly prized. Chocolate lovers from all over do pilgrimages to the Basque city of Bayonne, where the machine for milling chocolate was invented in the eighteenth century. Its numerous chocolatiers compete in excellence.

By the time that François Mitterrand, whose most devoted constituents had actually nicknamed him "God," had nonetheless passed on to his namesake, Antoine's reign at the l'Ami Louis cast-iron stove had also come to an end. The old man, as it was told to me, had an eighteen-year-old girlfriend who, after a lovers' quarrel, informed the tax people that his accounting was creative. He was obliged to sell to pay what he owed. One of the well-heeled regulars of the place stepped up and bought it. My ingenuous Cap Cities couple notwithstanding, l'Ami Louis had become a darling venue of rich Americans and their French friends.

Among other places for insiders to do pseudo-slumming, there was Chez Monteil, opposite Les Halles, both of which were still in full, swarming operation when I ate there. Like many Paris bistros, Monteil would have a boar nailed to its door in season, to announce that *sanglier* was on the menu. Subsequent sanitary laws aside, a boar on a door these days would hardly last long enough to age out there, and the door might likely be tagged when it disappeared.

Monteil was a very small hole in the wall with uncomfortable stools to sit on, but it had a great cellar and its tiny kitchen turned out good plain food, dishes that were *canaille*. The French sophisticate, taking pleasure in the idea of slumming, would add a note of endearment to the term. High on the list of *canaille* food are such dishes as breaded pigs' feet, or tripe sausage. My friend Jacques Rouët used to like to go to places like Monteil. "*On va s'encanailler*," he'd say. "We're going to brush shoulders with the rogues." I rarely noticed any roguish characters at Monteil, just businessmen. The wine cellar was over the heads of and beyond the purses of the Halles workmen who sometimes did drop in, to sip a Byrrh *apéritif* while Monsieur Monteil did likewise with his friend Jean Gabin.

Monteil was torn down, when they destroyed the Halles for a monstrosity to take its place in a big real estate scam, which included the considerable money made selling the cast iron frames of Balthard's historic buildings. Monteil's street, la rue de la Réale, has disappeared forever, along with this special place.

Before its destruction, Monteil might have merited a plaque outside. Pierrot, the waiter at Monteil, told me about the meal he once served at the restaurant when he was very young. That day, he said, the Swedish ambassador Raoul Nordling took Dietrich von Choltitz, German military governor of Paris, to a discreet, out-of-the-way lunch at Monteil and ordered a grand Bordeaux. Over an excellent and excellently irrigated meal, Nordling convinced Choltitz not to blow up Paris but to make contact with the Resistance. With their Cheval Blanc '29, they ate *entrecôtes marchand de vin* and those little potato balloons, *pommes soufflées*. Neither Nordling nor Choltitz mentioned this pleasant and momentous interlude in his memoirs, but I had never known Pierrot to name-drop about the numerous other celebrities who frequented Monteil *pour s'encanailler.*

Having capitulated, Choltitz was treated to his last meal in Paris before prison, at a much more luxurious restaurant. Pierre Taittinger of the champagne family, chairman of the Municipal Council, took him to Lucas-Carton, a Mecca of gastronomy for the lucky few during the war. (Alain Senderens, a self-esteeming, while true talent of *la nouvelle cuisine*, would scrub its name off the outside walls of that storied Belle Époque gem, and replace it with his own, after he bought it in 1985 and matched the interior wood paneling by the great *art nouveau* decorator Louis Majorelle with banal contemporary décor.)

My own favorite dish at Monteil was *haricot de mouton*. Mutton, with its deep flavor, is just about impossible to find these days in Paris, either in a restaurant or a butcher shop. People favor the delicacy of lamb. Perhaps there is a sociological revelation there in the victory of mildness. Great lamb is indeed great. Mutton is a more intense story. In any case, the next and last time I ate mutton was a long time later, in the tiny once-elegant cure town of Aulus, in the Pyrenees. There was a little spa still left there, where I experimented with taking the waters for the gout that had become the retribution for my lifestyle. Once rich French people came here yearly from the colonies to recover from the assaults of strange and inclement climates, exotic parasites, and the solicitude of barmen at the clubs. They stayed at a few stylish hotels that were all boarded up by the time Joanne kept me company down there. They'd been witness to a far worse moment of history: During the last war, Jews, having been rounded up else-where in France, were parked down here and forced to pay to stay in those hotels, awaiting their ultimate dire journey. Spain was just six hours on foot across the mountains, and a number of the townspeople honored themselves by guiding some of those victims, strong enough for the climb, to reach freedom on the other side.

Joanne and I rented an apartment for the time that I went through the routine water drinking and the being bathed and *schpritzed* at the adjacent spa. Below our window every morning a shepherd led a troop of sheep from one local pasture to another. In a while they would make the long climb to higher pastures, in what is called *la transhumance*. The good grass and good air give the lamb of the Pyrenees a merited great reputation. The town butcher, who sold us some of that excellent *agneau des Pyrénées* was the shepherd's brother. Having noted that we seemed to take a particular interest in what we ate, he urged us to try a *gigot de mouton*. We did. Roasted well done the Arab way, in contrast to the French predilection for rare or *rosé* lamb, our leg of mutton had a full but not heavy flavor. Try one if you can find one. . . .

Among the other Paris restaurants that my contacts favored, there was, and still is, a place at the opposite end of appearances from

Monteil: Voltaire, which is just below the gilded, wood-paneled apartment facing the Seine where Voltaire died. Voltaire is a comfortable cocoon of a restaurant that was once a café—part of it is still a café—where the owner would hold secret meetings of the Resistance during the war. The same family still owns it, the food, far from *canaille*, is a sophisticated version of *cuisine bourgeoise*—the very best lamb chops, a wild turbot in perfect hollandaise sauce. Among the starters there is a dish called *oeuf James,* named after an expatriate native of Englewood, New Jersey, writer and friend of the great Paris artists of the twentieth century. James Lord's favorite starter was a hard-boiled egg sauced with fresh mayonnaise, a classic French dish. In the late Lord's honor, the price of his egg has not changed since the fifties. Like all of Paris's best restaurants, Voltaire draws informed Americans, who rub shoulders with the local Fashionables and the publishing and antique people of the Quai Voltaire neighborhood. Once, when I'd moved on to write for *Condé Nast Traveler,* I took another executive in from New York to lunch at Voltaire. He was expecting me, as the great Paris insider, to take him to a totally French place and he was chagrined when I got into catching up on fashion with Nan Kempner, the socialite editor of *Harper's Bazaar,* who'd come to town on the Concorde, and was lunching at the next table.

Another unique place stays in mind. It was a very modest, though far from shabby, obscure restaurant in the Seventeenth Arrondissement, a becalmed bourgeois neighborhood, on a street near the lovely Parc Monceau, with its eighteenth-century pastiche Roman ruins. It was called La Mère Michel. Mother Michel did her own cooking, and she poached fish that brought aficionados from all over. Turbot, pike, John Dory, or sea bass, sauced with *beurre blanc.* It was the *beurre blanc* that was her monumental accomplishment. A successful *beurre blanc* is composed of the best quality butter and a reduction of white wine or wine vinegar with finely chopped shallots. The trick is to hand whip all that into an ethereal froth.

Not easy. Mother Michel's *beurre blanc*, which relied on nearly evaporated wine vinegar, was ethereal to the point of being heavenly. If you asked her for the recipe, she'd first say, "The recipe's in your hand."

There was Chez Denis, also in the Seventeenth, a little bistro very big for its aprons so to speak. The chef, Claude Mornay, practiced his craft in that modest place with old-style grandeur, and impressed a lot of people. His moment of glory and simultaneous opprobrium came in 1976, when Craig Claiborne, the food critic of *The New York Times*, ate a thirty-one-course dinner there with his companion Pierre Frany, running the gamut from caviar, past *foie gras*, chartreuse of pheasant, *ortolans*, wild duck, and beyond, "washed down," as critics sometimes unfortunately write, with a '29 Romanée-Conti, a '28 Latour, and an 1935 Madeira, along with six other wines. Claiborne, who learned to love to eat from the African American cook at his mother's boarding house in Mississippi, and who'd gone on to be a star food critic, was not totally impressed. Their check, $4,000, created shocks of disapprobation throughout the world. The pope pronounced it "scandalous."

You know, I ate once at Chez Denis, but all I can remember of the meal was Mornay's personal favorite: a whole black truffle cooked in aluminum on embers. Denis Lahane, the owner, closed Chez Denis two years after Claiborne's blowout was a splash in the press. A neighbor told the Associated Press that "the tax man" was involved in its demise.

In that pre-*nouvelle* era, the cooks in the best bistros in Paris were perpetuating *plats* of hallowed deliciousness; these people became renowned, yes, among serious eaters in Paris, and sometimes among sophisticated travelers in the wide world, because they had a talent to do each to a point of exaltation, if you will. Simply as good as it gets.

Anyone could, for example, cook up a *pot au feu*, but people flocked to a little place in the Batignolles quarter, where Madame

Gorisse had her way of making a humble *pot au feu* into a cherished memory. For extraordinary *cassoulet*, you went to Proust, up in Montmartre. You would not have eaten a pudding as memorable as the *gâteau de riz,* Chez Pauline, whose *blanquette de veau* drew the actors at the nearby Comédie Française in great number, every Wednesday. At Chez les Anges, you'd be treated to the starter, *oeufs en meurette,* poached eggs in red wine and meat sauce, a Burgundian classic. There were the renowned *quenelles de brochet,* airy pike dumplings, at Le Louis XIV, near la Places des Victoires. The *boeuf à la ficelle* simmered in stock at Le Grand Comptoir, which began as a noisy tavern for the Les Halles workers in 1868. And there were others. Forgive me for want of space to give all of those numerous bistros, each proudly distinctive, its due here. Were those great cooks artists? Maybe you could compare them, without taking the matter too far, to great musicians, interpreters—interpreting faithfully what they'd learned and revered.

Recently, I experienced a delicious rush of memory when I came upon a book called *Paris Bistro Cookery* in a second hand bookstore. The author, Alexander Watt, compiled 270 menus from fifty of those places, a greatly meritorious act of cultural conservation. The copyright of the book reads 1957. I ate many of those same dishes up to two decades later. Those restaurateurs were who they were, doing what they did, like no one else did quite as well. Things essentially simple but deftly done. They were never compelled to reinvent themselves, like fashion designers, to excite critics, so long as people who knew what they were eating kept coming back for more.

You can think of the selection below, put together from Watt's compilations, as a starter, a main course, and a dessert—a dinner menu that might have been drawn up sitting around the pool, in whatever Valhalla heroes of French cooking go to.

Here are: La Mère Michel's *beurre blanc* to garnish poached fish; Veau Marengo from Aux Rendez-vous des Camionneurs, once an honest little place beside the Seine, on the Ile de la Cité, cherished by truck drivers and cab drivers, hungry for lunch, before it died as a tourist trap; and Chez Pauline's *gâteau de riz*. I salivate remembering them.

Le Beurre Blanc of la Mère Michel

½ pound best available butter

2 tbs. finely chopped gray shallots

⅓ cup white wine vinegar

Salt, freshly ground pepper

Cook the shallots in the vinegar in a small saucepan until the vinegar has nearly evaporated. Remove the pan, and whisk in small quantities of butter, whisking constantly until you have a creamy sauce. Add salt and pepper to taste. Pour the sauce on poached fish, preferably pike.

Sounds easy, but Mother Michel would indeed insist that the "recipe is in your hand." The pan should not be allowed to get too cool. She would put it back on the fire in brief fits, but you might want to use a double boiler. Neither should it be too hot, or the butter goes very liquid. Keep whisking and whisking. Enough sauce for serving four.

Sauté de Veau Marengo
From au Rendez-vous des Camionneurs as it once was

2 lbs. breast of veal

6 tomatoes, peeled, seeded, and quartered

4 onions, finely chopped

2 tbs. of olive oil

2 tbs. of butter

¼ cup of flour

1 cup dry white wine

1 cup stock

1 clove of garlic, finely chopped

1 bouquet garni

chopped parsley

salt and pepper

Cut the meat into one-and-a-half-inch-cubes. Salt and pepper them and brown them in the butter and oil, along with the onions, which should become transparent but not allowed to brown. Crush the tomatoes and then add, along with the flour. Let the flour cook with the butter to make a roux. Warm the white wine with the stock. Add it to the saucepan stirring slowly, having added the garlic and the bouquet garni. Cover and simmer for one hour or until the meat is tender. Serve with chopped parsley sprinkled over the meat. Serves 4.

This hearty dish is no French adaptation of an Italian or Spanish dish. Don't be deceived by "Marengo". It was born of a simple, impromptu recipe that Bonaparte's cook put together for him in the field, after the Emperor defeated the Italian army at Marengo near the Italian Alps. The original dish called for chicken, but veal became the favorite version. . . .

Gâteau de Riz, as it was at Chez Pauline

6 oz. long-grain white rice

6 cups milk

1 whole vanilla bean

4 oz. butter

sugar to caramelize a mold

Caramelize a cold pudding mold, which will contain the rice after cooking. Place the raw rice in a sieve and pour boiling water on it. Throw the drained rice into a pan containing the boiling milk and vanilla. Cook uncovered, very gently, over a low flame. After an hour and a half, the milk should have evaporated. Add the butter and gently melt it into the rice with a spatula. Empty into the cold caramelized mold and leave to cool. . . .

Chez Pauline still exists, with some inspired classic French cuisine, whose pricy-ness might be rationalized by its rarity these days. But the *gâteau de riz* is gone. Try instead the dessert menu's *panna cotta*.

7

CHIC TO CHIC

Maxim's and the Relais Plaza were the two canteens of the Fashionables and they were where I lunched most frequently. The Relais Plaza, which was the actual canteen of the officers of the *Kriegsmarine* during the war, was the less formal, snack-possible restaurant of the elegant Plaza Athénée hotel, with a separate entrance, through which passed ladies shopping until hungry at the expensive boutiques of the quarter, which has come to be called the Golden Triangle. They would often come with their lap dogs. The waiters would set down a cushion at the feet of the owner, where the shiatsu or whatever was treated to lamb chops. I'm serious. The lady's eating her diet salad and the dog is chowing down on lamb chops. It happened all the time. A guy dressed in an idea of a harem eunuch, with flowing pants and a fez, would go around with coffee, brewed by a process since outdated by espresso called Cona. You could get a gourmet hamburger topped with a gently fried egg at the Relais Plaza, or a *paillette de veau*, a sliver of veal like a Wiener schnitzel without the breading. I was found of the *gnocchi à la fiorentina*, semolina gnocchi gorged with butter and cheese on a bed of spinach—as good as you'd get in Florence.

Maxim's was a less relaxed place. It was, along with the Brasserie Lipp, the cruelest restaurant in Paris. Roger, the headwaiter, knew and looked after His People, in contrast with the folks who allocated a good portion of their travel budget to have Been There. Their money was welcomed at this legendary place, a haven of the Tout Paris, *le monde* and *le demimonde*, since the Belle Époque—of which its décor was a precious testimony. Innocent aliens, they were sent directly to the bad room. By day the bad room was at the back of the restaurant and the good room was up front. These changed by night, when there was an orchestra in the back. In between was a sort of purgatory, a narrow strip known as the *"omnibus,"* where young businessmen not yet at the top of their professions and other almost-Tout were seated. Once an old garment manufacturer from New York treated me to lunch at Maxim's. We were led to his table in the *omnibus.* "You know," he said proudly, " I have been coming here for fifty years and I always get the same table." I wouldn't have dreamt of telling him it was not really a good table, but, in my shameful thoughts, I did feel uneasy sitting there.

I would be placed in the good room. I suppose it was because I was a regular, and John and Jim had made their importance as published social arbiters known to Roger, the headwaiter, before I was passed on as their minion. Roger was the successor to Albert, a darling of the Wehrmacht's resident elite in earlier history. At Maxim's, the Good People would get their orders sent into the crowded little kitchen with their names on the slips, to be sure that they got special care. I don't know what they dished up for the aliens. I was also among the desirables who got a reduced rate on my monthly bills. John had come a long way.

The crowd in the front room at lunch was an interesting group. Estée Lauder lunched there often when she was in Paris. After lunch,

I once saw her go from one table to another, not principally to kiss-kiss hello, but to give out samples of her wares. Chutzpah had borne this woman from Corona, Queens, whose forefathers hailed from the Dual Monarchy, to the high place that she held in the world of cosmetics. She began her career knocking on doors to sell her pots of face cream, and she was not too haughty to give out the latest versions of her line, among the very rich like her at Maxim's, decades later.

The best table in the front room was a little round one near the curtained windows. Here Mr. and Mrs. Aristotle Onassis would come to late lunch when they were in Paris. It was amazing to see that the crowd of the most sophisticated people in the city would suddenly go silent, their buzz of internecine gossip come to a sudden halt, when Jackie and Ari walked into the room.

Of the classic food at Maxim's, I remember most of all a dish of potatoes, which I ate often with perfectly roasted, perfect quality chicken. *Pommes Anna*. *Pommes Anna* are very thinly sliced potatoes, piled between layers of butter, as a bricklayer would, and baked in a copper pan. Potatoes and butter to match the quality of the chicken. Cholesterol city? That's another story. The story behind the name goes back to the nineteenth century, when ladies whose elegance exceeded their virtue, les *demimondaines*, frequented Maxim's with the gentlemen who kept them. Those men also kept their wives away from this luxurious venue of the well-heeled lascivious, with its private rooms for private pleasures upstairs. The chef who created the dish at the Café Anglais, a similar hangout, was Adolphe Dugléré, a disciple of the great Marie-Antoine Carême, and noted in the history of cuisine as the inventor of *sauce dugléré*, a complicated, creamy fish sauce. Which Anna, among those fetching *poules,* was the one whom he honored with the name of the dish of potatoes is a matter disputed in history.

Just as Pierre Cardin's wacko stretches of imagination as a clothing designer were considered nonchic by those who swore by the suave creations of Saint Laurent, Givenchy, Balenciaga, and Chanel, so Cardin's buying Maxim's proved the time to leave for the chic crowd. He has a museum there now, and Asians in jeans file in to dream of what was once Paris, and eat at *le grand* Maxim's.

Paris has another class of restaurants known as *brasseries*. The word means, literally, breweries. Originally these were places that brewed their own beer. That went out a long time ago, but they continued to serve roguish food all day and into early morning. The Coupole was the most storied *brasserie*—it was a hangout for the Montparnasse artists and intellectuals of the twenties and thirties, Picasso et al. As a contemporary writer, John Glassco, unkindly recounts, a young journalist and novelist called Ernest Hemingway used to work the vast dining room of the Coupole, shaking hands with whoever seemed able to give him a hand up. When I knew it, before it was bought by a chain and went less notable in clientele, La Coupole still attracted an arty crowd. I often used to see Jean-Paul Sartre, Simone de Beauvoir, and Sarte's mistress/adopted daughter sit down to a three o'clock lunch, when the place was almost emptied, while I was finishing, say, my curry. The Coupole was a restaurant to have a steak or a *choucroute* at any hour. Curry was an anomaly in a very French bill of fare, although it had been on the menu since 1927, the year the place opened. That was a time of fantasy, and the owners, Messrs. Laffont and Faux, thought it would be cool to dress a guy up like a maharajah and have him serve curry based incongruously on someone's Tamil recipe. The current owner, the Flo *brasserie* group, has taken to dressing up a waiter like that again. In my experience, the curry was tasty but nothing remarkable for the genre, nothing like what I'd had staying on a houseboat that came with a cook on Lake Dal, in Srinagar when Kashmir was heaven on earth instead of the opposite as it is now. But like James Lord's egg at Voltaire, the curry at the Coupole kept alive a memory of the place, embodying history. In its own way, a wafer of communion.

Joanne and I spent our first New Year's in Paris at the Coupole, and would, over the years, go there for Sunday lunch with our son and daughter. At age three, André, who would grow up to be an estimable trencherman, would polish off a half a dozen oysters at lunch at the Coupole.

The insiders' Paris *brasserie* was Lipp, which was and still is, as I said, a place to match the old Maxim's in cruelty. Its apparent informality adhered to a rigid drill that was its own version of chic.

While his headwaiter stood guard at the entrance, Monsieur Cazes, the owner of Lipp, would sit reading the extreme right-wing periodical *Minute*, raising his eyes to scan the arrivals. Monsieur Cazes would sometimes stand guard himself. Or he would retreat to a table to inscribe, in his own hand, the names of the celebrated who came to eat among their peers at La Brasserie Lipp that day. Famous politicians, film actors, artists, kingpins of enterprise would come to Be There and eat the banal, chiefly roguish food: pigs' feet, *blanquette de veau*, a *choucroute* notable for its frugality, crowned with a slice of industrial ham. Lipp made a truly good steak and a dessert hard to find elsewhere: *fontainebleau à la crème*. Le Père Cazes might have put it on the menu with a touch of irony, because, with it, he was serving his distinguished clientele nursery food. But it was delightful. A froth of whipped fresh cheese, crowned with a dollop of *crème fraîche*, on which you showered sugar. You can still buy *fontainebleau* at some Parisian cheese stores, but some benighted EU rule about sanitation has replaced the cheesecloth it came wrapped in with a plastic container, such as have lately been suspected of containing carcinogenic chemicals.

All in all, the food at Lipp was not up to the level of the people who were served it. But they were in with the in crowd, and, last I checked, many of them still come back, their egos stroked by being in that rare atmosphere.

At the door, potential eaters were sorted out with pitiless rapidity. I don't know what incident might have occurred if an unenlightened tourist tried to give the implacable guardian at the gates a bribe for a table. You don't do that in Europe; other beasts, other habits, as the French adage goes. Although once I saw an American guest, relieved to have been well placed and apparently used to the practice, slip a lire bill with many zeros on it into the handkerchief pocket of a snotty headwaiter in the dining room of the Sirenuse, that candy box of a hotel above the sea in Positano.

The first ranking of your importance at Lipp was how long you were told you had to wait for a table, since there were no reservations. Hungry and naïve wannabes were regularly told they would have to wait two hours, yes, while regulars brushed past them to be seated. Then there was the matter of where you were placed. Nowadays, tourists get seated on the terrace, not even allowed to enter the lair. In those times, many would wait, or come back when all the regulars had emptied their tables, only to be sent, nonetheless, upstairs to Siberia. Among those who qualified for being seated downstairs, there were those sent to the rear of the room and those seated closer to the front. The ultimate honor was the table to the right of the door, partly sheltered by a partition. Here people could pay you homage as they came in. I was sitting there with a notable client of Monsieur Cazes when the old man rushed up to us. "What does John Galbraith look like?" he asked. The great economist's hotel concierge must have phoned to alert Monsieur Cazes of his coming. Monsieur Cazes was all a-flutter about inscribing Galbraith's name in his *livre d'or* for the day.

"That's him," my friend said, pointing up to the lanky man descending the staircase, coming back, just then, from his lunch in Siberia, where, unrecognized—given the parochial knowledge of Lipp's arbiters of status—John Kenneth Galbraith had been relegated.

Mehdi Ben Barka, the important left-wing Moroccan dissident, was kidnapped leaving the Brasserie Lipp, to be tortured to death by Mohamed Oufkir, King Hassan II's sinister minion, later executed for his own treason. Is it heartless not to keep from wondering whether Ben Barka would know a moment of regret about his last banal meal as a free man, chez Lipp?

Recently, French president Nicolas Sarkozy's published habits have revealed Fouquet's on the Champs Elysées—whose terrace is a Mecca, for some reason, for tourists—as the lunchtime inner sanctum of people of power in business and politics. I knew it when it was where film producers did deals at lunch, when they weren't having drinks at the bar of the Hôtel Raphaël. The poorer, creative movie people settled for coffee and snacks at the café Le Select, on the Left Bank. The quality of the food at Fouquet's then was far inferior to the status of the crowd—a perverse elitism, like at Lipp or at 21 in New York.

People who were regularly photographed in those days enjoyed discreet and delicious lunches and good weather outside a place up a carless dead end near a garden not far from the Boulevard Saint Germain. The name of the place was Le Récamier, named for the lane it was on, itself named after a woman in French literature. The owner, Martin Cantegrit, would make up his tables with care about whom to place near or far from whomever else, but there was no Siberia at Le Récamier. His relationship with the nabobs was that of a polite friend, while he treated strangers with consideration. Le Récamier's wine cellar was enviable. Cantegrit chastised Robert Parker when he came to lunch one day, for making a big deal about the taste of oak. He gave Parker a road map to the Rhône vintages he favored, which Parker indeed followed. The food was impeccable and classic. I shall remember forever the thick, delicious *foie de veau* at Le Récamier. Martin's son sold the place to someone whose claim to fame was soufflés.

Although good food mattered to us, and we had our favorites where the food was simply as good as it gets, Joanne and I would more often go to where the food, the atmosphere, and the crowd, all combined, gave the place a certain authenticity. The food always seemed right for the place, part of the personality. And, whether with *haute cuisine*, or *cuisine bourgeoise*, or the simple, economic dishes that snobbish Parisians called roguish, eating put us in concrete touch with a segment of the life of Paris, whether inspired, shamefully vain, or absurd. In my own stance of privilege but not allegiance, I'd connect, by dining, with each place and also with the city's social texture. In any case, we never met in a restaurant to applaud a performance. But the times were changing. . . .

8

CAME THE REVOLUTION?

The French have a weakness for revolutions, with their history of five republics interspersed by two kingdoms, two empires, and a dictatorship. A revolution in French cuisine?

French cooking has enjoyed a long reputation as the best in the world, a renown that might have begun in the sixteenth century, when Catherine de' Medici brought her Italian cooks with her, having left Florence to marry King Henry II of France. Talk about *nouvelle cuisine*, Catherine was supposed to have brought a vast cornucopia of comestibles to the table that would change French eating habits forever. Practically Edible, the Internet food encyclopedia, mentions artichokes, aspics, baby peas, broccoli, cakes, candied vegetables, cream puffs, custards, ices, lettuce, milk-fed veal, melon seeds, parsley, pasta, puff pastry, quenelles, scallopini, sherbet, sweetbreads, truffles, and zabaglione. It is also fairly certain that Catherine taught Henry to use a fork.

What happened afterward could best be understood if you perceive the dichotomy that persisted in French cuisine, and how that

100

became more and more blurred as the society evolved toward greater democracy. There was the food of the commoners, who lived off the bounty of French agriculture, and had no reason to turn up their noses at dishes their forebears loved to cook. And then there were, into the early twentieth century, the cooks who served crowned heads and later, tycoons, for whom preparing formal meals was creating something like a dramatic performance that the diners attended. The food came out with the finery of an Elizabethan masque, in elaborate presentations; never mind that, way back, diners were poisoned by the lead used in the bright coloring of the sculptured *pièces montées*. Nobles and royalty were at one time served peacocks, because they made for a breathtaking table decoration. The mighty were beyond just eating, they wanted rare experiences that reinforced the notion of their power and might. Sounds a little familiar today?

Looking further back, we see that the beautiful birds did indeed become meat, as the oldest known French cookbook that dates to 1290 prescribes. The flesh of the peacocks or of swans was to be roasted on a spit, caked with a mixture of saffron, wine, egg, and white bread. To the host went the head, the rear, the wings, and the thighs, and the "remainder" to the others. Taillevent, who became King Charles V of France's cook in 1373, had a knack for slipping the carcass out of the skin of a peacock, roasting it on a spit, and putting the skin and feathers back on like a jacket for the royal guests to admire before dissecting. His recipe calls for one accompaniment, "aged pepper."

We learn in a cookbook called *Honest Voluptuousness*, published a hundred years later, that in the fifteenth century dolphins were the ticket for an upscale dinner. The author, one Baptiste Platine de Crémone, spends a long discourse about how dolphins, which love mankind, save drowning men and take pleasure in being called Simon. He next recommends letting their flesh go tender for several days, before frying and roasting, rather than boiling it. This contribution to *la cuisine, Dieu merci,* has not survived.

In the post-Italian era, François Vatel was a star to compare with today's culinary luminaries. Vatel's strength was *pièces montées* but he was also fanatical about the finest quality of his ingredients. The cook to French royalty, Vatel was so passionate about his calling that he ran himself through on a sword when a dinner he prepared for the Prince of Condé's reception for Louis XIV was ruined by the late arrival of a delivery of fish. Despite his fatally fervent devotion to his craft, Vatel's lasting contribution to the evolution of *la cuisine française* was just whipped cream.

Scholars of the history of French cuisine might believe that Louis XIV's court chef, Francois Pierre de la Varenne, Vatel's contemporary, deserves a more prominent place there than Vatel's dramatic farewell. La Varenne's noted accomplishment was to have created new taste sensations by eschewing strong spices and replacing them with a vast, erudite palate of subtler ones. Such was his *nouvelle cuisine* of the seventeenth century.

In the canon of lofty cookery, Marie-Antoine Carême is the next great name you usually find inscribed. Carême was called "the king of chefs and the chef of kings." Carême, who cooked for the consummate diplomat Prince Talleyrand and for Bonaparte, was known for his elaborate *pièces montées*, but, note well, he also favored the use of fresh herbs, simpler sauces, and he changed the way of serving from the equivalent of a smorgasbord of lavish dishes all laid out at once to a rational succession of limited courses, changing *service à la française* to *service à la russe.*

His preference for *à la russe*, which became the dominant way of serving in Western culture, would have an ironic overtone. Carême's mentor was the man he ardently called "Le Grand Laguipière." Dartois Laguipière, who was chef to Napoléon's brother-in-law Prince Murat, accompanied that swashbuckling warrior on Bonaparte's disastrous Russian campaign and froze to death in his carriage during the retreat from Moscow—leaving behind Carême to pick up the torch for lighter sauces. Carême, like that obsessive perfectionist in hostelry and luxe restaurants César Ritz, would earn his own death from exhaustion, which was not hard to do in the cramped, torrid, professional kitchens of France, which remained that way well into the twentieth century.

Auguste Escoffier, who was born in 1845 and died in 1935, is often called the person *la nouvelle cuisine* of our era turned its back on, but, in fact, it continues to follow some basics of his techniques, including the sauces he codified: *béarnaise*, hollandaise, and so forth. Escoffier further simplified and lightened Carême's style, while carrying forth his legacy. By then, high cuisine was no longer the domain of crowned heads and their banquets. Luxurious hotels and restaurants were perpetuating it for the grandees of the Industrial Age. Escoffier worked for César Ritz, pioneer of *les grands hôtels*, which came to be called *palais*. At the Carlton in London, one of his last accomplishments was training a pastry chef who would abandon the trade. His name was Ho Chi Minh.

The next great culture hero of French cuisine was Fernand Point, a cook who was no longer a vassal to the mighty. In the southern town of Vienne, Point opened La Pyramide, a restaurant tourists could afford to drive to, after World War I, where the hallmark of his cuisine was lightness, using delicately young vegetables and unfloured sauces. Point would become known as the godfather of the twentieth-century's *nouvelle cuisine*.

Looking back at this long tradition, it is harder to talk about today's grand chefs as revolutionaries. They indeed shook up the canon with more precise techniques and pushed the envelope of lightness, away from the heavy sauces that had dominated French food for centuries. And then, something else happened. Driven, like poor Vatel, to be at the top of their craft, they began doing weird concoctions, their versions, if you will, of the baroque presentations, the *pièces montées* of the exhibitionist chefs of yesteryear. You could call that a counter-revolution. Or call it decadent, like the Romans who fancied mice simmered in honey.

This notable change in French cuisine began in the sixties, when a whole lot of things about the way we lived and what we valued was being challenged. A reporter for a popular newspaper *Paris-Presse*, Henri Gault, teamed up with one of its editors, Christian Millau, to write a guidebook to leisure activities, including restaurants and upscale shopping, in Paris. They called it *Le Guide Julliard*, after their publisher. Their guide was also a spunky throwing down of the gauntlet to *Le Guide Michelin*, which had been the authority on the best places to eat and sleep in France since its inception in 1900.

Michelin was in the tire business, and the family was inspired by the realization that more tires would wear out if people took to the road more. To encourage travel, Michelin created a guide to where to get a decent place to eat or sleep in the sticks, or if you're a provincial, where best to eat or sleep in Paris. By the twenties, Michelin was distinguishing particularly good places to eat with one, two, or three stars. One star for good food, two worth making a detour, three worth the trip in itself. The starred ones got their owners' names mentioned and the names of a good dish or so that they accomplished. The criteria for ratings, beyond the stars, included more than just food, but also comfort or luxury in the surroundings. The Michelin man, in the old days often a tire salesman promoted to the gastronomy beat, was under strict orders to arrive without notice and remain anonymous.

In practice, the major restaurateurs would each make a pilgrimage to the office of *The Michelin Guide*'s director each year, to curry favor, before the new guide came out. Also, as soon as a single diner sat down in a restaurant to eat alone and touched his plate to see if it was hot, and checked out the toilet, the arrival in the region of a Michelin inspector would commonly spread from restaurant to restaurant. Gault and Millau, starting with Paris, took a radically new tack. Their guide concentrated on the cooking rather than the accoutrements and they ranked the chefs' performances on a scale up to 20. Rather than remaining anonymous, our two mavens stayed close to the latest happenings in the world of chefs whose celebrity they created. They were in the swim, attentive to any gossip or news that could affect the ratings. Theirs was the world of ambitious chefs, a fraternity bound together in freemasonry. They promoted the gospel of lightness, precise cooking time, and creative imagination at the stove. They had caught on to a generation's ambitions, and they called their shared revisionism of the canon of kitchen methodology "*la nouvelle cuisine.*"

Mimi Sheraton, the celebrity food critic of *The New York Times,* would call *la nouvelle cuisine* a "gastronomic revolution." She described "the verdant brightness and herbaceous freshness of its dishes with an emphasis on lightness and the elimination of heavy flour-laden sauces so typical of classic French cooking."

Nouvelle cuisine was French food lite, but it wasn't entirely a disavowal of *la cuisine française.* And as we said, the change was already long in evolving. The multicourse elaborate meals of the nineteenth century were a thing of the past. Nobody, anymore, was hanging pheasants on a string tied to a wall, until their necks rotted and they fell, ready for cooking, as was the prescribed way of flavoring and tenderizing game birds.

The most prominent nouvellers among French chefs—the Troisgros brothers, Alain Chapel, Paul Bocuse—had all been trained by that one man who is considered the father of *la nouvelle cuisine,* Fernand Point, of the legendary La Pyramide, in Vienne, a town south of Lyon.

Point died in 1955. He was an inspiration for his followers because of his deftness with light sauces, his precision in cooking times, and the use of the freshest local ingredients. His light touch had its limits. Point's motto was *"Du beurre, du beurre, du beurre, et encore du beurre!"* If you look closely in the plates of his disciples' preparations, you will find that they weren't always light either. If Point loved to soak his puréed spinach with butter to the point of saturation, today's star of new cooking, Joël Robuchon, was famous for his mashed potatoes that are also made to take as much butter as they can stand. In each of the main courses of a contemporary-style restaurant, odds are high that you will find a brown liquid that is none other than a *fond brun,* a base of conventional cuisine. It was once a decoction of long-cooked meat scraps and vegetables. Now, because of food industry–lobbied European Union sanitary rules, a *fond brun* is most often made from a powdered version of these ingredients, at the factories of the clients of the lobbyists. Two other things stand out in the cooking of today's star chefs: original combinations and skimpy portions—as if the money spent on labor in elaborating the dishes, before they get the last touch of the microwave, is made up for with chary purchases of ingredients. In any case, those little things on your plate, in a Japanese-inspired design, have the value-adding suggestion of being precious. A third thing, which shows indisputable skill, is precision in cooking.

Michel Guérard, whose restaurant Le Pot au Feu, which opened in the modest Asnières suburb of Paris in 1965—a restaurant that became a Mecca of the new style—is a master at cooking things to the point of their greatest savoryness. His thumb pressed on a grilling steak tells him more about where things are inside it than any thermometer. Guérard left Paris to open a spa-related establishment in the South of France with his wife, whose parents owned a chain of spas.

I ate at La Pyramide long after Fernand Point's death, when his wife was still running the place. I remember a great *côte de boeuf,* with a *sauce choron,* a butter-gorged *béarnaise* sauce altered by a touch of tomato paste. Madame Point was not charitable toward contemporary cooking, which she found flashy. "Some of these cooks don't even know the difference between a *ratatouille* and a *sydney,*" she opined. I didn't either, but she explained: A *sydney* is a dish of numerous vegetables cooked together; a *ratatouille* is made of all those ingredients, each cooked separately to its ideal state—since each takes different times arriving there—before combining them.

Gault and Millau, before they split up, went on to found a magazine and then a guide to France bearing their own names. They spawned other guides throughout the world, along with generating a whole race of guides inspired by them.

Gault died in 2000 and Millau has separated himself from the guide and the magazine. I asked Millau to look back on the epoch of French cooking in which he was so key an influence, and to bring us up to date on where we are with new cooking.

In the 1960s, "I was the chief editor of the leisure page of the newspaper *Paris-Presse*," Millau recalled, "and Henri was what we call a '*grand reporter*'—a reporter who does the important stories. He seemed to have nothing to do, and the director asked me to give him something to do. 'Why not ask him what he wants to do?' I said. We asked him and he said, 'I like to stroll about.'"

And that was how, for the first time, a review of what was going on among leisure activities in Paris, including what was happening in restaurants, got into the press, in the form of a weekly page. Not long after *Paris-Presse* was absorbed into another daily, *France Soir*, Gault and Millau took wing and started their own business, after having already been the authors of a guide for the publishing house of Julliard, which expanded on the same themes as their newspaper reviews. Their first annual *Guide Julliard* had come out in 1961 and sold, Millau told me, two hundred thousand copies. They launched their own magazine in 1968, the year that bobos still call the time of "the revolution" in France. The GaultMillau Guide soon followed.

"Something was happening," Millau said. "Going around France, we saw something happening. Our society was changing. Cuisine evolves in the same way as society. Cuisine is a reflection of life."

French cuisine hadn't changed, he explained, since before the war. Auguste Escoffier, an innovator in his own terms, had codified restaurant cooking techniques—from the details of managing a team in a kitchen to the ingredients of a sauce and what should be served with what. "Veal has to go with spinach," Millau said, "duck with peas. Escoffier's *Le Guide Culinaire* was as authoritative as Mao's *Little Red Book*.

"Several things in the culture were now coming together to create an important change. Up until now, there were only a very few celebrated chefs in France, who had begun their careers before the war and who were near the end of their lives. Curiously, they were all outside Paris: Fernand Point, Alexandre Dumaine, François Bise. In the great Paris restaurants, it was the owner who mattered and who hired anonymous chefs. Now we saw a lot of young chefs in France who own their own restaurants.

"France was now adopting to a new way of life. For one, people were less hungry. Up until the fifties there were ration tickets. Now we'd finally come to live normally. People had been gorging on food, and we were now at a time when they felt that they'd had enough.

"People had begun to travel. In France, in the rest of the world. If you can imagine, there had been only one Mediterranean restaurant in Paris. People found an appetite for new things. Our diet could not long be what it was before.

"The sixties were a time when people were experimenting in their personal lives. . . . It was the spirit of sixty-eight. And your chefs were trying new methods.

"It came down to cooking precisely and less long. Creating lighter, simpler, and closer to natural savors. We gave a name to combine all the tendencies in cuisine. *Nouvelle cuisine*. We didn't launch the movement, we accompanied it, encouraged it. We were journalists covering what was happening. Few other journalists were interested. Now there are more food journalists than war correspondents.

"We have come full circle and are now in a ridiculous period, ridiculous, pretentious, and stupid. In every movement, whether intellectual or literary, you can't stop imbeciles or shady people from following something that's happening. It's easy to fall into the folly. How can these guys who begin their careers at the age of fourteen, down at the bottom in some kitchen without having other than a manual education, not fall into this trap, when suddenly they're taken for artists, philosophers, thinkers. I heard this celebrity chef, darling of the press say:

"'You don't come to me for my cuisine but for the philosophy of my cuisine.' Imagine!"

In my mind I heard an epicure who earned his own way to celebrity on the strength of a lot of trite maxims. It was Jean Anthelme Brillat-Savarin, who wrote in the nineteenth century:

"The discovery of a new dish confers more happiness on humanity than the discovery of a new star." And I recalled the couturier André Courrèges's stellar modesty, when he replied to Mildred Custin, president of the upscale department store Bonwit Teller, after she gushed over one of his collections, the day after the moon walk:

"Ah, Mildred, I'm nothing compared to NASA."

Millau said he wasn't at all opposed now to originality, even though "new, new, new" has become a shrill refrain. "We communicate with history when we eat," he said, "not just past history but also current history. You need not be a great talent to not be an imbecile.

"I say, if you have something to express, do it as honestly as possible. There are a lot of little chefs who do admirably well what they know how to do. You can have the capacity to do something notably well, without saying if I'm not a genius, I'm nothing.

"Once again, what is happening in cuisine is a perfect reflection of what is happening in our society. I was in François Pinault's museum of contemporary art in Venice and I saw a bicycle leaning against a pillar. I thought a guard must have left his bike there, but that seemed pretty strange. Until I saw the label that said that this was the creation of a German 'conceptualist.'

"In the end, it all comes down to two things, the media and the money. The two are tied. The media and the money dictate everywhere in our times.

"But do you know about one big change that nobody talks about in restaurants today? You cannot imagine how unhealthy the kitchens were, cramped holes unhealthy to work in and a danger to health in the handling of the food. You cannot image how unbearably hot and filthy the kitchens of the fanciest restaurants in Paris once were."

Today, *la nouvelle cuisine* is no longer new, and it has undergone changes of its own. We have molecular cooking, made famous by Ferran Adrià in Spain. By then, a French name was no longer appropriate for what was going on. We had arrived at "fusion food." Fusion cooking meant mixing ingredients from various places on earth to create something even more exotic that is the chef's own achievement.

Globalization. I quote from a piece in *The New York Post* about a new delight at a restaurant called Resto:

"This strip of cured pig fat from the very rare Mangalista pig which general manager James C. Mallios notes 'was originally reserved for the Hapsburg royal family,' is served with grits and farm eggs to special friends only."

The esoteric pig fat, the foam instead of meat. . . . New creations for new sensations. Like the Japanese who play with death eating blowfish poisonous if wrongly cut, and like somewhere in Asia, if I recall, where they eat the brains of live monkeys, there is always someone combing existence for some ultimate luxury in dining. Someone told me that his brother frequents a secret place in Brooklyn, where gourmets gather to eat horsemeat, forbidden by law, smuggled in from Canada. Until more opulent recent times, this rare treat was a staple of the poor in France, just as the chorizo made of worn-out donkeys was its equivalent in the austere Spain of Franco.

In the quest for rapture in gastronomical experience, the exotic shades over into something like the erotic. I think of the slogan some advertiser for a coffee in America invented long ago: "a new taste thrill." The word kinky also comes to mind.

And I hear Christian Millau talking again, a man of great civilization, whose career is a tapestry of a legal education, war reporting, literary criticism, fiction, and . . . gastronomy.

He remembers Molière, the Shakespeare of French satirical drama:

"We're in a ridiculous period that would enchant Molière. If Molière were here, he'd surely do a play about the *cuisiniers.*"

Fusion food is what Alain Ducasse told me was "confusion food." He meant to describe eclectics less talented than himself, since the menu of at least one of his restaurants, Spoon in Paris, is extremely fuse-y.

Ducasse is the most successful of the culinary stars who have become big businessmen, much like fashion designers who license their names all over. Ducasse has saved a handful of old-fashioned bistros and restaurants in Paris that were no longer in fashion from a slow death by revising their menus with his contemporary style while still keeping their essential personality. Maybe he has acted out of a bit of a guilty conscience, but he's indeed a keen businessman, who has surmised that synergy was possible in reviving the popularity of a longtime favorite with his own culinary charisma. Viewed in business terms, in swallowing up places that had "brand" value, he has been increasing his share of the overall market, increasing the dominance of the Ducasse brand, as the the first name in restaurants.

I was at a lunch for the press that he gave at Rech, a restaurant that had been dear to Parisian seafood lovers since the twenties but which was far from trendy decades later. Ducasse had taken over Rech and installed Jacques Maximin, another celebrated French cook, as its chef. Lunch began with a "cookpot of asparagus tips and morels," served with a "tea of vegetables," a "milk-shake of peas and mint," in a large shot glass, and some barely cooked broad beans you could dip in sea salt. The "cookpot" is a round porcelain pot with an oval top that Ducasse has designed for cooking vegetables. You didn't get the pot in your plate but the vegetables, which were precision cooked. From there we each went on to a rectangle of sea bass that looked like my New Year's Eve *pièce de résistance* in Auvergne, accompanied by a tiny squash and a potato the size of a big marble, each stuffed with things I had trouble identifying. It was all tasty; was it worth all that jazz? Ducasse had preserved the 1925 décor of the place, but our palates were communicating with the dandyisms of our other age. I felt comforted reading the regular menu of Rech, which resembled the bill of fare of a serious seafood house, brushed up with touches of fantasy. At our lunch, on the other hand, Ducasse and Maximin had given what the newspeople needed to feed off: an original performance.

Ducasse, ever a man of his times, has also been creating his upscale version of fast food. . . . It's a response, no doubt, to the phenomenon known as "fooding" in contemporary French. Since the upheavals of 1968, antielitism has been a strong current in French society, and *Fooding* magazine has prospered under that banner. *Fooding* takes you to many places much cheaper than the famous French restaurants and fosters a less elitist approach. It writes about food from all over, prefers the exotic for its news value, and is not averse to judging junk food. With its "cool" graphics, a language full of slang, and the mixture of comic strips on its website, *Fooding* is a guide for those who would be "*branché*," or plugged-in. Although its omnivorous approach does not ignore authentic pedigreed cooking, it's still much about celebrating novelty and "being there."

Joanne and I were leading what some might call enchanted lives when I was at *WWD*, which was when the new wave of cuisine began getting attention. But despite raises, my salary remained ridiculous. Meanwhile, a crowd of *sans culottes* had invaded the fashion world, some with fresh talent, more bent on becoming rich celebrities above all, with freak shows to get the attention of a new breed of journalists coming to the collections. It wasn't in me to praise their pursuits, which, if they weren't cynical, were benighted.

When Régine's brother made me an offer I couldn't refuse to be his "communications" vice president and change his image as a predatory corporate raider, I took it, only to find the task worse than daunting. I left Maurice quickly, long before he went to prison. From then on, on my own, and together with Joanne, I devoted myself to writing fiction and travel narratives. Harry Evans tapped me to be his man in Europe when he founded *Condé Nast Traveler*, and it became an unforgettable privilege: taking people's vacations for them and being paid for it—while doing it in a provocative, honest way, conscious of the dirty footprints we travelers often leave on the planet, and how we could avoid doing that along with other damage. That mission was an extension of the journalistic ethics Harry had already demonstrated in a brilliant career in Great Britain, before he and his incisively smart wife, Tina Brown, crossed the ocean, bringing with them new bursts of energy to the profession.

Part of the fascination, for Joanne and me, in our extended travels for *Condé Nast Traveler*, was getting to know, more intimately, the extraordinarily varied and textured culture of France. To hear what people, whose ways of life made up the fabric of French culture, had to say.

In all that, of course, *la cuisine* is an essential part. That element, menaced by being cynically denatured, still exists. We'll take you on a voyage to meet people whom you might at first think would be "Primitives," but who are often people who've trained in their craft and gained kudos at it elsewhere, before going home to grow roots again: people preparing food that defines who they are and what they are, in the particular places they are. Artists? That word gets bandied about so easily by the hyperbolic arbiters of achievement, in our so-called antielitist era. La Rochefoucauld looked at the matter from another angle centuries ago. "Eating," he wrote, "is a necessity, but eating intelligently is an art."

Let's just forget that loaded a-word; we're off to some pleasurable and revelatory eating. And on our way, we'll more than eat, we'll visit the elements of nature and the landmarks of high civilization that make France, everywhere you go in its hexagon, an irresistible destination. We'd never turn our backs on being American, a country where our ties defy distance and to which our families owe a lot, having left behind the barbarism of Eastern Europe. But the Germans are right with their proverb: France is a very privileged place to live. "Like God himself."

9

PARIS THE OMNIVOROUS

Aside from the *goujons*, the little fish that people caught in the Seine and served up fried at the riverside *ginguettes* in the Paris that Hemingway knew, it is hard to think of an item of food that is native to the city. Once, the cherries of the now upscale suburb of Montmorency were renowned as particularly delicious, as were the peaches of Montreux, the suburb that has been gentrified, after becoming the neighborhood of Communist factory workers. The asparagus of Argenteuil were famous well into the twentieth century. Argenteuil, where impressionists painted, is now pretty much a ghetto of public housing, although there is a single farmer left there who sells his asparagus for more than nine dollars a pound in April at one Paris vegetable store. The bakeshops of the suburb of Nanterre do *brioches* in a different shape from those in the city, but they taste like they do all over. In Poissy nearby on the Seine, they do that fruit pit liqueur such as it has been distilled since 1698. The turnips of the Ile de France, of which Paris is a part, were once renowned for their succulent, firm flesh, but you rarely see mention of them in markets anymore, while truck farmers still do bring in lettuces and leeks from their plots a few miles beyond the Paris region.

I have heard chickens clucking in the backyards at the Goutte d'Or, the neighborhood of African immigrants, and of course there is still a vineyard on Montmartre, whose wine is a curiosity rather than a pleasure to the palate. Mushrooms are still raised in the former catacombs and are called *champignons de Paris*, and the most banal ham available bears the alibi *jambon de Paris*.

Otherwise, the French have a saying: Don't look for noon at two in the afternoon. A contemporary city is a city. What Paris has been as far back as the eleventh century, when they built Les Halles, is the place that drew a great variety of produce from elsewhere in the nation, because the Parisians had the most money to pay for the cornucopia.

The cuisine of Paris is thus made up of ingredients from all over—all over the world in recent times. Nonetheless, an eclectic but characteristic way of cooking took firm hold here. Parisian fare spreads across the three categories: *la haute cuisine, cuisine bourgeoise,* and those dishes that the Parisians call *les plats canailles,* the fare of people without a lot of money, dishes that their social superiors call— with patronizing mitigated by affection for the tasty food—roguish. The sophisticates of Paris love *les plats canailles* the way that they love the black-and-white, proletariat-oriented movies of the thirties.

But I won't get into nostalgia for nostalgia's sake:

Once Joanne and I, shortly after arriving in Paris, stumbled into a shabby restaurant near Les Halles that catered to *les forts des halles,* the rough-and-ready crate pushers of the market, working past closing, until lunch. The Michelin man would have turned heel. But what could have been more authentically Paris to a neophyte couple like us? The wine for everyone was a rugged red served in carafes, the *plat du jour,* a *boeuf mironton,* a second-day treatment of the beef in a leftover *pot au feu,* sauced with wine, vinegar, onion, a touch of tomato paste and flour, and topped with bread crumbs, before going into the oven. It is now almost impossible to find, in a restaurant, this souvenir of the nonjaded thrift of yesteryear, whose aroma you'd passed going by your concierge's *loge*—in those days in France when newspapers were cut in squares for a second life in the WC, when old pensioners steamed envelopes open and turned them inside out to reuse, when you bought a metal slug in a café to work a telephone beside the bathroom, and when the *métro* smelled of sweat and the movie houses of sweat and caporal cigarette smoke. A *boeuf mironton* is as *canaille* as you can get. Curnonsky called it "the concierges' triumph." I ate it only once again since. Frankly, I don't miss it. Any more than all of the above.

Haute cuisine has been at home for years in the handful of luxurious Paris restaurants that Michelin accorded three stars. Their ranks remained rather constant, with demotions and reinstatements. Gault and Millau, promoting creativity over luxury, enlarged and challenged the list. Michelin, meanwhile, recreated itself into a follower of creative cooking and became more laid-back about luxury.

It wasn't enough for members of Michelin's cast of stars to preserve and perpetuate their achievements. They had to come up with novelties. Jean Ducloux, who had a Michelin star since 1949 at his Hôtel De Greuze in the little Burgundian town of Tournus, and who earned a second one in 1978, was one of the most skilled chefs in France. Having been demoted back to one star, he was at risk of being old hat and starless, before doing riffs on his repertoire. We remember well his *oeufs en meurette*, Burgundian poached eggs in stock, his turbot *sauce béarnaise*, his terrines. . . . He died before we went back to eat there again for this book, and now his successor is doing *oeufs en meurette* with crushed candy and nectarine pie, and artichokes with tandoori oil. The star has been saved from extinction.

The end result is that the old stalwarts of grand classic cooking have become more and more creative to stay competitive and stay in business. The prices seemed to call for equal exaggeration in culinary prowess, and their stardom is in constant competition in the eyes of the novelty-hungry critics. Those who were slow to react to this saw their clientele growing older while fewer new ones, youngish followers of fashion, have been making reservations. There were two grand restaurants that preserved the character of traditional *haute cuisine* for a long time, Taillevent and Laurent. Now that Monsieur Vrinat, the owner, who dressed and comported himself like a distinguished civil servant, has died, Taillevent has been getting more and more into the art act. Laurent, a rendezvous of conservative people of power, might have been a better choice, probably, to illustrate this side of French cooking, but it, too, has become more inventive. Leaving the celebrated chefs to rival each other in imagination, Joanne and I headed elsewhere in Paris:

Cartet

"There has been no *brandade de morue* made here in thirty years," the man told me when I called to reserve a meal such as I used to have at Cartet. I remembered Madame Cartet's *brandade de morue* because it was simply unlike anything else I had been served, and it was the purist version, like the one that Prosper Montagné defines in just a paragraph in his venerable first edition of *Larousse Gastronomique*. Montagné wrote that encyclopedia of French cuisine in 1938, two years *after* Madame Cartet was doing her orthodox *brandade*, just one item on her palette of unforgettable, lovingly prepared *cuisine bourgeoise*.

Dominique Le Meur, whom I'd spoken to on the phone to order the *brandade,* informed me that Madame Cartet had died four years ago at the age of ninety-nine. He was the current owner. Marie-Thérèse and Raymond Nouaille, Madame Cartet's longstanding one waitress, and the waitress's husband, had assumed the place when Madame left thirty years ago and then sold it to Le Meur in 2003. They went on to look after Madame, accompanying her through her retirement, as she indulged in her fascination for eating at every touted grand gourmet haven in town, beginning with the Tour d'Argent, whose late owner, Claude Teraille, had been her loyal customer.

She'd enjoyed herself, but from my point of view, Madame Cartet was slumming. Her own food and restaurant, with seven or so tables and a storefront façade, made for an absolutely unique, incomparable eating experience. I went back once after Madame Cartet retired and it wasn't as good. I felt that the soul of the place was lost when she left, and I hadn't returned until Joanne and I decided to give the place another try for this book. We found out that Le Meur had been there for years. Le Meur is a forty-seven-year-old fellow, shy but jolly and a tad elfish, looking much younger than his gray hair—which may come from hard work—suggests.

Cartet, we discovered, after rapping at the storefront door, now kept locked to the unreserved, is perhaps even more wonderfully unique. So is Dominique Le Meur—who, alone, cooks, serves, washes the dishes and the glasses (twice) before they're rewashed in a machine, and goes to the Rungis wholesale market at 3:00 A.M. to be sure of the best fillets of beef before anyone else buys them.

Le Meur serves eight people at an average lunch and eighteen at dinner. Full nights can run into twenty-odd diners. There are, of course, never two servings, since it would be impolite to hurry people for the sake of the table. Since there's no one working in the dining room while he's in the kitchen, Le Meur keeps the door locked so that no one enters off the street without a reservation. This is not his snobby shtick. He likes to know how many people he'll serve in advance. Anyone can make a reservation, and among those few tables none are good or bad. There is no special treatment for the Known who know about the place.

Dominique has no answering machine. You have a good chance of his answering the phone for a reservation between noon and two in the afternoon, but some days he just closes the place to cook for a customer at the customer's home.

Once, he told me, a customer had put him up in a house on the grounds of his Normandy manor for ten days, while he cooked lunch and dinner. The kitchen of ten thousand square feet was five times the size of his dining room, and his kitchen is less than half that size.

And the food? The Nouailles had passed on Madame Cartet's repertoire, which they had followed with their understanding of faithfulness. He also kept the telephone, so if you want to call a taxi and you are without your cell phone and have to press a button on the phone, there is none, just the rotary dial. No affectation of old-fashionedness here. The phone works, and Le Meur—who doesn't own a TV; never, he says, reads a newspaper nor listens to the radio—didn't see the need to update the technology.

The *brandade*? A purist *brandade de morue* is not the potato and fish purée you will find everywhere. It is cooked dried cod, with some garlic—lots—a bit of milk, and olive oil added drop by drop while you pound the fish with a pestle until you have something close to mayonnaise. It requires long labor. The Nouailles chose to buy a ready-made *brandade* from a supplier in Nice, Le Meur explained, which their customers considered quite good. I later noticed that someone had put on the Internet "Madame Cartet's" *brandade*. It did contain potatoes, but anyone who ever ate the original would question its authenticity.

Dominique continues to serve the bought *brandade de morue* to whoever asks for it, while he devotes his labor to perpetuating Madame Cartet's achievements.

I started with a *croustade de morilles,* and Joanne prudently chose a salad tossed with perfect vinaigrette. The morels were tiny, dried because of the season, but I think that dried mushrooms, once reconstituted with water, are more intense tasting than fresh ones—unlike the insipid truffles that are cooked and jarred. At $69 for 3.5 ounces at my neighborhood vegetable store, dried morels are more than acceptable. Morels have become more and more rare, and the fresh morel season in the fall passes in a blink of the eye. With a sauce of *béchamel*, cream, a splash of cognac and of Armagnac, on an airy *brioche*, it was excellent.

"It's touching," Le Meur put it, when he came by our table, "touching. Nobody eats *béchamel* anymore." Flour in sauce, we agreed, has become a pariah in light cooking, but it has its moments of being the right thing in the right dish all the same.

Joanne and I went on to share a *boeuf à la ficelle*. This dish was invented back who knows when, in a household wealthy enough to buy the costliest cut of beef, one that was exceptionally tender while still being nearly fat-free. The dish is simplicity personified. You would never see a virtuoso chef wasting his talent on it, but done with its precisely right accompaniments, its subtlety is part of a memorable, elegant fugue of flavors. The recipe for the beef and its sauce is below. Dominique used a leaner version of a *sauce bordelaise*, without marrow, reserving a rich presence for the *pommes dauphinoises,* which, in Madame Cartet's version, are no more than sliced potatoes covered with *crème fraîche*, and grated Swiss cheese (*Gruyère*)—just enough to form a rich, thick presence with the firm potatoes, after baking.

The dinner was a concert for the palate.

At the other tables, people were delighting in breaded sweetbreads, roast leg of lamb, veal chops with morels and flamed kidneys.

I provoked Le Meur, telling him that his array of desserts on the bar was only half as extensive as what Madame Cartet used to serve, when she insisted that you sample everything from the two shelves on the caddy she'd bring out. Lunch at Cartet meant leaving the table at four thirty.

"The assortment is what the former owners passed on to me," he said, a little chagrined.

Joanne and I made do with little portions of lemon pie, chocolate mousse, rice pudding, floating island, cream puffs, French donuts (*beignets*), and tangerines.

It was now near midnight. Le Meur had washing the dishes of the evening's ten diners to look forward to next morning. I told him I'd be back next day in late afternoon, to talk.

We talked. He had met Madame Cartet only twice near the end of her life, but neighbors on the street knew her story. Nobody could say how she learned to cook to perfection elegant, classic food. She was an orphan who became the young mistress of a surgeon with means and later married a cardboard box salesman, who ran around on her and, to keep her busy during his affairs, he bought her this café near the Place de la République, which the whores of the neighborhood frequented and where you could also buy coal to heat your flat. Serendipity brought a fancy fellow from the well-heeled Sixteenth Arrondissement to the café, who found her lovelier than the ladies of the night. He redid the place, chased the whores, and set her up to serve his group of friends. She became his mistress and, once divorced, lived part of the time with him and his wife. Le Meur didn't know how that *ménage à trois* ended. Late into middle age, as neighbors reported to Le Meur, Madame Cartet, whose first name has been lost in time, received young men in her apartment above the restaurant. Madame Cartet's cooking, in any case, became a beacon for initiated gourmets. When I knew her late in her life, serving in her pink nylon smock, I had no idea of her sensual past, but sensuousness surely went into the food.

Le Meur does not like to talk about himself. "The thing that matters most to me is to be invisible," he said. He remembers working in the kitchen at Fouquet's, the lunch venue for the powerful, and seeing the headwaiter spend an hour deciding who deserved what table, before lunch began. He wouldn't dream of sorting people who came to eat his food.

Le Meur had had a fascination with food since childhood. He grew up in the big house of his parents in the Breton city of Rennes, where his father was a prosperous business consultant who entertained frequently. His parents fostered his bent by letting him cook for dinner parties, when he'd stay in the kitchen rather than come out for the accolades of the diners. He studied at a school for cooks in Paris as well as hotel school, and went off to work in kitchens in Australia, Tokyo, in Saint Tropez, on yachts in Italy, and in the homes of very rich French families. He did lobster bisque that earned him a reputation in Nantucket, and he trained in some of the most noted restaurants in France, the three-star restaurant of the Hôtel Bristol, the Ritz, the Closerie de Lilas. . . .

He would leave each very quickly. "I was never fired, but I couldn't stand staying on." Le Meur was an innocent in the hassle and harassment of French kitchen society. "I love to work," he said, "it's my big love. I can work eighteen hours a day without a problem. I was treated like a nut. I realized that I'd be happy only by working alone."

Dominique's father was a customer of long-standing at Cartet's and ate there whenever in Paris. When he learned that Madame Cartet's successors were selling, he bought the place for his son to settle down.

"I'm very happy here," LeMeur said. "My pleasure is giving pleasure, and to be totally discreet. The other night, I had a table of people who stayed until three in the morning. One of the women said to me, 'I never saw you all night.' It was the greatest personal compliment I could have."

I add mine to his prowess at the stove.

Boeuf à la Ficelle comme chez Cartet

For four people

  a fillet of aged beef of about two lb.

  beef consommé to cover the piece of beef

  salt and pepper to taste

Bring the consommé to a simmer.

Tie the beef with string, either attached to a wooden spoon that you can hold it on or tied to the handles of the pot, so that the beef is suspended in the simmering bouillon without touching the hot bottom of the pot. Some recipes call for adding vegetables and herbs to the broth, but a good bouillon has already had that experience.

Suspend the meat for two to three minutes. Slice it and put the slices in a medium oven for five minutes and serve with the following sauce:

  3 shallots

  2 cloves of garlic

  3 glasses of wine

  2 or 3 spoonfuls of veal *fond*, veal stock reduced to a thick concentration

Cook the garlic and shallots, minced to a paste, in the wine until the wine is nearly evaporated, then add the fond.

Le Meur uses wine left over in bottles after it has become slightly sour. The acidity is an improvement to the sauce.

Stella

The *brasserie* Stella is across the avenue from where Victor Hugo lived, but his house was destroyed in the late 1800s, when street after street of Belle Éqoque apartment buildings were built to

characterize the opulent Seizième Arrondissement. Yves Saint
Laurent's late aged mother used to walk her dog along the avenue
Victor Hugo, from her apartment nearby. This is not the kind of
neighborhood in which you might expect to find people chowing
down on some *plats canailles.* Yet night after night, seven days a
week, distinguished venerables and new generations of the successful fill Stella, consuming platters of fresh seafood and humble
but satisfying food. When we lived close by instead of across the
river, Joanne and I used to take a night off from the kitchen and
come here with the kids for some great steaks with fresh French
fries, and honest Beaujolais, when we weren't tempted by whatever else was on the changing menu that night, *hachis parmentier,* a
choucroute garnie, a steak tartare. . . .

The current owners have been there since 2001. They bought the
building, turned what was part of a little hotel above into a second
dining room, put in comfortable bathrooms, and redid the wood-
paneled walls. Nothing changed in the personality of the place. "If
I changed the food," Christian Philippon, one of the directors, told
me, "they'd tear out my eyes."

Philippon called Stella "artisanal." Almost all the other noteworthy *brasseries* in Paris have been bought up by the Flo chain,
which does much of the cooking in one central kitchen. Stella
remains independent and fills up with a crowd of regulars, with the
occasional exception of someone sent by the concierge of the Ritz
or the Plaza Athénée, who wants to eat among Parisians, not fellow
tourists. As with Lipp, there are no reservations, but here it's first
come, first serve for no matter whom.

The last time we were at Stella I ate *pieds de cochon,* as *canaille* as
you can get, and with them *frites,* freshly peeled from a variety of
potato called *voyager,* which, as Philippon pointed out, contains far
less water than the usual bintje variety for *frites.* They're bought
directly from a single farmer. The pigs' trotters come breaded and

first roasted, from a famous *charcutier* in the Loire Valley by the name of Hardouin. They were quite tasty, but nobody's perfect. *Pieds de cochon* are among the *plats canailles* dearest to the French, and they have a history as well as a pedigree.

They are sometimes called *pieds de cochon Sainte-Ménehould*. Sainte-Ménehould is a village in the Ardennes forest where in 1730 a cook in a hotel left a dish of pigs' feet on the stove all night by mistake and found out that they became more succulent than ever and that even the bones were chewable. That was the beginning of the *pieds de cochon* of Sainte-Ménehould, the town where Louis Seize was caught trying to flee France during the Revolution. Legend has it that he was recognized there, having stopped to eat some trotters, but Alexandre Dumas debunks that fatal urge in his authoritative dictionary of French cuisine. They are still cooked for at least eight hours in *court bouillon* before going into the oven breaded. I have never eaten the genuine article, but anyone so tempted can make the pilgrimage to Sainte-Ménehould, near Belgium, where they are still served all over the place.

For *pieds de porc*, Sylvain Warin's shop in the town is the consummate place to go. His trotters are made, according to the precepts of the Charter of the Brotherhood of Cochon à Sainte-Ménehould, from front feet only. "They're meatier," he told me, and he cooks them in *bouillon* for thirty—that's what he said—thirty hours on a faint flame, after which the marrow-filled bones are soft as meat. They're breaded and briefly roasted afterward.

Joanne had Stella's decent *blanquette de veau*. I couldn't convince her to order an *andouillette*, which ranks with *pieds de porc* among the most *canaille* of dishes. An *andouillette*, a tripe sausage with a strong taste, is the Rubicon foreigners often will not cross in going native in French eating. The *andouillette* at Stella is in any case the most distinguished variety, bearing the A.A.A.A.A. stamp of approval.

The five A's, L'Association Amicale des Amateurs d'Andouillette Authentique, is a body founded by food critics that now includes artisanal sausage makers and gourmands.

It bestows diplomas on those who make a proper *andouillette*, according to its standards. The most famous *andouillette* comes from the town of Troyes, but that's not its exclusive purview. And some towns are noted for *andouillettes* that include sheep as well as pork innards. The crucial criterion for a five-A diploma is that the sausage is done *à la ficelle,* which means that it is not stuffed with ground meat. The innards are cut in long strips, bound to strings, which are drawn through the casing, creating the authentic consistency, identifiable to the palate. I have eaten five-A *andouillettes* at Stella as well as at other self-respecting perpetuators of the genre. The diploma is well earned.

Stéphane Cailloux, Stella's chef, trained and cooked in some of the most prestigious gourmet venues: the Château de Mercuès, the Michelin-starred Sans Souci in Rome, and the Duc d'Enghien near Paris. He carries on the traditional cuisine at Stella because it's the food he likes to eat.

He gave us his recipe for a *blanquette de veau*. It is different from the one you're bound to find in a cookbook. It doesn't contain flour, but neither does he add egg yolk, a standard presence. It's the kind of *blanquette* you get in a bistro, where the dish is reheated each time before it's brought out. Reheating runs the big risk of curdling the sauce, if it contains egg yolk. "I add an egg yolk when I cook it at home," Cailloux said. He also does not use white wine but water instead: "The wine makes the delicate dish too acid." We didn't agree on that.

I was about to give here Stella's recipe for *blanquette de veau,* which I called decent—a treat enough, consumed in the authentic, convivial Parisian atmophere of this special place, but Joanne kept me back. "Hold it," she said. "It's not as good as yours. A *blanquette de veau* belongs in a book about French cuisine, but if you're going to put it in, put in yours, which is the best I know."

Forgive the self-promotion, reader. I cook fewer than a handful of things, but *blanquette* is one. I did not learn it from my grandmother, but not from a cookbook either. It is the result of many tries, some better than others. Take your chances with this. I feel confident that you'll like it:

Blanquette de Veau, à ma façon

Serves four to six people

    2 lb. veal short ribs (The bone enriches the flavor of the mild veal. Veal shoulder in cubes would also do.)

    a bouquet garni to which a sprig of fresh tarragon is added

    1 cup crème fraîche or heavy cream

    2 egg yolks (3 if you prefer more unctuosity)

    3 cloves of garlic minced to melt in the cooking

    two carrots cut in small strips

    a large onion, with a clove stuck in it

    a bottle of white wine, using enough to just cover the cooking meat

    1 ½ cups of chicken stock

    flour to coat the meat in browning

    a big handful of mushrooms (small brown ones are the best, or slice white ones in thirds)

    3 handfuls of small raw white onions, the kind you use to make a Gibson (if not these, small onions cut in half).

Brown the meat in oil, flouring it very liberally. The browned flour will disappear in the sauce, thickening it, without making it taste floury.

Boil off the alcohol of the wine you'll need to cover, say three cups.

Add the wine and the stock to the pot with the meat, a bouquet garni, and the garlic.

Bring to a small bubble and cook until a fork says the meat is tender, about a little more than an hour.

When the meat is cooled, skim off the fat.

Reheat the dish until it begins to simmer and cook the mushrooms, onions, and carrot sticks in it until they are tender.

Remove most of the sauce, keeping the meat hot.

You needn't strain the sauce. Combine the egg yolks with the cream, adding the mixture in small amounts, while stirring, to the sauce. Put the liquid back in the pot over the meat. Heat ever so gently so as not to curdle the egg yolks.

Sprinkle the dish with a sprig more of fresh tarragon and as much parsley, and serve.

Refrigerated and reheated ever so carefully, the dish can be served a second day, when it tastes even better. You won't regret the wine or the tarragon.

Chez Josephine

It was January, the opening of the season for the melanosporum, the best black truffle that French gourmets prize most among the six truffle varieties that exist in the world. Time to make a reservation at Josephine, one of the rare restaurants in Paris that changes a perennial menu to do suitable honor to that fabled tuber.

Chez Josephine, off the boulevard Montparnasse, has been around since the 1930s, when Josephine Duranton left off cooking alongside Marthe Allard, at chez Allard, and set herself up in what had been a *bougnat,* a humble café that sold coal when it wasn't topping up its topers with *gros rouge.*

(Chez Allard lives on as a landmark of French *cuisine bourgeoise*. A while before I wrote this, Fernande Allard, Marthe's eighty-seven-year-old daughter, moved out of her walkup high above the restaurant near l'Odéon, to return to her native Burgundy. The former owners of a small chain to whom she sold the place in 1985 continue to fill the dining rooms nightly with tourists, while nostalgic French come for lunch at a bistro that goes back to 1930.

Georges Pompidou used to come to Allard for the corned pork and lentils when he was prime minister before he was president, Juliette Greco gave her wedding lunch here, Catherine Deneuve and Jeanne Moreau have been known to cheat on their diets over the ample *plats du jour*.

Georges Braque liked Allard enough to design the roast fowl looking at a spur that is still on the menu. John Turturro was enjoying his braised beef with carrots at the table beside ours when we were there a while ago. But alas, we've gone back several times realizing that the following was true: Food so satisfying can at other times be terrible—for example, soggy, sweet fried potatoes with stringy *confit de canard,* burnt *bourguignon*. . . . Can the full house of foreigners every night make it either hard to get everything right in the little kitchen—or was there no need to try?)

Josephine created her kitchen but kept the décor simple, which has never changed since, except for the occasional paint job. The gaslight fixtures that were there before her time are still on the walls but no longer function. Yet the restaurant is far from decrepit, and it fills up nightly with assiduous gourmands, celebrities, and travelers in the know, all because it's been devoted for decades to some of the best *cuisine bourgeoise* in Paris.

Jean-Christian Dumonet's father bought the place from Josephine in 1962. At forty-one, Jean-Christian is both head chef and owner, a job he's held since his father handed the restaurant over to him when he was twenty-five, once he had completed

apprenticeships at such prestigious establishments as the restaurant
of the late Bernard Loiseau in Saulieu and the Jules Verne on the
Eiffel Tower. "I had to learn traditional cooking again," Dumonet
told us, "and it's been my love."

The seasonal truffle menu is a tradition that goes back beyond his
father's time, when Josephine's husband, who was her headwaiter,
used to come back, after retiring, every Wednesday to carve the leg of
lamb that was always, and still is, on the menu that day each week.

Since then, the price of the best black truffles has risen to the
league of caviar. "I buy mine directly from a supplier in Puymeras,"
Dumonet told us, "otherwise you can even pay two thousand euro
a kilo for it in Paris. A restaurateur could also buy black *truffes
musquées*, which look like the real McCoy but have far less flavor.
At eight hundred fifty euro a kilo, Dumonet still manages to serve
enough of the right stuff for diners to remember to come back next
winter. For starters: truffles in salads, truffle omelet or scrambled
eggs with truffles, soft-boiled eggs with truffles, truffles with fresh
pasta. Then there's a main course of the ultimate classic truffle-
garnished dish, *tournedos rossini*.

Joanne went for the *salade Rothschild*, a simple dish with watercress
and sliced fresh truffles—the kind of simplicity a coddled nabob of
finance could affect. Neither Jean-Christian nor I could determine
which Rothschild was its namesake. Google tells us that King Albert
of Belgium and his wife, Paola, ate a *salade Rothschild* as part of the
extensive menu of their fiftieth-anniversary dinner. I venture that
Joanne's *salade* was better than the royal couple's because Dumonet
substituted the classic hearts of lettuce with watercress, which has
much more to say to the palate.

I started with something more substantial, the fresh pasta with
cream and truffles, and went on to the *tournedos rossini*, a very tender
but richly flavored aged fillet, topped with fresh *foie gras* and a truffle
slice, in a *sauce brune*. The epitome of decadence, the modernist of

today's cuisine would call it, but wickedly delicious, the brown sauce being a rarity: made on the premises.

Joanne had something less grand: a half portion of the best *boeuf bourguignon* in Paris. Dumonet counseled us on a Languedoc red. It was one of those new-style punched-up reds and I was surprised by his choice, given the fact that since one of his brothers, who ran the restaurant before him, sold off the old cellar at auction, Jean-Christian has steadly built one of the best cellars in town— and among the costliest. Maybe he took pity on us, after the hit on our bank card the truffles made, by suggesting a modest-priced wine. I was ready to be happy without dessert, when one of the billowing soufflés that are a fixture of the dessert menu came by, and I was driven to have one, along with the shot of Grand Marnier accompanying it.

We completed our dinner with that special feeling of touching base with something rare, wondering what Sharon Stone, who had sat at our table a week before, made of the truffles. It would be hard to say that truffles are an acquired taste—it would take a lot of cash for such an acquisition. They do have a taste hard to compare with anything else. The white truffles that are the more common variety in Italy can recall garlic and a certain gaminess. Black melanosporum truffles, as best as I can describe, have a presence that makes you think of dark woodland. Exotic and alluring, like a unique perfume. I thought again of Henry James's ultrafine sensibility, which extended to truffles. I shared my Henry James truffle story with Dumonet. The great novelist, I recalled, liked to store fresh truffles with uncooked eggs, so that their evanescent flavor seeped through the eggshells, making for delicious egg dishes afterward. With that, Dumonet came back from the kitchen holding a basket of truffles and eggs.

"He didn't invent the recipe," Dumonet said. "Afterwards I do all the egg dishes."

"Henry James would throw the truffles away once all the flavor went into the eggs," I said. Jean-Christian made clear that neither he nor anyone he knew was throwing truffles away these days.

"But you know," he said, "truffles were once far more plentiful. When Baron Haussmann was rebuilding Paris, the workmen he engaged would sign on, providing they were not obliged to eat truffles at every meal."

We'd be back again before next truffle season, for the *côte de boeuf* with incomparable *béarnaise* sauce, the veal chop with its wicked rich, cognac-exalted sauce, the *confit de canard*, the *cassoulet*, and the *foie gras* . . . and especially the *boeuf bourguignon*, followed by the irresistible *soufflé au Grand Marnier*, or the house *mille-feuille*, which we for some reason call a Napoleon back home.

I went back next day, in any case, to take a tour of Jean-Christian's kitchen with him. He showed me the rapid cooling machine he uses to make his *fond brun*, that basic stock of a brown sauce I had savored the night before. Under the sanitary rules, the machine permits him to make it on the premises rather than buy some powder.

"It's designed to have the stock reach sixty degrees centigrade and then cool down to zero in an hour," Dumonet pointed out. "You're then allowed to keep it three days."

In the nearby meat locker were the fillets, the beef ribs, and the veal chops that Jean-Christian ages himself. From there we saw where his help makes the sausage for the *cassoulet* from scratch. A batch of fresh *foie gras* was about to be made into terrines. He showed me the backs of force-fed ducks, with a tender part of the legs that commercial *confit de canard* makers cut away, but which he keeps with the legs for the *confit de canard* he makes from the start. We passed where he had rolled out flaky pastry for the *mille-feuilles*.

I came away with an expression that encapsulates why I go back to Josephine: rare and deliciously authentic.

And the exceptional *boeuf bourguignon*?

I got nowhere asking Jean-Christian for the recipe. A lot of chefs keep their recipes to themselves, and I think that one of the reasons is that they have trouble sitting down and writing measurements for the household quantity of a dish that they cook in bigger amounts, relying on instinct and eye for the proportions. *Boeuf bourguignon* is, in any case, one of the easiest traditional French dishes to prepare. Dumonet, in speaking about his version of the dish, allowed that his major riff on the genre was different meat. "I used to use chuck but I got tired of handing out toothpicks to my customers after they ate the *bourguignon*," he told me. He uses beef cheeks, which are tenderer than chuck, richly flavored and not stringy. Some cooks use the more economical and still tougher shin. I've never seen beef cheeks on sale in America, but American chuck is tender enough to grill, so you can stick with chuck. The second phase that distinguishes Dumonet's version of *bourguignon* is that he doesn't marinate his meat in the wine in which he will cook it. The marinating is needed to tenderize tough meat. At the same time it is harder properly to brown the meat after it's been soaked. Dumonet browns his meat, tender enough not to be marinated, then adds the wine and a bouquet garni, the onion and garlic, and cooks it until fully tender. His sauce suggests that he adheres moderately to the classic adjunct of flour. You can do so sparingly, too, with a brown roux of equal portions of butter and flour, a scant tablespoon each, or you can flour the meat while browning it. Important to the dish however, are the bacon, mushrooms, and tiny onions that enhance a *bourguignon*. The wine? He didn't say. Although the dish originates in Burgundy, most Burgundies are too thin to stand up cooked with the meat, and the better Burgundies would go to waste in cooking. As you'll read ahead, I saw the late chef Georges Garin, one of the most famous pre-nouvelle cooks in Paris, pour Algerian *gros rouge*, inexpensive table wine, as he cooked his greatly appreciated *bourguignon* in his glassed-in kitchen. Choose an inexpensive wine with body and full flavor.

So, for six people:

Allow about a half pound of chuck per person cut in cubes. Braise the meat in butter. Put it in a pot with a couple of cloves of garlic, a bouquet garni, an onion stuck with a clove on each end, and cover with enough wine, having first boiled the wine to get rid of the alcohol. Dissolve the roux by pouring the wine on it slowly and stirring. Cook the dish gently until tender.

Before reheating, add to the pot two thick slices of slab bacon that you've diced and browned with the meat. Cured bacon can be used or smoked bacon, blanched to get rid of most of the smoke. Near the end of the cooking, you add also a scant handful of peeled small onions and an equal quantity of mushooms. The leftovers taste even better, reheated in the oven.

Le Rosco

This is not a place you'd walk into off the street. We did because, until the street sweepers arrived for their break of espresso or *ballons* of red wine at the bar, it was completely empty. We went on to write fiction daily here, around the corner from home, side by side with our two computers connected by the software Timbuktu. The coffee is good, and the place is silent for a few hours. We don't pay attention to the kitsch globed lights or the plywood walls trimmed with Burgundy-colored painted wood. Alain Martinez and his wife, Sue, are very congenial and don't bother us about lingering over a single coffee, and we leave when their daugher, Elodie, starts covering the tables with some of those time-honored bistro red-and-white-checkerboard tablecloths, which suddenly give the place a more charming allure. We'd leave to let the lunch crowd of local workers fill the place.

That is, we left every time until we spied Alain through the door to his kitchen peeling potatoes and whipping up mayonnaise by hand. The man cooks. He doesn't just work the microwave with wholesale, prepared food that he picks up at Metro. Soon we knew why the place was always full for lunch.

At a price about a third less than what the neighboring cafés charge for their microwaved food, Alain creates savory dishes from scratch. He's got the requisite diplomas, we learned, for a career in cooking; he spent a long time pursuing the role of a waiter in such fancy places as the Royal hotel in Deauville, the Grand Vefour under the fabled Raymond Oliver, and the Trois Marches in Versailles. "Finally," he said, "I wanted to be somewhere on my own." He bought Le Rosco with the money he'd saved. When the cook retired shortly afterward, he turned to his training as a cook at trade school. To be fair, the cafés that don't have cooks have a justification: The salary of a cook these days can be insupportably high. Alain, on his own in the kitchen, saves on that cost, and his modest but honest food is an attraction that makes the office people and the artisans, who rub shoulders at his tables, so fond of it that they bring him presents: wines and food specialities from the regions where they go on vacation. Flowers for Sue. As a sign of his attachment to value, the house "table wine" that comes in those heavy-bottomed glass carafes known as *fillettes,* is an honest *côte du Rhône* and not a *gros rouge.*

"I do the food that people no longer have the time to do at home, and nobody goes home for lunch anymore," he told us. From day to day it varies from the likes of a *blanquette de veau* to, say, a *boeuf aux carrottes* or a *boeuf bourguignon.*

We stayed for lunch.

Alain's *quiche lorraine* is a star attraction, and we shared one to start with—rich, smooth, and nicely enhanced with bacon cubes and a kind of custard on a puff paste. Joanne had the *boeuf aux carrottes,* respectably good, but I had something special. I say special because you never see *endives au jambon* on a menu anywhere. Dominique Le Meur would call the dish "touching," the way he speaks about the out-of-style *béchamel* sauce that is a major part of it. *Endives au jambon* are not so much *cuisine bourgeoise* as a thrifty main dish that households fell back on in poorer times, along with spinach topped with hard-boiled eggs and a macaroni casserole with ham. It was a staple of the years when France was recoving from World War II. It lost favor with the rise of prosperity, but for some it is still soul food. It originates from the North, where endives are common. The North is a region of obsolete mines and mills where, as Zola made clear, people were always poor. It was there that I first ate *endives au jambon*.

The scene was touching. I was accompanying the Socialist politician Michel Rocard on his trip around the nation to rally the faithful behind his ambition to become a candidate for the presidency. There was a dinner on his agenda with a humble family of Socialists to give him a touch of intimate contact with the grassroots. It was in one of those sad, brick company row houses built during the Industrial Revolution. The lady of the house prepared the authentic local dish, which happened to suit the austerity of the region. She'd taken great care. I found her *endives au jambon* quite delicious. The politician never touched his plate, and the look on her face was indeed touching.

At a later time, I was with the man at a book signing. He is very short, so he sat, looking serious, pen in hand, on a big pillow on top of a chair at a desk. Michel Rocard passed many good laws when he became prime minister, but he didn't seem to have the touch that made him close to the people. And he was never elected president.

Béchamel is a thick sauce, which improves the unctuousness of a dish, but, with its ingredients of milk, butter, and flour, it is also important in adding nourishment to thrifty dishes. Modern tastes associate it with being floury and are turned off it, but properly prepared it is an enhancement to a dish. *Béchamel*'s origins are far from poor. It is said to have been invented in the seventeenth century by Louis de Béchamel, Marquis de Nointel, the financier who was Louis XIV's honorary chief steward. Invented by him or by one of his cooks. Escoffier in his *Culinary Guide* and Prosper Montagné's

Larousse call *béchamel* one of the four "great" or "mother" sauces in the annals of cuisine, the sauces from which others are then made.

There are several versions of the *béchamel;* one begins with a previous "mother" sauce, a *velouté* containing a roux and stock. *Béchamel* for vegetable dishes is done without meat in the stock, while the roux remains a crucial element. A roux is flour and butter cooked together to take the farinaceous taste of the flour away, while keeping its thickening power. You mix the flour with slightly less butter, with a spatula, over modest heat until they combine into the begnning of a sauce. The cookbooks you read today often tell you that the roux is achieved when it is blond in color. Classically there are three roux: one for intensely flavored meats, such as game, a long-cooked *roux brun*; another for more delicate dishes such as fowl, cooked just until it is a *roux blond*; and third a *roux blanc*, quickly done before changing color.

Alain does a *roux blanc* for his *endives au jambon,* prepared as follows:

Endives au jambon at the Rosco

For four people

    12 endives

    12 slices of cured ham

    A qt. and a half or so of milk

    1 cup grated Swiss cheese (Gruyère)

    6 tbs. flour

    6 tbs. butter

    salt, pepper, and a bit of nutmeg

    1 lemon

Remove the outer leaves of the endives and cut off their tips. This avoids bitterness.

Cook the endives well covered with water in a casserole into which you have also put a lemon cut in half, to avoid discoloring the endives. Let them cook for ¾ of an hour.

Drain the endives in a big strainer and when they've stopped dripping, squeeze them each in a towel, otherwise they will be full of water.

Wrap the endives in the slices of cured ham.

Put them in a platter to go in the oven.

Prepare your *béchamel* by first making a roux of the butter and flour as follows:

Heat the butter until melted, sprinkle the flour on it, and take it all off the stove and turn with a spatula until you have a consistent paste.

Pour on the milk slowly, add salt, pepper, and the touch of nutmeg, put the mixture back on the stove, whisking constantly until it comes to a boil. Let boil two minutes more.

Pour the *béchamel* over the endives, cover with the grated Swiss cheese and a few tabs of butter, and brown the dish in a medium oven.

Thrift definitely has its rewards.

Alain's food will never be in the running for a star, but it's tasty, generously served, and inexpensive, factors that enhance the *bonhomie* of his luncheon scene. The eleven o'clock street sweepers, however, are no more at Le Rosco. Someone in the neighborhood snitched that their daily, convivial gathering at the bar, talking recipes and soccer, was happening during working hours. But the lunch crowd remains faithful. Sue told us they had been thinking of changing the name of the place. It comes from a cake in the Breton town of Roscoff, she said, where a past owner was born. They were thinking of Le Vieux Paris. But they decided to perpetuate the inherited name.

Along with a certain French way of eating. . . .

We had one more trip to do to outside Paris. Sylvain Vandenameele's rare chicken was on our minds, and we had a date for lunch in Houdan. The train gets you in about an hour to a peaceful town of thirty-two hundred surrounded by farmland and inhabited by many retirees. A tall, wide rectangle of stone looms over the streets that rise toward it. It's what's left of the castle that from its heights protected Houdan. Houdan is something like the word for "high" in Saxon. The town has been inhabited since the fifth century.

The Lord of Montfort built the castle between 1120 and 1134, and the dungeon, now partly a water tower, is all that's left of the castle. The Hundred Years' War between the Plantagenets, settled in England, and the Valois dynasties, over who owned most of France, ravaged much of the country, and Houdan wasn't spared. Houdan was occupied by the English through the middle of the fifteenth century. The Montforts later ceded it to the Dukes of Brittany, through marriage, and when Louis XII married Anne de Bretagne, it became royal property, until Louis XIV exchanged it with the Duke de Luynes for some land to build the Château de Versailles, twenty-seven miles away.

You're treated to a lot of interesting history wherever you go in France, even to the exurbia of Paris, and we were happy for that, but what we were also confronted with, as we left the little railroad station, was a horrendous downpour, which kept us from strolling around to see some of the historic houses and the flamboyant Gothic Église Saint-Jacques et Saint-Christophe, with its rare Renaissance apse. A cell-phone call reached a taxi nine miles away and before too long, we were away from the chilly station and sitting beside the brisk fire in the stone fireplace of the dining room of La Poularde. Sylvain Vandenameele stepped out of the kitchen wearing his chef's hat to get us a couple of glasses of white wine, while our Houdan

Chez Fonfon

à Fonfon gastronomique hommage

Une mer, des pêcheurs, un soleil qui réchauffe
Un imposant viaduc comme toile de fond,
Un passé qui survit grâce au "Vallon-des-Auffes"
Et, pour notre plaisir, le "Restaurant Fonfon"...

The legendary, "Fonfon", Alphonse Mounier, lives on, on the menu of Fonfon in Marseille, as does his famous recipe for Bouillabaisse.

Marguerite Laborde and her son Jean, two of the three generations at the Buvette de la Halle in Saint-Jean-de-Luz.

TOP: *Le Relais Gourmand's Sébastien Petit's riff on classic cuisine bourgeoise: his foie gras.* BOTTOM: *His homard à l'américaine under a balloon of crust.*

TOP: *Le Rosco's Alain Martinez and his popular quiche lorraine.*
BOTTOM: *Les Vapeurs, Trouville's favorite brasserie goes back to 1927.*

Patrick Vilfaillot, of La Boucherie de la Tour Eiffel, the day before our Thanksgiving.

ABOVE: *The menu of Trouville's favorite brasserie.* OPPOSITE (ALL): *The menu tells where on the Normandy map all the ingredients come from.*

Traditionnel - Copieux - Tout pur beurre à la minute
La qualité des produits de la mer et du terroir dans votre assiette

Ouvert tous les jours - Service continu

Les Entrées

Nos Spécialités

Les Salades

Les Coquillages et Crustacés

Suggestions du Chef

BADOIT

evian

BADOIT

Informations Client

Les Poissons

Les Viandes

Les Légumes

Pour les petites Faims

Les Œufs

Pour les enFants (-12 ans)

CAFÉ ou DÉCAFÉINÉ - 3,20 €

A découvrir

Nos vins en pots

Sélection du Sommelier

Côtes du Rhône

Sélection du Beaujolais

Vins Blancs de Loire

Vins Blancs de la Loire

Vins Rouges en Magnum (1,5 l)

Vins Blancs en Magnum (1,5 l)

Muscadet

Vins Blancs de Loire

Bourgognes Rouges

Bourgognes Blancs

Vins Rosés

Bordeaux Blancs

Champagnes

Vins d'Alsace

Champagnes Rosés

Côtes du Rhône Blancs

Cidres

Notre sélection de Bordeaux :

Traçabilité de nos produits

Moules de bouchot de Normandie

Huîtres de St-Vaast

Huîtres des Îles Chausey

Coquilles et Jacques

Raie et autres poissons de nos côtes

Crevettes grises

Bulots

Raie

Crème crue fermière

Crème crue

Viande de bœuf : une ORIGINE reconnue, une QUALITÉ garantie.

Les bovins nés, élevés, sélectionnés dans les herbages de Normandie sont engraissés au moyen d'une alimentation traditionnelle à base de fourrages.

Un contrôle constant du cahier des charges

Chaque étape de la chaîne est rigoureusement contrôlée et la recherche de traçabilité effectuée en continu, du producteur au consommateur.

VIANDES
MONTHEAN

TOP: *Here near the village of Camembert, Francois Durand lives and makes his own camembert cheese from the milk of his own cows.* BOTTOM: *Gérard Durand and his son Michaël fish for lampreys on the Dordogne River, which Michaël and his mother Mado can.*

"Main Street," Le Fel, in the Aveyron.

The Saint Sépulcre is a favorite, cozy Winstube in Strasbourg.

Strasbourg's 16th Century Maison Kammerzell still looks much like this.

At Maison Kammerzell ten varieties of delicatessen go into the choucroute formidable.

Sébastien Petit getting ready his lobsters.

BRASSERIE
Frites

Les Plateaux de Fruits de Mer

Le plateau du Stella *(2 personnes)* 118,60 €
12 claires n° 2, 6 spéciales n° 3, 6 belons n°3, 2 clams,
4 langoustines, 4 moules, 1 homard, 6 crevettes roses, 6 amandes,
20 bulots, bigorneaux, crevettes grises

Le plateau Mareyeur *(1 personne)* 46,80 €
6 claires n° 2, 3 spéciales n° 3, 3 belons n° 3, 1 clam,
2 langoustines, 2 moules, 3 crevettes roses, 3 amandes,
10 bulots, bigorneaux, crevettes grises

Pain, beurre, sauce échalotes, citron compris

Arrivage quotidien de fruits de mer.
Notre Chef écailler sélectionne la meilleure qualité d'huîtres spéciales entre les saisons
Gillardeau, Papin, Bordal et Ancelin.
Fraîcheur garantie

Les Huîtres, Coquillages et Crustacés

Fines de Claire n° 2	les 6	22,20 €	Praires *(les autres)*	les 6	16,50 €
Fines de Claire n° 3	les 6	19,80 €	Moules d'Espagne	les 6	6,90 €
Spéciales Marennes-Oléron n°2	les 6	29,40 €	Clam	la pièce	3,95 €
Spéciales Marennes-Oléron n°3	les 6	23,70 €	Bigorneaux	la portion	9,90 €
Spéciales Marennes-Oléron n°5	les 6	20,40 €	Bulots	la portion	9,90 €
Belons n° 00	les 6	27,90 €	Crevettes roses	la portion	14,00 €
Belons n° 1	les 6	23,40 €	Crevettes grises	la portion	9,80 €
Belons n° 3	les 6	19,20 €	Langoustines	la portion	30,70 €
			Oursins		selon cours

Demi-homard froid, mayonnaise 24,40 €

Les Hors-d'Œuvre

Harengs, pommes à l'huile tièdes 9,90 €
Œufs durs mayonnaise 5,90 €* 6,70 €
Salade de haricots verts frais et parmesan 13,50 €
Céleri rémoulade 7,70 €
Terrine de foies de volaille 9,80 €
Tarama et pain poêlan grillé 9,90 €
Foie gras frais de canard «maison» 19,80 €
Salade frisée, croûtons et lardons 9,70 €
Saucisse sèche de la «Maison Conquet» 9,90 €
Saumon fumé d'Écosse *(pané par nos soins)*, blinis et crème 19,80 €

		les 6	11,40 €	les 12	22,80 €
Gros escargots sauvages de Bourgogne			11,40 €		22,80 €

Les Traditions du Stella

Steak tartare préparé à votre goût 18,50 €
Andouillette tirée à la ficelle AAAAA 19,90 €
Saucisson chaud du Beaujolais, pommes à l'huile 18,50 €
Pied de porc pané «Maison Hardouins à Vouvray» 18,80 €
Tripes à la mode de Caen - Michel Rraull «Champion du Monde» 18,80 €
Tête de veau, sauce gribiche 22,00 €

Tous nos prix sont nets, service compris 15 % sur le H.T. - La maison n'accepte pas les chèques.
* Ces produits bénéficient de la baisse intégrale de la TVA.

STELLA
fraîches

Suggestions du jour

Arrivée du Vendredi 10 Décembre 2010 St. Romaric

Salade de Crevettes et Pamplemousse		11€
Potage de Carottes, crème aux herbes		10€
6 Huîtres Spéciales n°3 Triguy «la Venise»		19,80€
Moules de «Bouchot» marinières		10€
Suprême de Dorade Royale et Langoustines rôties		25€
Paré - Brest		10€
Tarte Tatin, glace vanille	7,50€	8,50€
Vin des rose : Bts Gaif de Lagrange (St. Julien 2007)		
La bouteille 75cl		54€
La Carafe 50cl		36€
Le verre 15cl		10,80€

Le Semainier

Lundi Hachis Parmentier 18,90 €
Mardi Petit salé aux lentilles 20,50 €
Mercredi Choucroute Stella 19,90 €
Jeudi Blanquette de veau à l'ancienne 21,50 €
Vendredi Aile de raie, beurre noisette et câpres 21,00 €

Les Poissons

Haddock poché à l'anglaise 21,00 €
Sole meunière ou grillée, pommes vapeur 34,50 €
Pavé de saumon à l'oseille 19,80 €
Quenelles de brochet, sauce Nantua 22,00 €
Homard grillé, beurre blanc 47,00 €

Les Viandes

Entrecôte charolaise *(env. 350 g)*, beurre Maître d'Hôtel 28,80 €
Filet de bœuf grillé, sauce béarnaise et frites 27,90 €
Pavé de rumsteck au poivre 21,00 €* 23,50 €
Foie de veau à l'anglaise 24,80 €
Carré d'agneau rôti *haricots verts frais* 34,50 €

Le Fromage

Saint-Marcellin de la «Mère Richard» 8,20 €

Les Desserts

Faisselle au coulis de framboises	7,50 €		Île flottante aux amandes	7,90 €
Profiteroles au chocolat chaud	8,70 €		Baba au rhum	9,40 €
Vacherin glacé, sauce caramel	8,70 €		Coupe de sorbets	8,00 €
Crème caramel	7,60 €* 8,70 €		*3 boules au choix : cassis - fraise citron vert - passion*	
Éclair géant au chocolat	9,50 €		Coupe de glaces	9,00 €
			3 boules au choix : vanille - chocolat - moka	

Ouvert tous les jours
Service assuré jusqu'à 1 h 00 du matin • Service voiturier 7/7.
Tous nos prix sont nets, service compris 15 % sur le H.T. - La maison n'accepte pas les chèques.
* Ces produits bénéficient de la baisse intégrale de la TVA.

OPPOSITE and ABOVE: *At Stella, the sophisticates of the neighborhood enjoy the simple food on that menu.*

*Chez Marinette in Le Fel, lodestone for regional gourmands
who relish Sunday lunch in an ordinary house next door.*

Jean Ducloux, first on the left, was an apprentice cook in 1933. He would be a star perpetuator of Burgundian cooking for 63 years.

Le Fel, population 171's one hotel.

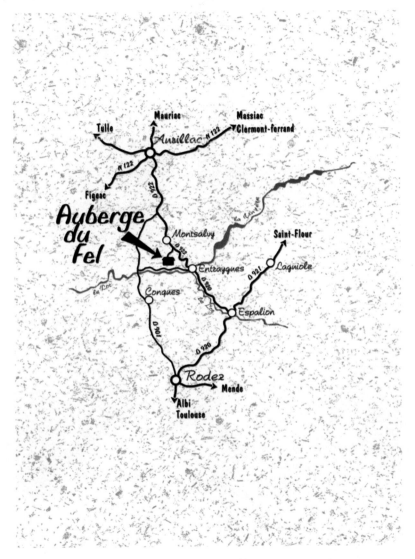

Finding Le Fel.

OPPOSITE: *Elisabeth Albespy and her crew at the Auberge du Fel.* TOP: *Guy-Pierre Baumann passes on a way with his native Alsacien dishes to Hubert Lepine in the kitchen of the Maison Kammerzell.* BOTTOM: *The Prix Fixe on the menu of the Auberge d'Achtal in Arcangues hasn't changed except for the price since 1927.*

LE GARS NORMAND

TOP: *Nobody knows why—as here on the Winstube's sign in old Alsacien—Le Saint Sépulcre is named for Christ's tomb.* BOTTOM: *Edward McClain bottles his cider when the moon is in decline.*

TOP: *Bayonne chocolate, a pride of the town for centuries.* BOTTOM: *The Maison Adam, which supplied the sweets for the wedding of Louis XIV and Marie-Teresa of Spain in 1660, specializes in old-fashioned macarons.*

RESTAURANT BAR SALON DE THÉ
POTTOKA

64250 **ESPELETTE**
Tél. 05 59 93 90 92
e-mail : francoise.aguerre953@orange.fr

RESTAURANT - HÔTEL
MODERNE

Poissons - Fruits de mer - Cuisine traditionnelle
M. & Mme CAUCHEMEZ
50760 BARFLEUR - Tél. 02 33 23 12 44 - Fax 02 33 23 91 58
http://www.hotel-restaurant-moderne-barfleur.com
Fermeture hebdomadaire le mardi soir et le mercredi sauf du 14 juillet au 15 septembre 7/7
Salle de banquets - Repas de familles

Restaurant LE POTTOKA

64250 **ESPELETTE**

bouchon lyonnais
Daniel et Denise
Joseph VIOLA
Meilleur Ouvrier de France 2004
156, rue de Créqui / 69003 LYON
Tél. 04 78 60 66 53
www.daniel-et-denise.fr
FERMETURE SAMEDI ET DIMANCHE
PARKING BONNEL SERVENT

CONSERVERIE TRADITIONNELLE
DURAND Mickaël
Pêcheur professionnel à St Terre
05 57 47 17 14 - 06 30 91 42 87

LAMPROIE A LA BORDELAISE

Ingrédients
Lamproie 80%
Poireaux
Vin
Sel Poivre Laurier

Préparation
10 min. à feu doux

Poids : 800 gr.

Nos spécialités en conserve
Soupe de poissons de rivière
Gattes
Œufs de gattes

En saison
Lamproies vivantes
Gattes
Anguilles
Crevettes blanches
Poissons blanc

TOP LEFT: *The Aguerres' Basque restaurant in Espelette is named for the wild horse as endemic to the region as their cooking.* TOP RIGHT: *The Hôtel Moderne in Barfleur, where William the Conqueror left Normandy to conquer England, is just a restaurant now, still worth a stop off.* MIDDLE LEFT: *The Pottoka as it once looked.* MIDDLE RIGHT: *Joseph and Françoise Viola serve dishes the old mères of Lyon would be proud of, at a little place still called Daniel et Denise.* BOTTOM: *The Durands' classic lamproie à la bordelaise, that comes out of their tiny cannery with this label, gets sold in local markets.*

chicken was roasting. Two other chickens had already come out of the oven. At the one other table being served that rainy afternoon, three generations of what was obviously a family had come to have a long lunch together.

They were enjoying, Sylvain explained, free-range chickens from Les Landes, in the Southwest. "They're a black-feathered breed, like the Houdan," he said. "It's a fact that black-feathered chickens have a fuller taste than white-feathered ones, even if the white chickens look better."

Some naïve words have been spent in print about French eating habits. For example, someone who hasn't looked around very much has made a lot of money with a book and a diet, declaring that French women don't get fat. Nonetheless, UNESCO hasn't been off the mark in declaring French gastronomy meal a cultural heritage. It's a less frequent thing, these days, but when it brings a group of French friends and relatives together, it is a rite with reverberations of bonding, and even the tone of talk assumes a purr that sets the moment off as significant in the flurry of life's moments. And noteworthy in this moment of exceptional conviviality is the close presence of people of different ages. At the risk of also sounding naïve, I'd say that the French practice a lot less segregation between ages in their social lives than other people do. There they were, a boy and a girl not yet teens, a teenage son, the parents, and their parents, together around a table laden with food, in lively rapport.

The white wine while we waited for the food was a Mâcon *viré*, a chardonnay, but without the opulence of the chardonnays nearby in Burgundy. The town of Mâcon, with the long reputation of being an important place for selling wines, is surrounded by a region of vineyards that is a poor neighbor to Burgundy and even Beaujolais, but in recent years its reputation has come up with a new generation of vintners. The Mâcon *viré* was respectable, dry and clean, and stimulating to the appetite.

Our lunch began with Sylvain's own *foie gras* and a mussels and cream soup with bright, flavorful little orange mussels. The slab of the *foie gras* was layered with *pain d'épice,* the spice cake the French call bread, rich in cinnamon and cloves and some extra notes, and it was garnished with a fig chutney.

Michelin gives La Poularde two humble forks, although its prices—justified, we'd finally say—suggest more luxury than that does. "Traditional recipes," Bibendum notes, not without a tone of kindness. But we were already learning that Sylvain's style of precise, clear cuisine, instead of showiness, strikes notes of grace that could fall on some critics' deaf ears.

The spice cake was made by Sylvain himself, using a combination of spices that his father had chosen, when he owned the restaurant before Sylvain.

He was away from his stove and back again beside us with that information. Sylvain pointed out that the chicken at the other table was what he usually served, a good free-range bird. The Michelin guide said that "the famous Houdan chicken is on the menu, to be sure," but it surely, alas, was not, and Sylvain said that he had to buy a bird from a fellow collector who knew how to kill his chickens, in contrast to Sylvain's relationship with his own pet flock.

"I couldn't find anyone who was raising them commercially anymore," he explained. "It's too expensive for the farmers to keep them to the mature age. Plus that, people say they want plump birds. People would turn up their noses at the *poulet de Houdan* in a supermarket. They're wiry, long-muscled. They don't look like they melt in your mouth."

Vandenameele said he stopped serving Houdan chickens a couple of years ago, when the farmers who raised them had given up, but he keeps thirty or so in his garden, where they fly around among the trees, and sleep on the branches. He's become a historian of the breed, pointing out that it was brought into France in the fifteenth century, was the chicken

Louis XIV ate, when His Majesty moved into nearby Versailles. In the 1830s, he said, there were more Houdan chickens sold in France than *poulets de Bresse* are sold now. Houdan growers today couldn't compete trying to sell their lean but delicious birds at a premium price, while fat, round-breasted chickens, more glamorous, stopped eating expensive feed and went on sale a full month before the Houdan birds.

Sylvain said he'd been at La Poularde since not long after he was born. His father had bought the place fifty-four years ago. His father took over a restaurant that had been closed for five years, because of failure, charmed by the long garden that went down to the little Vesgre River. Houdan chickens were still being raised for consumption in those days, but more than just adopting a brand, his father brought to the place the refined skill of a chef who had cooked at Café de la Paix when it was a stylish place to eat before the war, as well as at Claridge's in London. Sylvain credits his father for most of what he learned as a cook, although he left Sylvain to apprentice under Michel Guérard and chez the late Jean Delaveine, another great figure of the *nouvelle cuisine* era, with his restaurant l'auberge du Camélia, on the Seine, near Paris, in Bougival. Sylvain credits Delaveine, who became his great friend as well as mentor, for his understanding of what *la nouvelle* essentially meant. For Delaveine, Sylvain explained, the soul of *nouvelle cuisine* was "purification," the stripping away of everything overrich, heavy, and hard to digest, that had developed during the Belle Époque. Instead it strived to give each presence in a meal its own personal, bright flavor.

The excesses of searching for new tastes that characterize our own times leave him cold. Searching for "astonishment," he said, "can get pretty shrill. Thirty years ago I was modern, today I guess I'm old hat." Or cutting edge? Sylvain indeed sounded on the declared wavelength of Le Grand Ducasse, whose latest period of his art is, as we've noted, what he calls "simplicity."

The chicken came out. It was not a *poularde* but a male, and not a *coquelet* or baby cock, but a young rooster that had not yet reached the age of a cock of the yard. It's called a *garçonnet*. With it there were mashed potatoes, and a sauce he called his *"sauce secrète."*

"It's not really a secret," Sylvain explained. "I learned it from Jean Delaveine, who called it a *sauce trouble."*

Trouble, in French, when it comes to a liquid, means cloudy.

He said, "Anyone could do it."

It was, he said, the juice of the roasted bird, along with a bit of fat that was under its skin, and a spoonful of butter.

"Anyone can do it, and you can't do it better."

It was, we attested, excellent.

The *garçonnet* was too. Tender, but not flabby, with no flavor lost for tenderness. Sylvain said the bird, nonetheless, wasn't given the period of confinement that the best *volailleurs* of the past—the middle men who would buy fowl from the farmers—would give their chickens before selling them in turn to the *volaillers*, the storekeepers. The practice, a little like force-feeding, was called *mettre à l'épinette*, he explained: the putting in coops, for at least two weeks.

"The chicken gets claustrophobic," he said, "and it makes up for its anxiety by gorging itself.

"The best roast chicken I ever ate, and I only ate it once," he revealed, "was for a lunch I did for a group of chefs. It was a rooster five months old that I'd confined for four more months."

An old bird? I had never heard of eating a nine-month-old chicken.

"It was superb," he said.

The white meat of our *garçonnet*, Joanne noticed, resembled good turkey, the dark meat very faintly gamey. Sylvain is no reactionary in his craft. He brought out one of those cellophane roasting envelopes. "It comes from the States," he said. "It's ideal. The chicken stays moist while the skin is crisp."

I remembered Julia Child's recipe for roast chicken in *Mastering the Art of French Cooking*, written with Simone Beck and Louisette Bertholle, with their turning and roasting and turning and salting in instructions that run nearly four pages. Here was a man who has raised chickens to eat, lives with them now, so to speak, to preserve their breed, and has a restaurant named for chicken that chicken aficionados flock to. And here is his simple answer for roasting a chicken—free range, of course—that I pass on:

Sylvain Vandenamele's Roast Chicken at La Poularde
"Anyone can do it, and you can't do it better"

Vandenamele serves it for two. A chicken classically serves four.

Salt the chicken inside, leaving in it a clove of garlic, a sprig of thyme, and a bay leaf.

Rub salt on its skin.

Place the bird in a cellophane roasting bag and roast it for two hours at a very low temperature (240 degrees Fahrenheit).

Remove the bird, drain off the juice, leaving an amount of fat that suits you.

Add a spoonful of butter, stir over a fire.

Pour the warm sauce that was drained off over each serving of chicken.

The rain beat down outside. The fire near us was warm. The Crozes Hermitage 2007 wine, from the vineyard of Michel Chapoutier, was sturdy to match the harsh weather but didn't overpower the delicate fowl. Joanne passed on dessert. I allowed Vandenamele to indulge in a touch of cosmopolitanism, with his *panne cotte* with currants: creamy and sharply fruity.

It was a very pleasant afternoon, thirty-six miles from Paris and definitely elsewhere. We decided we'd come back when the garden was sunny and chickens were flying in the trees—those five-fingered, double-crested birds like no other, and uniquely delicious. . . .

10

NORMANDY

The Vikings knew where they were going.

The right words for Normandy, much as they risk sounding gushy, are plenteous and breathtaking. Here, where the generous earth and a still-bountiful sea provide some of simply the best food to be had, the lush countryside changes as you drive, while one version of loveliness follows another. Two hours or so northwest of Paris, the narrow back roads of the Pays d'Auge take you through old villages in timber and mortar. You pass manors, with great stables, settled among pastures: the *haras* or horse-breeding farms, famous worldwide. French horses breed in Normandy and train in Chantilly, where, in the nineteenth century, English trainers introduced the Sport of Kings. The breeders claim that the grass in the Pays d'Auge is among the best in the world, similar to the bluegrass of Kentucky, for strengthening the bones of horses. South in the valley, among those big estates, one of the most impressive you could pass, is Fresnay-le-Buffard, in the hamlet of Neuvy-au-Houlme. Fresnay belonged to the man who turned his purchase of cloth left over from

World War I plane fuselages into a textile empire, and whose cherry on the top was the house of Dior. The brother of a photographer I worked with was an executive, if that word really fit, of that aged tycoon Marcel Boussac. Monsieur Boussac liked to call his minions to meet in his office during lunchtime, and would consume a yogurt while the others, bellies growling, listened to his orders. Once he called the manager of his *haras* asking if the hay had been brought in. The answer was yes, but when Boussac had a plane fly over the property to check, and found that it hadn't, the manager had to look for another job. After *le patron* went bankrupt, Stavros Niarchos bought Fresnay and willed it to his daughter.

The Pays d'Auge is the most luxuriant region of Normandy, where there is much delicious poultry, native beef, cheese, cider, and redolent calvados (apple brandy) to be had. La Race Normande, prevalent here, is a breed of cattle that produces both exceptionally cream-rich milk and excellent meat. Further west, small plots of farmland still form the dominant theme of the landscape, where high shrubs separate the farmers' parcels, in the region called Le Bocage. Below the northeast peninsula of the Cotentin, which ends in a rocky cape, Normandy stretches west to Mont Saint Michel, just at the border of Brittany. That island monastery that dates to the eighth century, just offshore, is a wonder of Western civilization, but like what Graham Greene once said about Bruges, it is a "much trafficked jewel." The single street is forever dense with tourists, as is the restaurant La Mère Poularde, where Henry Adams, who wrote his classic *Mont-Saint-Michel* and *Chartres*, enjoyed one of those fluffy omelets that La Mère herself began beating up in 1879, and which now costs a minimum of forty-five euro a serving. We haven't gone back to Mont Saint-Michel in years.

Such is Normandy, where several towns knew the scars of World War II—Caen was more than seventy-five percent destroyed, Le Havre even more so—but where the land has changed almost not at all since the ninth century, when the Scandinavian marauders arrived and settled into the idyll, endowing future generations of the population with a strain of blond hair. Those tortured cities, incidentally, have since known some interesting vernacular architecture, and Le Havre's geometric modernism is now classified as a cultural treasure.

There are innumerable architectural achievements in Normandy: eight cathedrals as well as manors and châteaux wherever you drive. It all attests to when agriculture was the prime form of creating wealth along with commerce on the sea.

The other side to Normandy is the shore of the English Channel. From the fishing port of Dieppe to Fécamp, a bustling little Mister Hulot-ish old-fashioned summer haunt, the Alabaster Coast is a long continuum of white cliffs, with little sandy beaches nestled under them. Someone recently in a magazine called Étretat a "secret weekend escape" in a piece of travel writing that fits a salesmanlike genre widely employed, called "best kept secrets." I'm reminded of the day I stood before Nicolae Ceaussescu's huge, megalomaniac palace in Bucharest, while hundreds of soldiers were building it. My photographer took out a camera and a guy from the Securitat in plain clothes came up to us. "It's a secret," he warned. "A big secret," I agreed. There are no secret havens of loveliness on the French shores of the Channel, but some towns have kept a dated if worn charm, others have been developed with banal new buildings. The backstreets of Étretat are not the best of what Flaubert's Norman country towns have to show for themselves, and the port has been badly scarred with ugly contemporary construction, but the white cliffs, with their unique arches, remain as impressive as when Claude Monet and Manfred Schwartz painted them.

Further southwest, the land flattens out toward the water. There are more good beaches, backed by resort towns that sprang up in the nineteenth century, and where, now, fading villas, old fishermen's houses, and rows of contemporary, medium-rises are the faces on the

Norman side of the Channel. And there are the bunkers and some rusting portable piers at the landing beaches of D-day.

You drive past Cabourg, Caen, and Bayeux, with its famous ancient tapestry, a comic strip–like account of William the Conqueror's invasion of England—toward the peninsula of the Cotentin, where the houses change from mortar and timber or brick in checkerboard patterns to solid stone-roofed granite. You can keep on going to the point, among rocky cliffs that lead to a nuclear plant. Cabourg offers you another gloss on the life of Proust, at the Grand Hotel, where the room he took during some summers has been faithfully reconstituted in a hotel otherwise dolled up.

On the whole coast, the loveliest town is Honfleur, so famous for its handsome mortar and timber architecture that it has been completely denatured as a tourist haunt. The most interesting resorts are the twin cities of Deauville and Trouville, towns that make the seashore of Normandy well worth the two-hour train ride from Paris. Yes, Deauville gets crowded, particularly on weekends. For some reason it's become a favorite venue of the Parisian clothing makers and sellers, after having been very upper crust. Of the two, my heart belongs to Trouville, where recently Joanne and I went back to a long lunch at Les Vapeurs, a restaurant with as much character, as much anchorage in a place, as one could hope for.

A bridge across the narrow Touques River, which shortly after empties into the Channel, separates the two towns. To get a sense of the difference in character between them, think of the Upper East Side and the Upper West Side of New York City. One sleek, the other less preening, more welcoming to bohemians, each with its loyal devotees. In July, Deauville is still fashionable in an Establishment circle, many of whose members have country houses nearby, manors and thatched-roof farmhouses rendered chic, with manicured grounds. They're in Deauville for the polo season, which ends with the Gold Cup at the end of the month, and the yearling sales that draw the gentry of the horse world from all over. Creative people come to Trouville to "recharge themselves," as the French like to say, to charge their batteries, get back in touch with their inner selves in the sea air and "chill out," as we Americans say, in a relaxed environment among ordinary people. Gérard Depardieu, for example, is among the Trouville devotees.

Trouville has more history than its sleeker sister. It was a fishing town, and is still full of tiny fishermen's houses in its narrow streets. In the 1820s a crowd of artists and writers discovered it and its deep sandy beach. People sat on the beach or dipped themselves in the sea, rather than seriously swimming in those days. In August 1838, a beautiful twenty-six-year-old woman was sitting there with her child when her cape blew away. Walking by, a man saved it from the wind, and when he looked into the woman's eyes he fell in love, platonically, for the rest of his life. Her name was Elisa, common-law wife of Maurice Schlesinger, a Prussian music editor in Paris, who, along with her, would become Arnoux, man and wife, in *Sentimental Education*, this lone walker would write. He was Gustave Flaubert. After Maurice once saw him admiring his wife, Maurice himself took a fancy to Gustave, and Gustave would tag along with the Schlesingers on sailing trips and walks, while he mooned over Elisa in private.

Whistler and Courbet walked the beach here together with their sketchpads. Monet and a whole colony of other impressionists were charmed by Trouville. Before long, Trouville was drawing a richer crowd rubbing shoulders with *les artistes*. In the 1860s, Napoléon Trois's half brother the Duc de Morny, who had a villa in Trouville, looked across the Toques at marshland and decided to create a more upscale venue, and Deauville, with its racecourse, casino, and big villas, came to be a Mecca of style. A gentleman of the Tout Paris would deposit his wife for the sea air in Deauville and, rather than catching the train back to the capital, hole up for more excitement with his mistress in a onetime fisherman's little house in Trouville. It was actually a custom.

As for another, for the past forty decades and more, Deauville fashionables have been crossing the bridge to eat at the unpretentious but excellent *brasserie* that is Les Vapeurs. Opposite where the Toques is about to join the Channel, separated by a thin strip of land, Les Vapeurs is a few feet down the quay from the pharmacy that was a pharmacy in 1853, when Flaubert rented a room above it to look out at the water and remember the faraway day of the cape. In good weather Les Vapeurs' tables spread out onto the quay. The air flutters gently with bracing sea ions. Gulls cry overhead. The waiters bustle with their trays laden with pleasure. Life is bright and bountiful.

Les Vapeurs

This restaurant's brass-and-polished wood décor has changed very little since the place opened as a café in 1927, and the menu, which the noted poster designer Savignac, a Trouville habitué, graced with a cover, is much the same. Several examples of the produce that make up the dishes have come from the same suppliers for about a half century. But the place is far from ossified. Four hundred customers enliven Les Vapeurs on a weekday, and a weekend day caters to fifteen hundred, according to the current owner, a lanky, blond thirty-eight-year-old named Jérôme Meslin. When the American film festival is on in September, Les Vapeurs is a must for the Hollywood crowd—Spielberg, Harrison Ford, et al.

Meslin's family is the third of three that have owned the place successively since it opened. His father, Gilbert, bought Les Vapeurs having done well in the wholesale meat business, in 1996. After working for his father for four years, Jérôme took over the place in 2002. The Meslins come from generations that tilled the earth and raised cattle near Carteret in the Cotentin. Jérôme's grandfather was one of the last Norman farmers to have the right to produce apples for making calvados. For centuries, itinerant distillers, les *"bouilleurs"* would travel with their horse-drawn machines from farm to farm in Normandy, distilling people's crops. With alcoholism a chronic problem in the region, where mothers put calvados in babies' bottles to calm them, a series of restrictive laws finally limited the right to distill to those having it before 1960, with the franchise ending with their deaths. Making moonshine calvados in personal stills still exists, at a rare level, all through Normandy. I've had my taste of it. At 110 proof alcohol, freshly distilled, it is a formidable thing. . . .

"People come here seeking the immutable," Meslin explained. "We do a great volume, but everything is done at the last minute and no three-star restaurant can buy fresher ingredients than we do."

He went down the list:

His mussels come from Briqueville-sur-Mer in the Cotentin, from the same supplier to the restaurant for the past sixty years. His cream comes from a rare small group of farmers doing their exceptional cream and sending it to Les Vapeurs and other selected sources since 1982. The *tripes à la mode de Caen* served at Les Vapeurs, a dish that restaurateurs procure from specialists, has been coming from a man whose shop began supplying the restaurant in 1955. Meslin doesn't go about boasting about the pedigree of his basic products, but the back of his menu gives you a map with all the sources: oysters from Saint-Vaast-La-Hougue and from off the tiny Chaussey islands; shellfish from the west coast of the Cotentin; cod from its north coast; turbot, sole, flounder, and sea bass from the small boats that come to Port-en-Bessin; scallops from near Caen; and the tiny gray shrimp that have been a hallmark of the menu since 1927 from near Deauville.

People who've lunched on the sole at Ciro's on the boardwalk in Deauville, a magnate of chic at corresponding prices, come and come back again to Les Vapeurs for the big sole.

A sole worthy of his menu, Meslin told me, is a sole of at least five hundred grams. "I drive to Port-en-Bessin," he said, "and I get the fish from the boats that have been out no more than twenty-four hours, not your six- to seven-day boats. Each boat, with maybe a hundred kilos of sole on it, will have about five fish of five hundred grams; the rest will be no bigger than, say, three hundred grams. I take as many as I can get. Afterwards I keep them in the refrigerator for forty-eight hours. It's a fallacy to believe that fish right off the boat tastes best. That's true of sardines, but the freshest white-fleshed fish gain flavor with a short spell in the refrigerator. It's the same with beef, when it's too fresh."

I told him that his story of the sole corresponded to my eating experience—size determined flavor. Big fish and older beef are far better than younger versions. The opposite is true of vegetables.

Joanne ordered a *sole meunière* and I chose Caen tripes and we settled into a leisurely lunch. *Moules à la crème* opened the meal for Joanne, and I had room-temperature steamed *bulots,* the fat sea snails that I've never seen in America, with fresh mayonnaise. The mussels were a great combination of flavors: the subtext of white wine, the subtle sea taste of the mussels, the unctuousness of the cream. The *bulots* were plump and like the mussels, a combination of sea and the noncloying, delicate sweetness and buttery quality of fresh seafood. The mayonnaise was richly what it should be, so different from the "real mayonnaise" that people buy by the jar in the States, and which, too often you get in France as well.

What to drink? There is no wine made in Normandy, but cider has been the local beverage for centuries. Meslin chose us a bottle whose label bore the farmer François David's name. The Davids, father to son, Meslin informed us, have been making that cider since 1871. It was, at three degrees of alcohol (six proof) faintly fizzy and full of the flavor of apples. Americans would call it sweet cider, but it wasn't sweet enough to give an alien presence to the food. The color was rich amber. It drank splendidly. Later we would learn that David, with his one-man press in the Pays d'Auge had earned a great reputation and we'd find out how.

The plump sole, lightly floured and bathed with a butter sauce, had all the delicate quality of that fish. The tripes had a great dense flavor from the meat cooked with spices thirteen hours. I recently read that tripes were the buzz food in New York restaurants, what *quiche* once was, but I know that Americans have not been keen on innards. I think that the *tripes à la mode de Caen* of Michel Ruault, whose father began supplying Les Vapeurs with the dish in 1955, would change their minds. I was made to think, in any case, of how much innards are a part of French cuisine, and the way in which the preparation of *tripes à la mode de Caen,* a long and laborious process, is left to specialists rather than to chefs or home cooks these days. The local cuisine long believed by the French to be the best in France is the food of Lyon, which relies very much on a lot of innards.

Joanne passed on the Les Vapeurs desserts, and I had a *tarte tatin* topped with the special *crème fraîche.* The *tarte tatin* is not a Norman dish; I ordered it to have a dessert with that cream. Legend says that the dish, like many in the annals of cuisine, began an illustrious career as an accident. It was created, in any case, in the deep country of Sologne, the wooded area below the Loire, where hunters have big estates, but where life is poor for the locals. Two sisters named Caroline and Stéphanie Tatin were running an inn in the village of Lamotte-Beuvron down there, and getting ready a big lunch for a party of hunters. Caroline or was it Stéphanie dropped the apples for the tart they were baking, and with a hardscrabble adversity to throwing out food, picked the lot off the floor, put it in a deep pan with butter and sugar, and covered it with a thick layer of pastry. This upside-down tart, having been a hit with the distinguished trenchermen at lunch, made its way into the annals of French fare, thanks to these Parisians who spread their praise of it. Ideally, the dish is made of whole, peeled apples crowded together, but what you usually get is big apple chunks. Joanne and I have eaten the *tarte tatin* at the

Tatins' inn, still in operation, twenty-two miles from Orleans, where the sisters' stove decorates the bar. It was average for the genre. So was the tart at Les Vapeurs. Quite tasty, mind you, but it was the cream that was celestial, from a supplier in the village of Beuzeville, who has five farmers producing it in the most careful, artisanal way. It has a butterfat content of fifty percent; it's nearly twice as rich as the *crème fraîche* commonly sold.

Before we drank a glass of calvados from one of Meslin's small suppliers, we wrote down the phone numbers and addresses of the man who made the tripes, the cream supplier, and the person whose excellent cider we'd enjoyed, for its full, mellow taste of apples—without being the equivalent of a jammy wine.

We went off, as well, with a recipe from Meslin for Les Vapeurs' way with *sole meunière*. *Sole meunière* takes its place among the great favorites of French fish dishes, a very simple dish as appealing as those graced with such difficult sauces as *beurre blanc, hollandaise,* or *sauce mousseline.* The French prepare the fish gutted but whole and, in restaurants, fillet it at the last minute in front of the diners on a chafing dish, a virtuoso performance with knife and soupspoon. If you can't get whole soles where you live, you can do it with fillets from the start, but I think that sautéing with the bones in adds flavor. Here is how Meslin's cooks do it:

Sole Meunière at Les Vapeurs

Served filleted beside your table for one person;
two would not go hungry sharing it.

a sole of at least a pound and a quarter

3½ oz. of butter

1 lemon

flour

chives

Remove the skin on each side of a gutted sole. (The fish-store man could do this, with a ripping motion.)

Flour the fish on both sides.

Melt half the butter in a pan and cook the fish at a high flame for four minutes, turning once.

Melt the rest of the butter; pour the juice of the lemon into it.

Place the sole on a hot platter, pour the above sauce over it, and sprinkle it with chopped chives.

That's it.

The Right Moon,
A Half Day in the Pot, and the Cream of all Creams

François David's farm, near Pont L'Evêque in the Pays d'Auge, source of our excellent drink at lunch, has been making cider since 1860. His grandfather bought the property in 1871, and the Davids have been supplying Les Vapeurs with cider for nearly sixty years.

When we spoke with David, he was surveying the ripeness of his apples in his orchard in Blagny-le Château. His land borders a stream called Le Chaussey, in the most beautiful part of the department of Calvados, sometimes called "the garden of the coast." David's grandfather lived on it until 1923, raising veal, and with a fascination for making the best cider he could. His son succeeded him and then passed on the 430 trees with ten varieties of apples to François.

"I start pressing when it's eight or nine degrees centigrade outside," David said. "If you wait until it's five or six degrees, you don't extract enough tannin and you lose color. I press just after the full moon. In that phase called *le décourt*, the cider is much better behaved. It's less nervous, less change-y, easier to control, and it ferments more slowly."

I didn't raise my eyebrows at David's story of the moon. Many European farmers follow the rhythm of the moon in their planting and sowing. Just ask, as I have, Anne-Claude Leflaive, who runs a vineyard producing Montrachet. Montrachet, which was Thomas

Jefferson's favorite wine, is tied with Corton Charlemagne as the most celebrated white wine in Burgundy. Madame Leflaive follows the phases of the moon as part of an overall organic process called "biodynamics."

The fundamental difference between David's cider and industrial varieties is a process of decanting, or *soutirage*. He scorns the cider makers who filter their product. Instead, he decants his cider, removing sediment that keeps producing itself in fermentation, pouring the cider from barrel to barrel, leaving the must behind, six times. "After the third time," he explained, "we start to see the cider clearly." Each time he leaves behind expired yeast.

"When they filter," he said, "they get clear cider right away, but the cider is dead. So they put yeast back in to make it fizz. They wind up with a taste of iron from the yeast. Their cider will go bad in six months."

David employs old port *pipes* for his barrels. These chestnut wood barrels of 564 liters are used by port makers in Portugal to send their wine on a sea voyage. For centuries, this has been one way the best producers age port. New wood would give too bold a wood flavor to his cider, David explained. "It's got a lot of useful tannin, but you have to avoid too much of that taste." The memory of the port adds a highlight to the taste of the cider. I recalled that the effectiveness of the port's sea voyage is no more folklore than following the phases of the moon. Before the high-speed trains came into service in Europe, I would take the train from Paris to Brussels in the morning and be there after a long lunch on wheels. The waiters in their starched white jackets would serve those four-course meals on the jerking trains with the self-control of ballet dancers. The French cooks and the Belgian cooks, each doing one end of the voyage, would compete at delivering a more satisfying lunch. I salivate recalling the braised endives that accompanied the roast veal, a common vegetable in Belgium and Northern France, soaked in butter, caramelized.

And there was the wine. They were half bottles of wines, either Burgundy or Bordeaux, none with glorious labels, but very drinkable. Half bottles age faster than whole bottles. An explanation that you get is that the wine breathes through the cork, and the oxygen that enters, in relation to the volume of liquid, is greater in the half bottle than the whole bottle. Ah, but my waiters would assure me that the vibration of the train formed a still more beneficent aging process for the wine. Like the port in a rolling sea, it got better after several voyages.

David ages his cider in barrels sixty days before bottling. "Afterwards, it's best after two to three years," he said. "Something happens after it gets very dry: It starts to get fruity again." Like wine, as David explained it, cider has a life and even a second one.

David's quarrel with the run-of-the mill cider makers extends to the bottles. You see cider with wired caps like champagne, supposedly to hold back the carbonation, which he dismisses as showiness. His own caps are cork conglomerates, and it's the glass, he says, that makes the difference. "I use heavy glass and those people who filter use cheaper, light glass; it's a matter of seven hundred grams compared to five hundred grams." Why thick glass? "It insulates the cider better; it protects it against noxious temperature shocks."

Madame Leflaive, at her celebrated Burgundy vineyard, would approve of David's organic cider. It's nothing as rare as Montrachet, but *Marianne*, the French magazine, calls his sweet cider the "Château d'Yquem of the cider world," comparing it to the world's greatest Sauternes. Word of mouth among gourmets and the restaurant owners whom he supplies have made the product of David's little farm beside a stream a landmark for connoisseurs.

Great to drink as it may be, Michel Ruault, Jérôme Meslin's supplier of *tripes à la mode de Caen*, would have no part of David's cider nor of any cider nor calvados in his tripes. The unenlightened, in his eyes, write about cider's or calvados's presence in the dish, but Ruault made clear to me on the phone that tripes, rightly, and laboriously prepared, have their own savory identity that doesn't need an adulterating enhancement.

Ruault reminded me that the *code de la charcuterie*, the government's rule book of ingredients in food items, contains neither cider nor calvados in *tripes à la mode de Caen*. "And anyway," he said, "I've been doing my dish the same way my father learned it as an apprentice, before he began doing his own tripes in 1955. And my father won the world gold medal for them in 1966." William the Conqueror might well have enjoyed some kind of tripes while drinking apple juice, as it is written, but that doesn't excuse putting cider into the dish, in Ruault's eyes.

The world medal, he explained, is awarded by the La Tripière d'Or, a brotherhood of tripe lovers. That *confrérie*, with its feasts, its medieval robes, and initiation ceremonies, is based in Caen, but, Ruault said, it would be inaccurate to believe that the purest version of the dish can be had in that town. *Tripes à la mode de Caen* is the invention of a Benedictine monk named Sidoine Benoît, living in the fourteenth century in the Abbaye-aux-hommes in Caen.

The abbey, along with its twin Abbaye-aux-femmes, are world-renowned splendors that, in any case, make seeing Caen more worthwhile than a dish of tripes. The two abbeys, founded in the eleventh century by William the Conquerer and his wife, Mathilde, were miraculously spared the bombardment of Caen during World War II. The town also has numerous churches that represent the glory of High Gothic, a fine arts museum perhaps second in national importance to the Louvre, and a World War II war museum. All that makes Caen worth a visit.

Tripes à la mode de Caen, though, have traveled. It was in Paris that I had the best of them, before Les Vapeurs. The restaurant was Pharamond, near Les Halles, where they'd been serving the dish since

1832, after a Norman family brought them to the big city. Pharamond fed such tripe fanciers as Ernest Hemingway, F. Scott Fitzgerald, and Charles de Gaulle. In its history of the dish, the brotherhood of the Tripière d'Or honored Pharamond, as "the Parisian temple of tripes." Despite its polychrome ceramic walls, classified as a national treasure, it had been transformed into a banal restaurant, in recent years. But it has come up again, owned by a former wine steward at L'Ami Louis. Gone, though, are the little cast-iron warmers with pieces of live charcoal in them that used to come with the dish. They've been named a fire hazard. Tripes get gluey if they get cold. At Les Vapeurs, you get electric plate warmers with the dish.

Ruault has a *charcuterie,* a delicatessen, where he cooks the tripes, in the town of Vire, forty miles from Caen. *Tripes* in French has a meaning that happily goes beyond what we call guts. Ruault's recipe includes four different parts of a cow or steer's complicated stomach. To the tripes are added a steer or cow's foot. Some tripe makers include the cartilage of the heel, but Ruault considers it too sticky and he wouldn't think of adding beef fat, which some tripe makers fancy.

Salt, pepper, carrots, and a mixture of aromatic spices are mixed with the meat, before Ruault puts it all into big cast aluminum vats with sealed lids—but not before Ruault has spent three to four hours cleaning his fifty-five-kilo batch of tripes. And then it cooks for twelve to thirteen hours.

In the days when homemakers had the time for all that preparation, they would prepare *tripes* and put them in a *tripière,* a special pumpkin-shaped clay pot, with a small opening at the top that they sealed with flour paste. The dish then went to a baker after he'd banked the fire of his oven for the day, and it would cook there overnight, until he began his early-morning baking.

I told Ruault that I'd heard that *tripes à la mode de Caen* tasted best in autumn, because the cattle eat a lot of fallen apples then.

He called the explanation charming, but false. "How many cattle pastures have enough apple trees growing in them for that?" he asked. But he agreed that the tripes do taste better in the fall: "Why? By the end of the winter, the cattle have eaten silage. Not very good. In the spring, the new grass is very strong tasting, and that's not good either. The grass they've eaten by autumn is far better. It's all about the condition of the grass."

I had read so much about cider and calvados being essential in *tripes à la mode* that I called up another notable of the tripe-making world to get his take on the matter. He was Jean-Claude Plumail, a butcher in Urville, in the Cotentin, a town that was a battleground in World War II. Ruault never competed for the gold medal after his father had won it, but Plumail was the world champion of Caen tripes two years in a row.

Plumail came down definitely against either beverage in his tripes. "I was naïvely adding cider for years and coming in second or third, until I sat down with Jean Le Hiré, rest his soul, the founder of the Confrérie de la Tripière d'Or, and he gave me his recipe. No cider. No calvados. And that was it, I won the gold *tripière* in 1983 and 1984, and I could retire from competition."

Ruault had told me that he had never cooked with a little earthenware *tripière*, while he believed that tripes gained flavor being cooked in greater quantities. Plumail said he'd squared the circle. He had twenty-five-kilo earthenware *tripières* made for him, and he'll do you an earthenware-cooked dish, on order, without looking for a baker's oven big enough. "It's better for getting the full aroma of the tripes," he confessed, but his business requires him to do much bigger batches in, yes, cast aluminum. . . .

We thought again of the incredible cream at Les Vapeurs, and we called up Emmanuel Borniambuc, in the town of Beuzeville, near Pont L'Evêque. He is not a farmer but he had the idea of getting local farmers to do the cream of all Normandy creams, starting with one farmer in 1972. That was shortly before he began supplying cream to Les Vapeurs. He now sells to shops in Paris as well for five farmers.

"We start," Borniambuc explained, "with cows only of the race *normande*, that give richer, if less, milk. They're never fed silage. They get hay, beets, and carrots for color. We use unpasteurized milk—pasteurization loses flavor—and we skim it purely by gravity. We wind up with a cream that is fifty percent butterfat."

Borniambuc looks down on the creameries that collect milk and beat it in tank trucks and beat it again to keep it all fluid while it is pumped out, only to separate the cream mechanically afterward. "By then," he said, "the milk that has already been kept refrigerated on the farms four days is just about dead. The pasteurization finishes the assassination. Afterwards they have to add bacteria strains to clot the cream."

His cream, which has far less buttermilk left in it than commercial creams, stays far sweeter, while being thick and unctuous. He calls it naturally matured rather than fermented, and with fifty percent butterfat, it is nearly twice as rich as the *crème fraîche* commonly sold. At eighteen percent butterfat, sour cream, fermented longer than the latter and full of thickeners, is a poor cousin to both. Slavic *smetena* can be anywhere from fifteen to thirty percent butterfat and is more runny.

Borniambuc told me that his cream sells for thirty percent more than the market price for *crème fraîche* in Paris stores. I think it's worth it.

What Year Are We?

We drove west into the Cotentin, heading for the little port of Barfleur, where we'd spent many weekends and part of one summer in the placid *vallée de la Saire* nearby, in a village called Anneville-en-Saire, through which a tiny river runs.

In Barfleur we liked to stay at L'Hôtel Moderne, whose modernity was the case in 1900. The Moderne, when we went there, was cheerily furnished with heirlooms, the dining room particularly lovely with its walls covered with paintings of the region. The bathrooms were down the hall, but the new owner would tell us that, when the Moderne was built to attract bathers using the railroad between Paris and Cherbourg, it was the first hotel in the region to have running water in the rooms—accomplished by servants relaying each other at a hand pump in the cellar.

Barfleur, population six hundred-odd, was where William the Conqueror and his army set sail for England in 1066. Richard the Lionheart passed through it again to go home, after his release from Austrian captivity, in 1194. Paul Signac, the pointillist painter, lived and worked here part of the year among the seventeenth-century granite-and-schist-roofed houses. When we strolled among the empty streets before dinner at the Hôtel Moderne, a fog hovering over the waterside, we were back in the same little horseshoe port that we've known, with a tiny granite, mostly seventeenth-century church where the sea once reached, and lined with small, granite, ex-fishermen's houses. A British yachting crowd sails over in the summer, giving sophistication to an otherwise humble village. On the weekend, an enterprising butcher used to set himself up with his van near the water, grilling local lamb on an open fire. Joanne and I had become acquainted with Barfleur through our friend Victor Marengo, who sold advertising for Fairchild Publications in Europe and kept a small sailboat in the port. His native home was an ancient granite house in Saint-Vaast-La-Hougue, the next little port over. One morning as a child, he opened his bedroom window and saw the sea entirely crowded with ships from one end to another. It was the day that would be called D. . . .

Victor introduced us to the man who embodied so much of the character of the region. His name was Edouard Boisart. His French was mixed with Norman *patois*, and he sometimes wore on his chest not the usual red ribbon but the corresponding medal he had earned: the Legion of Honor. Edouard was the corpulent retired head of the life-saving station of the port. "How many persons did you save?" I once asked him. "Fourteen," he said, "not counting Germans."

Edouard was a fisherman. During the First World War, when he was very young, he had a fishing boat with a camouflaged cannon. German U-boats would surface, having detected it, and when they came up, Edouard opened fire. His actions in the Second World War were limited to saving shipwrecked sailors. Edouard had a friendship considered unusual in the region. In Normandy there is a form of alienation, distantly like the impulse of racism in the wellspring of human behavior, which keeps farmers and fishermen, each rooted presences there, from being friends. Each considers the other's activity an inferior form of endeavor for human beings. But Edouard had a friend who raised carrots—and who had another activity that made his friendship attractive. Bébert made calvados, "*derrière les fagots,*" as the expression goes, behind the woodpile: moonshine. And we were Edouard's friends. I confess that we enjoyed much of his hospitality drinking Bébert's loving-hands-at-home *calva*. At 110 proof, it scorched your throat, having first filled your mouth with the effluvia of fresh apples. Once Edouard got out an old bottle with tan liquid in it. He was fond of our son André, who was just a baby, and the bottle was for him, not to drink but to open on his twenty-first birthday. It was calvados that Bébert had bottled in 1919. He began to write the dedication and paused: "What year are we?" he asked.

Barfleur was the kind of offbeat village where you could lose track of what year it was, and, going back, we found the face of centuries past still on it, although time had gone by since we and André had drunk the 1919 *calva,* toasting the late Edouard's memory. It was memorably mellow and rich; alcohols age little in the bottle, even though some restaurants do a number about bottles of Armagnac with old dates on them. But this calvados had a good life in the wood before bottling.

L'Hôtel Moderne

Barfleur's Hôtel Moderne, small, endearingly awkward-looking, was now entirely a restaurant. The handful of bedrooms was being transformed into an apartment. Once they had accommodated the Parisian whores installed by German officers billeted in town. Now it would be a convenient place for Frédéric Cauchemez and his wife, Roslyne, to live.

Cauchemez, the thirty-eight-year-old current owner, assured me that a regular customer, a ninety-seven-year-old woman, tells him that she enjoys the food as much as she did a half century and more ago. It has, she believes, retained its character, and we went away from lunch believing Cauchemez wasn't making that up and that her taste buds were likely intact.

Cauchemez explained:

"I don't complicate things. Each taste has its place and I don't mix them. I don't like restaurants where everything is mixed together. Is it worth the while to take a good product from the sea or the land near here and complicate it?

"I have a four-wheel handcart," Cauchemez said, "and I go down to the port when the fishing boats come in. I cook what they have. Today we have soles; tomorrow there may not be any. When they have something especially nice, a pretty bass or a turbot, the fishermen at sea telephone me: 'We'll be there in a three-quarters of an hour.' I push the cart back to the restaurant. It's a thing in Barfleur—only some tourists go around using motor transportation."

We had called days ahead for Cauchemez to do us a *Saint Pierre à l'oseille*, John Dory fish with a cream and sorrel sauce—an old

Norman recipe that we used to enjoy at the Moderne. He bought
what John Dory fish were available in the port, four fish, and put
them on his menu.

Cauchemez's Norman idea of an *amuse-gueule* began our meal:
No foam nor baby food, but a small slice of faintly smoked tripe
sausage from the town of Vire, over a slice of locally dug potato
and melted Pont L'Evêque cheese. Not very sophisticated, but
appetizing.

We stayed in the territory.

Joanne had another of Cauchemez's Norman-inspired creations.
A paper-thin piecrust the French use for apple pie, but with local
scallops, a julienne of leeks and carrots, topped with *beurre blanc*. A
simple but intelligent combination, she pronounced.

I had oysters from the next town over, Saint-Vaast. Number
three *speciales fines claires*, which can be decoded as medium-sized
oysters that have been parked in pools to purge impurities, before
going to market. They were deep-shelled, deep green, lean, and
briney. Cauchemez made a confession: He didn't care that much for
Saint-Vaast oysters, but his customers expected him to serve local
oysters. His own favorites were oysters from off Isigny, a town farther west, otherwise famous for its butter; they were plumper and
subtler tasting.

The Saint-Vaast oysters were *triplots,* he said, the term for oysters
unable to reproduce. They never reached the plump, milky quality
of the Isigny variety, he said, but they kept a deeper taste of the sea.
Both, Cauchemez reminded me, are grown from micro-oysters
brought over from Japan, or similar, infantile local descendents of
Japanese oysters.

The only oysters in France that are native are my own favorites,
the flat ones, with a nutty, subtler flavor. Raised chiefly in Brittany, as *belons*, they account for two percent of total production in
the nation. The flat oysters were rendered rare, after a Portuguese

ship, the *Morlaisien*, sank in the estuary of the Gironde River, near Bordeaux, on May 14, 1868, bringing its load of oysters to the bottom with it. The Portuguese oysters prospered there, fed more voraciously than the natives they edged out. Oyster farmers found them hearty and full, and they raised them along the different coasts, until a parasite attacked them and the oystermen turned to importing the infant, "seed" oysters of a more resistent Japanese breed. The *belons* had been ravaged by the parasite as well.

Cauchemez serves his oysters on a bed of sea salt. He used to serve them on iced seaweed, until the food inspector declared that unsanitary, along with his boxwood rolling pin. So it goes.

The St. Pierre was excellent. It's an ugly gray, flat fish with a flabby skin, but once it's filleted and served with the sauce of cream and egg yolks—its unctuousness set off by the acidity of sorrel—it's an exceptional dish. Although it's no longer something on his regular menu, Cauchemez did it well enough to please the ghosts of the Hôtel Moderne, where once a railway station, across the road, disembarked hungry customers, after their journey through farmland on a train nicknamed the *tuvac*, dialect for cow killer.

We looked over the menu with the temptation to stay on in Barfleur for some more of Cauchemez's achievements. There was a simple brochette of several fish with *beurre blanc*; there was a baked chunk of big flounder with little vegetables—flounder is a fish less esteemed by the French, but when it's fresh with the flavor of the sea, not faintly muddy-tasting, I think it is exceptionally eatable. There were other dishes that spoke of a chef of his generation's wanting to keep up with the times. I couldn't hold back a wince at the mention on his menu of wild bass minced like a hamburger and roasted and combined with an array of vegetables.

For dessert we both had shortbread-crusted apple pie with a caramel and calvados sauce.

Cauchemez did it for us. We didn't reach out for his most imaginative dishes, which represent an impulse of his that we could understand, but his self-expression was also a felicitous expression of his heritage. We were in Normandy in communication with the place at table.

Cauchemez is a Norman from near Cherbourg, who was fascinated by his mother's cooking as early as age three. He entered the craft by cleaning the oven and the racks for a local baker at age thirteen, became his apprentice pastry maker, beginning with rolling croissants, learned chocolate and ice-cream making in school as part of his diploma as a pastry man, then switched to cooking, serving in the kitchen of a variety of restaurants in Paris and elsewhere until homesickness for Normandy drove him to buy the Moderne.

Four years ago he met a woman who had worked there before. She'd come to the restaurant, when friends gave a party for her 102nd birthday. "You're the chef? Congratulations," she said, "I worked in the kitchen when I was thirteen. I plucked chickens for the chef who earned a Michelin star here in 1933. He won it for his *poulet Léonie,* named for his sweetheart. A man eating alone ordered it and, having eaten the chicken, he dipped a slice of bread into the sauce and ate it. Everyone looked at him; in those days polite people didn't do that in public, but he explained afterwards that he was the Michelin inspector and the sauce was irresistible."

The kitchen maid grew up to marry a rich man and bought a manor near Barfleur after he died. After her birthday dinner, she sent Cauchemez the recipe for *poulet Léonie:* breast of chicken, sauced with cream, morels, and calvados. He served it in the restaurant for two years. The Michelin man these days gives Cauchemez's achievements just two forks. I would have awarded him a star—if those classifications were indeed worthy of stars themselves.

Saint Pierre à l'Oseille

Since the dish, prepared for us for old time's sake, was not on Cauchemez's regular menu, he demurred about proclaiming his own invention of the recipe, but it was, to our taste, totally the delicious dish, of which the classic recipe follows. Americans who have trouble buying whole fish can still accomplish this with fillets. A whole Saint Pierre is filleted in any case and the fillets are poached in a *fumet*, a variety of stock enriched with the carcasses minus the skin. If you buy fillets from your fish store, ask for a few fish carcasses as well; any will do for the *fumet*. The *fumet*, the recipe for which exists in any good cookbook, can be prepared in advance.

four fillets of John Dory (or another white-flesh fish if it is unavailable; the sorrel sauce is sometimes authentically used with salmon)
a generous fistful of sorrel, with the stems removed, washed and chopped
15 oz. of crème fraîche (if unavailable, heavy cream will do, if not quite as well; in this case use half as much wine)
1 large glass of dry white wine
the yolks of two eggs
salt and pepper
½ stick of butter
generous sprinkling of flour

Poach the fillets in the *fumet* to a degree of doneness that suits you. They should in any case be all white.

Remove them and keep them in a warm place. Melt the butter without burning. Add the chopped sorrel, lightly sprinkled with the flour.

Cook and stir the sorrel in the butter until it becomes close to a purée. Combine the egg yolks with the cream.

Remove the pan of sorrel from the stove. Slowly add the liquid onto the sorrel; stir it all into a thick sauce. Pour the sauce over the fish arranged on a hot platter. Salt and pepper to taste.

L'Auberge des Deux Tonneaux
Tommy Lee Jones Knows Where He's Going

There are 168 souls who live in Pierrefitte-en-Auge in the heart of Haute Normandie, where Parisian weekenders rub shoulders with dairy farmers. Among the few thatched-roofed mortar-and-timber farmhouses and manors, and the rolling pastures, there's a Gothic church, a village hall, and the seventeenth-century Auberge des Deux Tonneaux, once a *bergerie*, or sheepfold, on a farm that was part of the local lord's vast property, back then. Today it's a place where the locals and the city crowd come together, to eat the food of the region, and in particular a *poulet Vallée d'Auge*. When Tommy Lee Jones comes to Normandy to buy quarter horses for his ranch, I'm told that he eats at the Auberge as often as he can with the driver who takes him there. Out of tact, nobody takes notice.

A black iron pot was simmering above burning logs in a big fireplace when we arrived on a cold day, with a *poulet Vallée d'Auge* on our minds. We were alone in the dining room, the weekend crowd was gone; the locals were no doubt beside their own fires. Hervé Amiard, owner and chef, told us that the pot contained what was his own lunch of a local version of soup, to which we were welcome as a starter. The aroma coming off the pot as he lifted the lid told us that would be a pleasure.

Hervé has been living and cooking in Pierrefitte since 2005. He began life as a photographer in Paris and shifted from fashion photography to doing books involving food, working with the renowned chefs of France. Joël Robuchon and he became fast friends, and he's hung out with Ducasse, Alain Senderens, and the much-regretted late Bernard Loiseau, among other stars of the kitchen.

"They're great talents," Amiard told me, "but the young chefs with lesser talents whom I see coming along are on the wrong track. People don't want their Japanese-style creations. It was of the moment ten or fifteen years ago. And they give their dishes these names like the titles of the soupy romances on sale in the railroad stations. I do a true and generous cuisine."

Hervé brings his cast-iron *cocottes* to the table, and people serve and reserve themselves to the *poulet Vallée d'Auge* or, say, a *poule sauce suprême* with rice. This exercise is not an affectation. Those pots are common in French households where someone still cooks. Serving with them adheres to Hervé's belief in generosity in cooking. Meanwhile his roast stuffed baby pig sells out fast while others regale themselves with the black pudding with applesauce.

That blood sausage apart, those are festive dishes for French peasants. On the other hand, the local soup we had was so typical of the daily fare of people with a long tradition of living piously and charily, killing a pig in the fall and making that one pig, along with barnyard fowl, their protein until the next year. The soup was nothing more than a medley of vegetables and some bacon. The smoke of the fire added seasoning. It was lean but not watery, and savory. We had Hervé dip into the pot on the fire again, before we undertook the *poulet*, which was, in contrast, unctuous and full-flavored. Hervé gets his meats from a butcher in nearby Pont L'Evêque, in contact with the local farmers, and his vegetables partly from his backyard garden. The chicken in our pot was a free-range Norman fowl, butchered after 120 days, in contrast with the 90-day free-range fowls sold on a big commercial scale. Joanne and I shared a dessert after our copious and rich chicken. We did our duty to the cause of this book and ate a *teurgoul*. The name of this dessert of milk, rice, sugar, and cinnamon, baked for five hours, comes from Norman *patois* for tearing the mouth—because it is sometimes served very hot.

"Rice and cinnamon aren't native to Normandy," Hervé pointed out. "It was the pirates patented by the crown in the wars against the English who brought them from other climates to Normandy and Brittany, where they had their home ports." *Teurgoul* became Norman soul food, and homemakers used to bake it by bringing it to the ovens of the bakery shops to simmer overnight.

Before we left, we took with us Hervé's simple recipe for *poulet Vallée d'Auge*. The purists' antipathy to either cider or calvados in *tripes à la mode de Caen* notwithstanding, they are essential to this dish.

Poulet Vallée d'Auge at Pierrefitte-en-Auge

For four people
    a medium sized free-range chicken
    a small handful of diced bacon
    a handful of minced shallots
    two cups of thick cream
    enough butter in which to brown the chicken
    enough dry cider to cover the chicken
    a glass of calvados
    three apples

Brown the chicken cut in parts in a thick pan, along with the shallots and bacon and butter.

Heat the calvados until it simmers, pour it over the chicken, and flame it. Deglaze, adding a little water and the cider. Pour in the rest of the cider and cook for an hour.

Halfway through the cooking, add the apples in slices with the skins retained.

When the dish is cooked, reduce the juice, retaining enough
for sauce to go with the chicken. Add the cream, heat gently,
and serve with mashed potatoes.

The cider we drank with our *poulet* was a delicious match—dry,
but fruity. The label read Le Gars Normand, and we wrote down the
owner's phone number to know a little more about it. A *gars* is a lad,
but the Norman lad turned out to be a Canadian of Scots descent,
who retired at fifty-five to the 1636 *manoir* he'd owned for thirty-five
years, having been an international financial executive for a variety
of companies, including Paramount, United Artists, and Universal.

"I got tired of working for other people, " Edward McLean told
us. He added a few hundred trees of twenty-two varieties of apples
to his existing orchard, and has been making cider for a decade. He
lives near François David, the cider guru we'd spoken to, and he
actually became interested in making cider helping David haul barrels and learning everything he did. Like David, McLean clarifies
his cider through *soutirage*, but he does a final filter to get rid of the
remaining yeast that builds carbonation.

"François sells his cider to restaurants," McLean explained, "and
they know how to open his bottles carefully. I sell to shops in the
region, and the people who buy the cider would have it splash all
over when they opened it, if I didn't filter."

And did he follow, like his mentor, the phases of the moon?

"The phases of the moon definitely affect air pressure," McLean
said, "but we control things scientifically through a microscopic
count of yeast spores. This said, scientifically, I ignore the moon,
but culturally, I'm loath to bottle unless the moon's in decline. It's
like superstition. . . ."

About three miles away from the bucolic loveliness of Pierrefitte-
en-Auge, the Touques River flows gently through the town of Pont

L'Evêque. Pont L'Evêque was two-thirds destroyed when it was bombed during German occupation in 1944. Miraculously, the oldest part of town, the Vaucelles quarter, was spared, and its mortar-and-timber houses that go back to the sixteenth century have since been brightly restored. The town is worth a long stroll. Pont L'Evêque is famous for its square, unctuous cow's cheese. When I asked a café owner in town where we could buy the best cheese, he told me that there were no more cheesemakers such as his grandfather in Pont L'Evêque. The sanitary rules of the EU had made their conversion to norms too expensive—the fully tiled walls and so on. Outside of town, a number of factories were making cheese they call Pont L'Evêque.

A Cheese Worth a Statue

We didn't tarry long in Pont L'Evêque; we headed to another area not far away, the home of Camembert. I had once, as I've said, interviewed the last farmer making his own cheese in the area who hand milked his cows. Now, I had learned, there was only one farmer left in the neighborhood of the village of Camembert making his own cheese. Big companies all over the world, including Normandy, were producing a cheese called Camembert. We went to visit the farm of François Durand, where, below his Tudor house, at a location called *le lieu dit* La Bonnerie, he has a modern creamery. Both Durand and his wife, Nadia, knew the story that Daniel Courtonne, the hand milker, had told me.

As a youth, Courtonne was in Vimoutiers, the market town near Camembert and near his family's farm, when a man by the name of Joseph Knirim arrived, able to explain in French that he was a doctor who made the journey from Brooklyn. The year was 1926. Knirim told the young man that he had cured himself of intestinal problems eating Camembert with the rind on and he had subsequently cured patients with Camembert rind. He asked

Courtonne to aid him in raising money to the statue of Marie Harel, the farm girl from the hills near the village of Camembert who is credited with inventing the cheese in the eighteenth century, changing the recipe from the Brie of the region in the east from which she or a priest with whom she collaborated came. There are some doubts about her actually inventing the cheese that would become famous. But at a lunch given for him in town, Dr. Knirim put down twenty dollars to start the ball rolling for the statue in Vimoutiers. The good doctor left, the statute was built, and the locals kept on making Camembert, spraying it with a penicillin mold to create the crust. A decade or so after Dr. Knirim's peculiar success with his patients, Alexander Fleming won the Nobel prize for discovering the therapeutic wonders of penicillin. The statue to Marie Harel was damaged in the fighting during World War II. The Borden Company of Ohio paid to have it restored, making sure that its name was on it as well as hers. So it goes. . . .

François Durand was in the middle of the careful process of molding his cheeses when we were there, so we spoke with Nadia.

François doesn't hand milk his cows. If you took great precaution, washing and rinsing, you didn't contaminate the milk with detergents, she insisted, Courtonne's attachment to his good old days notwithstanding. François's way of making Camembert was still largely one of great care. François has been doing it for twenty-nine years, having done nothing else, after taking over the farm from which his parents sold their milk to the dairy companies. As for his wife, Nadia's been the bookkeeper, handling delivery and receiving visitors for that long. François's brother takes care of the upkeep of the property and they have a hired hand who milks and packages. The making of the cheese is the responsibility of François and François alone. Together they produce three hundred cheeses a day from the milk of sixty cows—not nearly enough to keep up with the demand of upscale cheese stores in Paris, Nîmes, and Toulouse. They often run out of stock.

The evening milk is left to "mature" she said, and partly skimmed with the next morning's batch. Heated to 90 degrees Fahrenheit, with rennet added, it coagulates within an hour. Salted, it's lifted with a dipper by hand, and dropped into molds, each mold getting two and a half liters of milk. This process is distinct from the industrial one, whereby the curds are pressed in the molds. Durand molds each cheese by creating five layers, each dripped into the mold forty minutes apart.

"What you get," Nadia pointed out, "is a very supple cheese, aerated, and not sticky. You get the right taste and texture."

The taste of authentic Camembert, she said, is also a matter of the local grass the cows eat. "It has great diversity."

I told her that I thought that Camembert from the region had a faintly garlicky undertone. "It's the wild garlic," she said. (I'd known wild garlic in pastures in Massachusetts: the leaves like chives with little white bulbs for roots.)

The cheeses, Nadia explained, are allowed to drain for a full day naturally, before stainless steel plaques are put on them to keep them straight. Unmolded, they are sprayed with penicillin, salted, and kept in a cellar two weeks and turned regularly until the crust develops. They stay in the cellar three weeks more before they're wrapped and boxed, and sold to dealers who have to ripen them another month.

"It's all not very profitable," Nadia said, "you can't sell the product at a high enough price in comparison to the cost of all your time and ingredients." The Durands do what they do because it gives their lives purpose and satisfaction. There were no cheeses left to sell chez the Durands when we were there. Neither for the stores to ripen further nor fully ripened ones that they could sell to visitors. Out of stock. We had to find a cheese store in Paris, some time later, to be among those who love what the Durands do: an unctuous, not sticky cheese, with a complexity of flavor.

We took a back road when we left. On it, we knew, was the house where Charlotte Corday, the famous virgin of the French Revolution days, was born. The house a few minutes away from Camembert, which had gone into ruin, was now fully restored, but instead of a museum, it stood behind locked gates labeled "private." Someone had bought the place, a small brick, timber, and mortar house with three gables, fixed it up and closed it, privately honoring the calamitous young lady.

Charlotte's father was an *hobereau,* a country nobleman who never got to court and was particularly poor, working his own farm, making his own cheese. Her noble lineage got her an education at the Abbaye-aux-Dames in Caen, the city where she later lived with her female cousin, until, at the age of twenty-four, she set forth in a coach to Paris on a mission. The revolutionaries had been perse-cuting and slaughtering priests and had beheaded the king to whom she felt allegiance fraught with deep emotion. In Paris she bought a new hat and a big knife for the occasion, near the Palais Royal, and from there she got herself admitted into the home of Jean-Paul Marat, the leading demagogue of the Reign of Terror. While he was soaking his eczema in a bathtub, she planted the knife in his chest. Mademoiselle Corday was beheaded shortly afterward. Normans have the reputation of being strong-willed people. The lingering strain of the Viking personality?

11

LYON

Motherland

I went down from Paris to Lyon to have lunch at the restaurant of a fellow whom the government had officially acclaimed to be one of the best cooks in France. Wearing his honors ever so lightly, that same year he bought a little neighborhood place and decided to perpetuate faithfully the vernacular food of Lyon, with all the technical skill and refinement that had earned him his accolade. Gourmets and gourmands weren't long in finding him.

Joseph Viola was paying allegiance to the achievements of a roll call of cooks who, for centuries, had made the down-to-earth cuisine of Lyon a renowned presence in cultural history. I'm not talking about a dynasty in the vein of Vatel, Carême, and Escoffier. Let feminists give three stars to this city, in honor of those far more modest women restaurateurs, who, over the centuries, became the celebrated culture heroines of *la cuisine lyonnaise*. *Mères,* mothers, they were called. The French sometimes use that term for a mature woman endearingly, expanding the plain meaning to express character: often benevolence and warm generosity. I'll risk the rap for political uncorrectness to declare what my own experience tells me: Men cook to impress, women to please. But then, there are some Lyon types like Joseph Viola, owner and chef of a little place called Daniel and Denise, who manage to do both.

The fast train takes you from Paris to a city with a remarkable hush to it in just two hours, and the relative quiet of Lyon, compared to the clamor of a weekday in Paris, is a pleasant surprise. Lyon spreads alongside two big rivers, the Rhône and the Saone. Little of it is fascinating to the eye; it's a lot of usual nineteenth- and early-twentieth-century construction, until you stroll inward, into the centuries-old interior neighborhood or up into the old quarters of the hills that edge the city.

Lyon's charm is discreet, to paraphrase the title of Buñuel's film *Le charme discret de la bourgeoisie*. Bourgeois is an equally informative term for this third-largest city in France, after Marseille. France was the earliest large nation in Western Europe to have a central government. Germany and Italy were gaggles of kingdoms, principalities, and dukedoms late into the nineteenth century, while in France, Paris made up the navel of power and had all the related trappings; i.e., the standards of style and manners, originated by a nobility attached to the court at nearby Versailles. As in the other provincial cities, a middle class whose fortunes were rooted in industriousness dominated Lyon. The bourgeois townsmen were not far removed, in the sphere of their existence, from the workers they depended on, and they established criteria for sensible excellence. The Lyonnais worked to earn money, the Tout Paris and its ostentatious wannabes lived to display it. Bonaparte perpetuated the centrifugal nature of the power and the elite lifestyle in France, and despite government attempts at decentralization, such is still the case today. Paris may always be in-your-face Paris, while Lyon remains down-to-earth, shy of superficial splendor, no place for competitive showiness.

This said, Lyon was the luxurious silk fabric center of Europe for centuries. Not far away in the countryside, you can still visit villages with peculiar three-story constructions—top floors with slatted open walls, where French peasants labored like coolies, trying to keep up with silkworms, cleaning their racks and supplying their voracious appetites for mulberry leaves.

In Lyon, making silk cloth was also very labor intensive. It became less so after Jean-Marie Jacquart invented a machine that could make silk fabric with the patterns and colors woven into it. His punch-card system would be a forebear of early computers. A lot of workers lost their jobs in that early part of the nineteenth century, but the work still required skill and discernment. An understanding of quality plus sensory perceptiveness, otherwise expressed as taste, characterized the silk entrepreneurs of Lyon and their workers. The best of their houses supplied the most prestigious clothing makers in the world, the Paris *haute couture*. Our friend Pierre Schildge was a Bianchini on his mother's side, and his family business, Bianchini Ferrier, catered to the best *maisons de couture*. The Bianchini people had hired Raoul Dufy the painter to design collections for them. By the 1970s Lyonnaise luxurious silk couldn't compete against equally good Italian cloth made with cheaper labor, and a few years after that, Japanese silk replaced the Italian, for the same reason. I haven't kept up with whoever since out-competed the Japanese.

It would not be an exaggeration, then, to think that the old silk world of Lyon nevertheless left an enduring stamp on the character of the town. Taste is taste in every form of aesthetic contact. Thus an understanding of what the matter at hand really is, its qualities, carries over to the world of food, where, as elsewhere, pretension is distant from good taste.

Paul Bocuse, Lyon's most famous contemporary chef, long considered the most famous chef in the world, is probably also the least flashy among the stars of his profession. One of his defining words for great cuisine is probity.

"An impression of work, order, and probity, of serious and thought-out power emanates from their city," he once wrote about the Lyonnais. To which he added, "Serenity and sureness.

"It is this probity, this sense of measure," he wrote, "that I love to find in the honest and healthy cooking of Lyon. . . . It never tries for effects."

Curnonsky, that legendary gourmet and critic, whose real name was Maurice Edmond Sailland, dubbed Lyon in 1935 "the world capital of gastronomy"—here where a writer, Joseph de Berchoux, first propagated that word. Erasmus, of Rotterdam, who lived in the fifteen and sixteenth centuries, called Lyon's frank cooking "sumptuous."

The culture of fine food in Lyon is married first of all to its serendipitous geographical location. Before road transportation made it even easier to supply the city with food from nearby, the rivers brought in their bounties. From the Louhans region to the east came their famous fowl, the *poulet de Bresse,* not personally my favorite chicken but one raised with exceptional care. Decades ago, farm girls force-fed *poulets de Bresse* with their fingers to fatten them up. Bugey, a territory nearby, has streams full of crawfish, a favorite presence in Lyon cooking. The nearby Dombes area is full of lakes with pike, which, ground and combined into a heavenly light *quenelle,* and sauced with crawfish from the region of Nantua, contribute to *quenelles de brochet sauce Nantua,* the town's most honored dish. The Saone River was once the source for tiny fish for deep frying. Carefully raised hogs among the Monts de Lyonnais provide distinctive varieties of ham and sausage. The *rosette de Lyon,* named for the pink color of the portion of the gut that encases it, gets aged for two to three months. The other Lyon sausage appreciated by gourmets all over France is the *Jésus*. This particularly fat, pear-shaped salami gets wrapped in gauze, looking slightly like a swaddled child. It is sometimes called *un petit Jésus* and maybe the association accounts for the peculiar name. Both are made from pork, the *Jésus* from the "noblest" cuts, fillets and chops. Lyon sausage with pistachio nuts in it, braised and served with lukewarm potato salad, form another local dish, as well as does the same sausage baked in a *brioche*.

Along with these hearty cold cuts, from those hills, and from the neighboring regions of the Dauphiné and the Ardèche, farmers bring excellent cheeses to Lyon. Just to the north, the Beaujolais region supplies an easy-to-drink, relatively-easy-on-the-purse wine, with a few distinguished vintages that, while of a humbler grape, approach the suaveness of the prestigious vineyards of Burgundy farther north. The vintners of the Rhône, near Lyon, do robust wines a little out of style these days, but revered by trenchermen for centuries.

Eating well is not just a privilege of the well-off in Lyon. Statistics show that the inhabitants of Lyon and its region frequent outdoor markets for fresh products twice as often as the average Frenchman. Nearly half of each household in town receives friends and relatives for a festive dinner at least twice a month.

In all of this, there is the most important human presence in the food culture of Lyon, a phenomenon about which sociologists and feminists have much to chew on: the mothers, the revered *"mères."*

In contrast with the famous restaurants that came into being to cater to the Tout Paris, with their splendid decoration, of which Maxim's and La Pérouse remain museum-worthy examples, and their private rooms that enriched gastronomy with sexual adventure, the restaurant culture of Lyon is a story of *bouchons,* the simplest of restaurants once recognizable from the exterior by a *bouchon*, a ball of straw hung outside as a sign of an inn for hungry silk workers or for the journeymen of all trades traveling through France, on the compulsory trip that allowed them to be accredited masters.

As of the eighteenth century, the *bouchons* became the province of women who would excel themselves at memorable cooking. The women, dubbed *mères*, were the cooks of rich families, who, showing permeability of class in Lyon, became independent, moving on in life by creating a *bouchon* open to all who could pay for a meal. Paris had its striving master chefs, while Lyon was delightfully, simply mothered.

The first recorded *mère* was La Mère Guy, mentioned in writings in 1759. Her granddaughter with the same name shows up for her much-admired eel stews in writings of the next century. Her contemporary, La Mère Brigousse, was famous for her *quenelles de brochet*, which would become a star of Lyon fare.

The most revered cook among the *mères* was La Mère Fillioux, creator of the dish that either carries her name or that of *Poularde demi-deuil*, a neutered young hen, poached in a broth with vegetables and with the distinctive presence of slices of black truffles under its skin—hence "half in mourning." Samuel Chamberlain, whose "Bouquet de France" commissioned by *Gourmet* magazine in the fifties is a landmark of empathy with the food cultures of France, ate at La Mère Fillioux's *bouchon*, a meal cooked by her last successor. He enjoyed her *poularde,* her *quenelles*, and her artichoke hearts garnished with *foie gras.*

La Mère Fillioux was not known for her imagination. Her menu was always reduced to a very few choices each day, and those three of her repeated successes remain at the heart of Lyon's own restricted menu of authentic local delights. Chamberlain also cites La Mère Guy, once the *bouchon* of a descendent of that eighteenth-century namesake, as still "a small intimate restaurant with the very highest standards."

Understating while overachieving then might be the key words for defining the culture of Lyon *bouchons*.

La Mère Brazier, who apprenticed under La Mère Fillioux, finally earned an honor that fits into the annals of women's liberation. In 1933, Michelin awarded the good mother of gourmands a star; she was the first woman cook so anointed.

Gone are all the famous mothers now. La Mère Brazier, the last survivor among the celebrated *bouchons,* having fallen onto hard times, was taken over in 2008 by Matthieu Vianney, who already had earned two stars from the epicurean tire people.

The name of the place has been kept alive, in his unquestionably competent hands. Yet, looking for where to commune with the cooking of Lyon, I was apprehensive about Vianney's fare; it comes out designed like a Japanese composition, and consists of such imaginative things as oysters with green apple jelly and French caviar, or John Dory garnished with summer truffles (I have never eaten summer truffles that had taste worth remembering) and Spanish Iberico ham.

Where then? There are a total of seventeen stars that Michelin has distributed in Lyon, including those, of course, of Paul Bocuse, outside town, who has had three of his own since 1965. Bocuse does some local specialties on his eclectic but still French menu. He does a *volaille de Bresse en vessie mère Fillioux,* which he poaches in a pig's bladder, and he also has *quenelles sauce nantua* in his quiver. I thought that the Fillioux *demi-deuil* chicken would be tempting, although at 170 euro for two people, offered when fresh truffles were out of season, I hesitated. The thought—the rationalization?—that risking spending about twice per person for a full meal chez Bocuse seemed, with all else, not typical of a Lyon experience, made me put another meal at Bocuse on the back burner.

I could be tempted, instead by a lobster *tagine,* a riff on a Moroccan tradition at one doubly starred restaurant, or maybe a grilled duck *foie gras* with mango chutney and hibiscus juice at another starry establishment. The choices in the kaleidoscope of prized food fantasies in Lyon are a plethora. Not what I was there for, though.

All but motherless, but still very much loyal to its antecedents, Lyon's world of eating out has a vast number of *bouchons* still pleasing hearty and demanding eaters of all ages. Arriving a little early for lunch on my train from Paris, I stopped for a coffee at a place that had been *relooké*, redecorated to the nines in the style of minimalist, contemporary design. The young crowd that had already arrived for lunch was eating what? Either sautéed calf's liver or *quenelles de brochet* at every table—the most traditional Lyon fare.

Still how to choose my own Lyon lunch? I had decided to phone up someone who is a Lyon cuisine connoisseur although he bears the nonendemic name of Dos Santos. He hadn't pondered long before suggesting that we have lunch at a place called Daniel and Denise, owned and run by a couple named Joseph and Françoise.

Dos santos in Portuguese means "two saints" and Georges Dos Santos, consistent with his name, has been a devotee since childhood of food and, as of early adulthood, of wine. The latter devotion has led him to be one of the world's great resources today for buying and selling rare wines. You can Google to verify the achievement of this forty-year-old, who is dealing with wines far older than he is, in a little shop in Lyon.

"I'm one hundred percent Portuguese," Dos Santos told me, "and a hundred percent Lyonnais.

"People approach me from all over the world," Dos Santos said. "I've sold wine to a number of rich and famous people, including Bernie Madoff."

Dos Santos assured me that the bulk of his customers buy those precious old bottles to drink. In particular diners at the luxurious establishments that he supplies: the restaurants of Alain Ducasse and

Lasserre, the dining rooms of the Crillon and Ritz hotels in Paris, to name a few.

His success is the achievement of the son of Portuguese immigrants who quit school at age fourteen. Afterward, inspired by a passion for cooking that he acquired from his mother, he literally took the blows, going from the sadistic environment of the kitchens of one restaurant to another, the small, young Portuguese boy at the bottom of the heap.

George Orwell's *Down and Out in Paris and London*, based on his experience in the thirties, revealed the cruelty in the pecking order of French kitchen teams. I'm told that things have become more civilized since, but Georges remembers being burnt and pushed around, while he hoped to learn to rise in the profession while cleaning stoves, washing dishes, and being allowed to do garnishing, working from 8:00 A.M. to one in the morning. This happened at what was one of the most touted restaurants in Lyon, Vettard, in the year 1985. Jean Vettard was a chef with a generation of culinary glory behind him. His father, Marius, had served crawfish in *Nantua* sauce to Curnonsky in 1934. It was after wiping his mouth of the Vettard sauce that the grand gourmet declared Lyon *"la capitale mondiale de la gastronomie."*

None of that prestige rubbed off on the seventeen-year-old Dos Santos in the kitchen. He quit, worked around some more, turning into a prodigy behind the stove, until at the age of nineteen, a backer set him up in his own restaurant, where three times in a row Gault and Millau's guide anointed him among the best young hopes in French cuisine. Dos Santos got restless and went off to London, where he cooked at Terrance Conran's Bluebird and Ducasse's Monte's Club. From there he traveled and cooked throughout the world, as a private chef to the rich, or in restaurants in Spain, Portugal, and Cuba.

"All that time I was building my interest in wine and buying. By the time I was twenty-five," Dos Santos explained, "I owned four thousand bottles of rare wines. I decided that wine would be it for me instead of aiming to be a great chef. I was young; I didn't want to claw my way up the totem pole. I was a little Portuguese guy without the needed talent for showmanship."

So Dos Santos wound up high on another totem pole. I often admire the success of Portuguese immigrants to France. I remember the big community of them parked in the Paris suburb of Nanterre, living in corrugated steel shacks, much like a Brazilian *favella*. In a very few years, the shanties were gone, the immigrants and their children had contributed a host of artisans to society who owned their own businesses and paid taxes. A Portuguese concierge, near where Joanne and I had once lived, dwelled with her husband and son in one room. He grew up to go to the best law school in France and on to a great law firm.

Dos Santos brought a bottle of Hermitage Paul Etienne, 1964 with us to lunch at Daniel et Denise.

Daniel et Denise

Georges and I let the chef choose our menu. Would there be a *Poularde demi-deuil?* Joseph Viola, the jovial forty-five-year-old chef and owner, with a premature gray beard, reminded me that truffles were out of season, and he only worked with fresh truffles, so there would be no *Poularde demi-deuil.* That was a little confirmation for me regarding the government's appreciation of Viola's merits. Joseph Viola had been dubbed *"meilleur ouvrier de France"* in 2004. "Best Worker in France" is an honor the Ministry of Education bestows in each case on a great variety of artisans, from masons to chocolate makers, bakers or cooks. It is an honor that does not come easily in any case. Some eight hundred cooks in all of France applied for the competition of 2004. After their credentials weaned down the group to fifty, the great cook-off began. "It was a challenge about mastery, not about inventiveness," Viola explained. "Everyone had the same dishes to prepare."

Viola's cook-a-thon took him through a timbale of sweetbreads with mushrooms and chicken *quenelles,* a saddle of lamb, a zucchini soup with tomatoes, a duck deep-dish pie with *foie gras,* and *sauce royale,* and an apple soufflé, made to rise in a carved-out apple instead of a mold. At the end of the ordeal, seventeen cooks were chosen to be named best in France, Joseph Viola among them.

Viola's credentials were already impressive. He was born in the East, near Germany, where he began his career as a cook. That eventually took him to the kitchen of Michel Guérard, at Eugénie-les-Bains. After his five years with Guérard, word of mouth about his prowess in the chefs' community earned Viola an offer from Jean-Paul Lacombe, who ran one of Lyon's famous restaurants, Léon de Lyon, to come and cook with him and make the place still better.

"He had a Michelin star when I joined him," Viola said, "and two when I left him, after ten years.

"When I got the best chef award, I made a choice. The chance came up to buy this restaurant," he said, "and I wanted at last to be in my own place. Traditional cuisine by a best chef in France didn't exist. There was a place for me I felt right about. "

Sounding a little like Proust, Viola added, "I was looking to touch base with the reality of the past.

"With an eye to the future," he said. "Every cuisine defines its moment. I think that it's the moment now for tradition." In 2010 the Guide Lyon Gourmand voted Viola chef of the year.

We began lunch with the "2010 world champion" *pâté en croute.* This honorable dish wasn't another prize of Viola's, but the creation of his second-in-command, Florian Oriol. An international organization of chefs called the Toques Blanches du Monde, with five *meilleurs ouvriers de France* on the jury, chose the twenty-eight-year-old Oriol over eleven competitors for the five thousand euro prize. Oriol had been an assistant to Viola at Léon de Lyon. After going off to the nearby region of Doubs to work for a caterer for a year, he came to Daniel et Denise.

It was Viola who taught him the crust, a puff paste whose dough benefits from a day's "repose" to avoid bubbles developing in baking. The contents are Oriol's idea: sweetbreads, chicken liver, the throat meat of pork, and wild mushrooms, side by side. Fifty minutes in the oven.

We told Florian that it was indeed world-class. It went superbly well with the first of the three wines we were sampling with our food, a simple, open Beaujolais in a carafe. Well, not so simple as the carafe suggests. Beaujolais, once the favorite modest wine in France, has come upon hard times, a result of its popularity, which spread worldwide after the war. Statistics showed that the vintners in this region between Burgundy and Lyon, driven by the demand, were selling more Beaujolais than they vinified, thanks to the vineyards of North Africa. The public also responded with a pernicious taste for wine stronger than Beaujolais's properly delicate nature, and the next Beaujolais scandal involved *chaptalisation*. This is a process abused by vintners who pour more sugar than they are allowed to into their vats, which produces a higher degree of alcohol—a hot mouth and a very hot throat for the drinker, which enough people like for shady vintners to get away with it. Those seem to be the same people who perpetuate the rite of drinking Beaujolais *nouveau* in cafés in November, subjecting their digestion to a raw drink that hasn't known a second fermentation, *la fermentation maléolactique*, which wine must undergo to be truly drink-worthy.

Beaujolais is classified into four categories, all of it from the same *gamay* grape: just Beaujolais; Beaujolais Villages, which comes from a group of villages a notch above in quality; and then the wine of two groups, one classed better than the other, that bear a place name other than Beaujolais. Think of Moulin au Vent, Fleurie, Brouilly. . . .

The Beaujolais Villages we drank *en carafe* had borne the label of the merchant Georges Duboeuf, who has the most famous name in Beaujolais. I think that Duboeuf is a great marketer, who manages to cover a whole range of quality in Beaujolais, giving the low end of his wines the rub-off of his name on the high ends. I have drunk quite ordinary, even not good wine by Georges Duboeuf. But the wine Viola puts on his list *en carafe* proved worthy of many a delightful bottle: light, fruity, an easy ride down to the stomach. With it we sampled Viola's best Beaujolais choice, a Morgon 2009 bottled by Martin Lapierre. Morgon belongs to the next best tier of Beaujolais, and this one, of a particularly good year, was worthy of tier one, in our opinion. The Burgundy winegrowers, with their frail *pinot noir* grape, look down on the Beaujolais's *gamay*, a hardy and more frank varietal. Lapierre's Morgon had a suavity many Burgundies never achieve. In the region of Beaujolais as well as in Burgundy, some wine is sold as bottled where the grapes have grown, but most are also the choice of *négotiants*, middlemen whose reputations immediately tell you something about quality. The Morgon spoke eloquently of flowers rather than fruit.

The wine Dos Santos brought along was another wine from nearby, an Hermitage 1964, a wine from the Rhône from the house of Paul Etienne. For the lusty trenchermen of the nineteenth century, the equally robust Hermitage was prized more than the best Bordeaux. Our wine had grown far shyer with age and had a new personality very unlike a Rhône wine. It still had something to say, if close to a whisper: an ineffable, floral perfume.

The more proletarian, simpler, fruity Beaujolais went particularly well with the *pâté en croute*, a hearty combination. The Morgon's depth enriched the presence of the *tête de veau* that followed. Viola's deft and refined manner came through with his choice of the portions of the veal's head, the precise, bright cooking of it and the *sauce gribiche* accompaniment. That's often a tasty while runny and lumpy combination of vinegar, hard-boiled eggs, pickles, capers, and herbs. Viola's sauce had the unctuous quality of a mayonnaise with the bite of the other ingredients still there.

Our main course with the discreet Hermitage was subtle and sublime: a *quenelle de brochet à la sauce Nantua*. The *mères* of Lyon would have applauded Viola's achievement with that dish they were famous for. Ever so light, subtle, with the full flavor of the pike coming through all the same. Eggs, butter, flour, the fish, and little else, together almost as light as a soufflé. The sauce was the classic accompaniment, a cream made with crawfish.

"In Paris they would eat lobster, while in Lyon we worked with crawfish," Viola said, explaining the difference between the down-to-earth culture of Lyon cooking and the Parisian striving for luxury.

There was, in a large sense, nothing down-to-earth about Viola's *quenelles*. Heavenly is the appropriate cliché. Viola served us two more examples of Lyon soul food, a *gras double à la lyonnaise* and a *gâteau de foie de volaille*. The *gras double* was strips of beef's stomach, breaded, braised, deglazed with vinegar. The *gâteau* of chicken livers with egg and beaten egg white was as light as a soufflé, but deep tasting, like the *gras double*. We were down-to-earth again, heartily so.

I asked why so much of Lyon cooking involved innards. The *quenelles* had reigned over a company of liver, sweetbreads, stomach, and veal's head, which, with its tongue, is classed among *abats* or innards. They told me that until the 1970s Lyon had been a major national center for slaughterhouses. The meat was shipped all over; the very perishable innards were bought cheaply. The mothers knew how to turn economy into gastronomy.

The French as a whole are not a profligate people; modest and even poor farmers dominated the nation's population up into the twentieth century. They made the best of everything edible. Think of snails. Louis Diat, the great French cook of that century, who emigrated to the States, mentions somewhere in his writing that the greatest virtue, perhaps, of French home cuisine is the ability to cook something cheap and transform it into something sublime. I remember what a woman whose *ferme-auberge* we'd once visited near Deauville told us. A *ferme-auberge* is a farm that belongs to a group that the government created to help small farmers earn a living. They have a restaurant serving food they produce or food produced by accredited fellow farmers. The woman told us that she would savor in her mind, late into life, the dish her mother made, reusing the well-cooked soft vegetables of a *pot au feu*, and, with one of those Moulinex hand-grinding purée makers that were in almost every kitchen in France, puréeing the vegetables, to recreate a tasty dish baked with *béchamel* sauce and a sprinkling of *Gruyère* cheese.

Tripes, kidneys, sweetbreads, brains, and liver are everywhere in French cooking, where a taste for them has left behind the inexpensiveness that they once represented. Nowadays, at the butcher's, calf's liver costs about twice as much as steak. Viola informed me that cocks' combs had become very expensive, since the old-fashioned starter, the *vol au vent,* was becoming fashionable. A *vol au vent* is a puff pastry filled with sweetbreads or chicken dumplings, mushrooms and cream, topped, as aficionados have it, with cocks' combs.

Joanne and I ate calf's brains first of all at Larré, way back in New York: *cervelle au beurre noir.* The brains were, as they should be, very fresh or they'd taste a little fishy. The recipe calls for them to be sautéed, the butter sauce on the calf's brains brightened with capers. In recent years, the burnt butter gave way to a mellower light brown version in French restaurants, until fears about cholesterol made the whole dish, chuck full of it, a no-no. The mad cow epidemic in Europe kept it taboo. But it has come back now in the humble *bouchons* or bistros of Lyon, and it has a deserved place in the culture.

Viola told me that there was one thing in his restaurant that was not made from scratch on the premises. The bread. But the baker, of course, was also a *meilleur ouvrier de France.* It was crispy-crusted, yeasty and chewy, a baguette as it should be.

We ended our lunch with a floating island and a *crème brulée*. Devotees of grand restaurants might have taken us for naïve, with these plain old-fashioned things, but each was precisely delicious.

Viola's prices are as reasonable as many an ordinary café-restaurant in Paris. He does what he does, getting obvious pleasure out of it. "People these days want to go into a restaurant knowing what they're going to wind up paying," Viola said. "They want a real product with a real taste."

So who were Daniel and Denise in this story?

"The former owners," Viola said. "The place had a name and we kept it."

I thought of Viola's decision. He was one of the best chefs in France, an honor bestowed by a jury in objective competition, unlike the subjective guidebook appraisals that give and take away honors, and thus keep themselves in the public eye. He took over this little place with an old-fashioned bistro look to it, and kept the name, making his own known through word of mouth, in gourmet circles. I thought again of Alain Senderens, one of the celebrated chefs in Paris who bought the house of Lucas-Carton, famous in culinary history, and scraped away its name, to inscribe his own. When Francis Carton bought the place in 1925, he saw fit simply to just add his name to that of Robert Lucas, the owner who founded the venerable restaurant in 1732.

Françoise, Viola's wife, who used to care for people as a nurse, runs the dining room of their bistro, caring for the regulars and nonregulars with equal warmth. She's an important part of the personality of the place, while totally okay not having her name on it.

Back home, I could dine on no more than some grapes and a glass of Bordeaux. Joanne, who had foreseen a dauntingly rich encounter with the cuisine of Lyon, had let me go off on my own on this culinary caper. Truth to tell, it was hearty but no cause for fear of heartburn. Viola has a light but strong touch. And the motherly ghosts seemed to have been at his shoulder.

Quenelles de Brochet

Having telephoned Viola several times, recalling that I was anxious to pass on the recipe for his airy *quenelles*, and having got pleasantness and promises, I had to conclude that revealing the recipe might have, in his eyes, rendered Daniel et Denise vulnerable to nonindustrial espionage. Georges Dos Santos told me that, while his onetime boss Jean Vettard's kitchen was hell to work in, his celestial *quenelles* were the most renowned in Lyon. But Vettard's recipe was lost with his death. I turned to my 1938 first edition of *Larousse Gastronomique*, written by Prosper Montagné, the book that is a bible for French gastronomes. The *Encyclopedia Brittanica* calls Montagné "one of the greatest French chefs of all times." He wrote the *Larousse* book at the age of seventy-three, having run several famous restaurants in Paris and Monte Carlo. Here, translated and as spelled out, is his recipe for those *quenelles*:

Prepare in advance, so that it is cold, a panade of bread or flour equal to ⅔ lb. [A panade is a classic paste used to combine with ground fish. For flour, Montagné recommends boiling ⅜ pt. of water with 1¼ oz. of butter and a pinch of salt, and throwing 5¼ oz. of sifted flour into it while it boils. Stir with a wooden spoon, until the mixture comes away from the sides of the pot. Put it into a buttered dish, and cover to cool with a buttered paper.]

With a mortar and pestle, pound 1 lb. 1½ oz. of Pike, devoid of bones and skin, with a pinch of pepper and of nutmeg and a little less than a ½ oz. of salt. Pound in the panade, until it's all smooth. Add 7 oz. of butter and pound it all until it's all united and then add one by one two eggs and four egg yolks. Pass it all through a fine sieve.

Mold the batter with a big buttered spoon and place the *quenelles* on a buttered platter. Put them in water lightly simmering for ten minutes. Drain them on cloth napkins. They should be thus poached just before serving with the sauce already prepared.

Montagné doesn't do this, but allow me to pass on a secret weapon of a *quenelle*-loving friend: Separate the eggs, beat the egg whites stiff, and fold them carefully into the rest, before poaching. The *quenelles* seem to float on air.

Sauce Nantua

Reduce by half, 3½ oz. of *béchamel* sauce. Add 3½ oz. of the water the crawfish were cooked in and 3½ oz. of cream. Add 1¾ oz. of *beurre d'écrivisses*, made of crawfish shells and flesh, pounded fine and mixed with an equal weight of butter, strained through a fine sieve. Add a pinch of cayenne pepper and a few drops of cognac. Strain it all again through a fine sieve.

Pour the sauce, after heating gently, onto the freshly poached *quenelles*.

12

THE BASQUE COUNTRY

As the Dove Flies

C rocuses, dandelions, and clover were blossoming, the sky was clear blue above green mountains, it was shirtsleeve weather at nearly November, and Joanne was in distress. "Doves," she insisted, "are lovely birds of peace." We had come down to the Basque Country for an annual dove hunt, a traditional *chasse* without guns that exists beyond memory. It goes back perhaps as far as when Charlemagne's army, retreating in 778 from having fought the Moors in Spain, was ambushed and butchered by booty-minded Basques in the mountain pass of Roncevalles. A pass similar to the one where our current Basque friends had strung their huge nets for the dove hunt.

The Basque Country is to my mind the part of France that matches only the heartland of Auvergne and the island of Corsica in loveliness. Down here in the Pyrenees, green mountains, lush valleys, and ample white-and-red-trimmed chalets with carved wooden balconies form

196

an extensive, visual harmony of mankind and nature, more uplifting than what you sometimes get elsewhere in the nation, where villages can be tired-looking gray faces lining the roads. The Basques are proud of their ethnic identity, of which their cuisine speaks clearly. The road signs are both in Basque—a harsh-sounding ancient language like no other—and French. A café in the village of Sare, where we were staying, had its walls lined with independence slogans and posters siding with the violent ETA Basque movement across the border in Spain, but it might have been a matter of decoration. Few French Basques are interested in having a new nation without the social advantages of France.

Our host for the hunt was Henri Dutournier, whose family roots go back into the nearby region of the Landes, as well as to the Basque Country. Like his father and grandfather before him, he has hunted the dove. He is president of the nineteen-member club called Les Palomières de Sare and of the ten other hunts in the region.

"I don't know when exactly hunting doves our way got started," he said. "The story is that it was invented by a monk of the Abbey of Roncevalles, who realized that if you threw a stone at a flock of doves, they imagined that they were being attacked and would dive low into waiting nets to avoid what they thought was a predatory bird."

Our hunt, we learned, after we climbed a mountain on a two-kilometer dirt road, consisted of six nets strung from tree to tree in a pass. Ahead the *chasseurs* wave white cloths and scream when a flock of migrating doves fly by, driving the birds toward the nets. As they pass, the *rabatteurs* throw white paddles at them, confusing the birds into believing that they're being attacked by sparrow hawks. The doves then fly into the nets, the nets are collapsed around them, and the birds are then scooped up, and killed with a blow on the head. They are no longer bitten at the neck, as they once were, Dutournier assured.

A cruel sport? The hunt began as a hunger for protein among poor people. The doves were kept alive in coops, after being netted, and eaten in the months ahead. Or they were cooked as a *salmis de palombes,* which was jarred and kept. The *salmis de palombes* still happens to be one of the most delicious things you can eat in France. It would be a gastronomic highlight of our trip.

Dutournier defended the hunt. "The doves are not an endangered species and we are not endangering it. Yesterday we saw a hundred and fifty thousand doves, and we netted seventeen. In four counting stations last year the counts ran to a total of about two million migrating birds. Net hunting all told caught about ten thousand doves."

The counting, Dutournier soon showed us, takes place a few minutes away, at the Col de Lizarrieta in Spain, where members of the League for the Protection of Birds and of the Hunting Federation of France, along with environmentalists of several organizations, were sitting in the sun on folding chairs, notebooks in their laps, while they peered through binoculars. I didn't venture to disturb them to ask someone how they could count thousands of birds.

"It's like counting crowds at a demonstration," Dutournier said. "They sort of extrapolate."

In any case no doves were in sight at the *col,* which means pass, so we enjoyed some *tapas* of Spanish mountain ham at the nearby café. We'd been out very early, before the sun had risen, and we were hungry, but had we known the repast that was ahead, we would have gone easy on the *jamón.*

They count fewer and fewer birds, Dutournier said, but no one has claimed that the species is declining. "The doves have become more and more sedentary, spending the winters in Scotland or Russia or Scandinavia, when premonitions of harsh weather used to drive them south."

Global warming? He shrugged. "In any case, the doves have also become destructive. I won't say they're as bad as locusts, but woe to the Scots farmer whose crop they settle on, eating seeds or sprouts."

Back at our own *col,* there were still no doves in sight. A flock of dark-winged *grives,* thrushes, passed in the distance, and we heard gun hunters firing at them. Thrushes haven't quite the culinary cachet of doves, but they reign in the form of the best *pâtés.* I would enjoy a memorable house-made *paté de grives* a couple of days later at a Basque *auberge* called Achtal. These little birds are esteemed enough to be the desired presences in the French equivalent of the adage "If you're hungry you'll eat anything." It goes, *Faute de grives, on mange des merles.* Which is: For want of thrushes, you eat blackbirds.

Across the canyon and the frontier, at Etxalar, the beaters for Spanish Basque hunters, soul mates of our friends from Sare, were making noise. A flight of doves had passed their way. Our way was still neglected, even if a lot of white feathers below the net in front of us attested to the catch of previous days.

The day went on. Joanne was relieved. No doves our way today. Someone blew a horn that officially ended the pursuit. "You'll stay for lunch? Please do," Dutournier said. It would be a lunch that, in itself, made our trip.

We were twenty-six people at the same long table in the cabin of the Palomières de Sare. Along with the hunters of the society, a group of men had come for a fraternal lunch from the town of Hendaye nearby. They were members of Le Vieux Château, a club dedicated to choral performances in French, Basque, and Spanish, and, as José Luis Alli, the club's president explained, to gastronomy. On the latter score they were well served that day.

The guys had begun eating mountain ham and scrambled egg canapés, while waiting for Etienne Aguirre to perform. We had known him to perform before. Aguirre, a devotee of the hunt, was also the owner of the restaurant Pottoka, down in nearby Espelette, where he's been at the stove for thirty years, having turned his back on being a chef in Paris, including at the exclusive Jockey Club and what was the Continental, one of the luxurious hotels in town. He'd gone home to perpetuate the cooking that his parents had made notable in Espelette. His twenty-eight-year-old daughter was now at the stove too, and we were going to re-savor the results of her prowess the next day, having eaten that summer, at their Pottoka, a simple place named after the stubby wild horses that roam the nearby mountains.

Aguirre came with a great quantity of venison, from deer also in season, which other hunters had shot. While the meat was being marinated, he served a red bean soup with ham and carrots, tasty and substantial, but that was just to whet the appetite for a *civet* of venison, which he'd had prepared, having stewed marinated venison with the blood of the deer and spices. Dutournier informed us that there was unsweetened chocolate in it, to render mellow the sauce. We remembered that the introduction of chocolate was a presence in the history of the Basque Country. It was quite delicious, more refined than the earlier peasant soup. Yet had Etienne served that *civet* to the lofty members of the Paris Jockey Club, each with his required four quarterings of nobility, they would not have passed on it. That was course two.

Now the other lot of venison was well marinated and Etienne began to grill it *à la plancha*. We went on to grilled venison and hand-cut French fries, and then to Basque hard sheep cheese, served, as is the custom, with jam from the black cherries from the illustrious orchards of the village of Itxassou. The Hendaye guests had brought the common French apple pie, which we passed on. We'd have Etienne's own homemade *gâteau basque* next day. Having drunk strong coffee ladled out of a pot, Joanne and I passed on the impressive array of *digéstifs*. And so I made my sober but sated way down that hairpin mountain road back to Sare.

It had been a savory, rustic meal appropriate for the hunt. Sabine Aguirre proved to us next day that the cooking she'd learned from her father, which he had learned from his parents, could be country cooking and refined at the same time.

She too had left home to cook elsewhere in the wide world before returning to her roots and her family's stove. She'd cooked in British Columbia, having apprenticed in the kitchens of a few of the most celebrated chefs in Paris—Eric Frechon, Michel Rostand, and Christian Constant. She confessed that what truly brought her home was a Basque, who still is the great object of her affection.

Cuisine had to be the next great one. Sabine's deftness was on par with the best you get in Paris. Joanne started with a pumpkin soup containing chestnuts from trees in the nearby village of Ainhoa. Subtle, smooth, and rich. I was more adventurous, having chosen something called *Tripotxes d'Espelette*. Espelette is known worldwide, among those who follow such things, for the red pepper it produces, similar to Hungarian paprika, but with a more complex, earthy flavor and aroma. Some of it had gone into this dish, a version of black pudding, using the blood and meat of mutton. Sounds strong tasting? In this dish done from scratch at Pottoka, it was rich but mellow. Sabine served this unpronounceable delight with a fresh peppery, Basque tomato purée, which becomes a *pipérade* when poached egg is added. Joanne's main course, equally strange sounding and equally delicious, was a *poulet xilindron*. A sautéed chicken with onions made blond in the oven and using yet another pimento, a mild *piquillot* from Spain.

My main course, the one we principally came for, was a *salmis de palombes*. A classic *salmis* is a dish made of game or fowl that is two-thirds roasted and then gets cooked again in a wine sauce. In the book that I have on Basque cuisine by Huguette Couffignal, you'll find the Basque version, which actually takes its name from Sare, called *le saratar*. I've never eaten a classic *salmis* such as Carême promulgated among gastronomes of the nineteenth century, but Sabine, sticking close to her roots, produced a sumptuous *saratar*, the meat still a bit rare. I'm not sure that Carême, who cooked in the days when gaminess was more favored than freshness, would have convinced us about the virtues of doves roasted and cooked again. Sabine's sauce, in birds just browned in advance, was unctuous without being strong and funky.

The *gâteau basque* that she'd baked from her father's own recipe rounded out our lunch. A *gâteau basque* is a white cake that can be very heavy, but, filled with custard, this one was light and delicious. Joanne passed on dessert, while she helped me finish our bottle of 2007 Ohitza Irouléguy red wine.

Irouléguy is a wine you never hear about outside the Basque Country, although the Romans implanted it there in the third century, and its presence was perpetuated by the monks of the Abbey of Roncevalles, to quench the thirst of pilgrims on their way to the tomb of Saint James at Compostella, in Spain.

Irouléguy is vinified from tannat, cabernet franc, and cabernet sauvignon grapes. Tannat gives astringency and an assortment of antioxidants, to red wines, in particular, as I mentioned earlier, Madiran. The cabernets are more elegant varietals that go into Bordeaux. Our wine was of a lovely violet color and, with a long, faintly floral bouquet. It gained body as we drank, while, in taste, the cabernets began to dominate. It was not a peer of luxurious Bordeaux, but it drank very well.

When we dined in Saint Jean de Luz on the Basque coast next day, we had another Irouléguy, or so it was still called: Ametzia Irouléguy, pumped up to 13.5 degrees of alcohol, in one of those trendy, skinny half bottles for contemporary wines, a lot of heat in the mouth and nothing else pleasant. The fad of juicy alcoholic wines had reached the Basque Country, in a restaurant remembered as a great family tradition for three generations.

Sabine Aguirre's Salmis de Palombes

Serves four to six

  4 quartered doves (the recipe would work with squab)

  4 slices of country bread

  ½ lb. mushrooms

  ½ lb. peeled carrots

  I large peeled onion

  5 oz. of cubed bacon

  3 ¼ qt. of veal stock

  I ½ bottles of dry red wine (Irouléguy, if possible)

  I oz. of butter

  I ¾ oz. of flour

  2 squares unsweetened chocolate

  pimento (Espelette, if possible)

  salt

  some duck fat

Heat the wine, while cutting the onion and carrots very fine. Caramelize them gently in the butter on a low fire. Add them to the wine and cool for twenty minutes, being sure that the wine has been reduced by half.

Brown the birds in the duck fat or oil, and then put them in a casserole with the vegetables. Sprinkle on the flour and mix on a low fire, then add the wine and the stock and cook for one and a half hours.

Remove the birds and set them aside. Add the mushrooms and bacon, the pimento, salt, and chocolate.

Fry the slices of bread and put them on a paper towel.

Serve the birds well heated. The bread can sop up the sauce, as can some fresh pasta or boiled potatoes.

As we left our hotel in Sare, to head for Saint Jean de Luz and dinner, Jean-Baptise Fagoaga, the owner, complimented Joanne. He was impressed that the members of the Palomières de Sare had received a woman for lunch. "An honor," he said. It seems that men of the Palomières de Sare, with their selective nineteen-man membership, enjoy in Sare, population 2,271, prestige equivalent to the standing of Paris's Jockey Club.

Fagoaga's Hôtel Arraya, which began as a hostel for pilgrims on the road to Compostella in the seventeenth century, is as pleasant a place to spend the night as any, full of lovely old things, and once again a family story, one of three generations. The restaurant, we thought, was worth less praise, but more than the one that we were heading to on the coast.

The pastoral Basque Country has also three noteworthy cities on the Atlantic shore: Biarritz, Bayonne, and Saint Jean de Luz. Biarritz changed from a simple village to a chic watering place, after Napoléon III's Spanish wife, Eugénie, took a liking to the place, and had a castle built there, which long after became a luxurious hotel. Fancy people kept coming down there until about the 1960s and some still go to lose weight and gain tone at the town's noted thalassotherapy center, but only the arrival of surfers in the past few decades has given a youthful presence to the aged gestalt of this town.

Bayonne, which brings to mind the regional ham that takes its name, is more industrial, while it has a charming old town and a fine art museum—with paintings by Goya, Delacroix, Géricault, and Degas—well worth the visit.

Saint Jean de Luz is the most alluring of the three. It was once a whaling port, and, in the wars of Louis XIV, pirates, patented by the crown for a share of the loot, sailed out of the harbor. Small boats still bring in tuna and sardines caught off Africa, but the town, with its cobbled streets and handsome, red-trimmed white houses, still

has also a good touch of the chic it acquired in the nineteenth century as a bathing resort particularly favored by the British, including
the fashionables around Edward VII. Right in the center of town,
a few steps from the lovely Square Louis XIV, the narrow rue de la
République, lined with Basque restaurants and ancient houses, leads
to a fine, sandy beach. Real estate prices in Saint–Jean–de–Luz recall
those of Paris.

The chic personality of Saint–Jean had its curious and pathetic
counterpart: Up until the twentieth century, a portion of the population resembled Indian untouchables. No one was sure where the
Kascarots came from. Some say they were Goths who settled here in
the first century, but the name comes from the Basque *kaskar*, which
means worthless. They settled in a ghetto, while they were forbidden
to drink at public fountains, marry outside their group, or touch
other people's food. In 1320 King Philippe Le Long ordered them
massacred, claiming that these people, said to spread leprosy, had also
been poisoning wells. The survivors turned to ship carpentry and
barrel making, because wood was supposed to be free of transmitting leprosy. After Louis XIV abolished the laws against them, they
became the town's fish merchants. Nowadays, they are mixed into
the population and haven't survived as an ethnic entity.

The last time we were here, we'd come on a reportage for *Bon
Appétit*, to write about the restaurant Mattin in Ciboure, a humbler community, just across the river Nivelle that empties into the
Atlantic. That was in 1994. This time, the two elderly women who
were in the second room of this pretty, rustic place—were they
peeling potatoes?—were gone. In charge was their grandson and
son respectively, a very hospitable and amiable man. I had written
about *ttorro* (pronounced in Basque "tchorro"), a fish stew that had
made the place a stop-off for gourmets.

I began dinner with an upscale version of Bayonne ham, a *jamón
ibaïona de la maison Ospital*. It was pink, while Bayonne ham is reddish,

and the color spoke of a subtler flavor. It was just okay, no better than the Bayonne ham I had with our Etap hotel breakfast. In my book, *jambon de Bayonne*, no matter what history it has, is nowhere as good as a lot of country hams. This pale version couldn't compare with a delicate San Daniele or Parma, or with any other good Italian prosciutto. At the same time, the usual darker French versions have nothing of the special full flavor of a Spanish *jamón belota,* from small black pigs that feed half wild on acorns. The best we've had of that *jamón* was in the town of Jabuco, where the nutty smell of the ham in all the shops fills the air. In Ciboure, I was presented with something that sounded fancy on the menu but was nothing extraordinary.

Our anxiety heightened as the owner urged Joanne to begin with a dish made of raviolis stuffed with a *brandade* of cod, in a sauce of squid's ink. Politely, she accepted his recommendation for this con-coction, and it proved a mistake; the only thing with an enticing flavor to it was a version of *brandade*—of potato, puréed salt cod, and garlic. It was garnished with fat mussels in their shells that had lost all flavor. By now she had also agreed to his suggestion for a sauté of scallops on a bed of soft spaghetti, which had something like a Chinese sweet and sour sauce on it.

I took the *ttorro.* The room was full of people eating *ttorro,* and everyone looked happy. The fish in my *ttorro* were nearly disin-tegrated; the broth was tasty but not memorable. I ventured to myself that the need to keep heating this dish to satisfy the big orders ruined it.

Such, as we saw it, was the result of the success of Mattin. You can't begrudge these hardworking people their success. A restau-rant is a business, and it is a successful business when it pleases the greatest number of customers. And who could have begrudged the people enjoying their evening around us? But the sight of a couple and their obese twelve-year-old-or-so son, across the room from us, seemed a quintessence of what people's understanding of food had become, as much in the town of Ciboure as anywhere. The parents were enjoying the insipid scallops, while the kid was pouring ketchup on his *confit de canard* and on the *frites* that accompanied it. He was drinking Coca-Cola. The wine served with our dinner, as we mentioned earlier—too juicy and over-alcoholic—was its mate for finesse. We thought again of our New Year's Eve dinner in Auvergne, in the hands of a well-established cook turning to the contemporary flaw of inventive food of diminished quality. But a restaurant is a business, and giving as many customers as you can what they seem to want is *good* business.

In the morning we walked around the old town. The Church of Saint John the Baptist where Louis XIV was married to Maria Theresa, *infanta* of Spain, on June 9, 1660, is a handsome example of Basque architecture inside, with its rows of carved wooden balconies and a choir with a gold altar and rows of gold saints and angels behind it. The elegant interior of the basilica is a shocking contrast to the exterior built like a fortress, as churches were, in these parts, during warring times. A few steps away on an elegant square is the seventeenth-century manor where the king was the guest of a rich shipbuilder between May 8 and June 15 of his wedding year. At that square, the Place Louis XIV, you're drawn to a confectionary store founded the same year as the Sun King's nuptials. La Maison Adam indeed dates to 1660, and its owners claim that the king and his bride ate the *macarons* of the house at that time. We ate some. They were delicious: wafers made of ground almonds from Valencia and Marcona in Spain, reputably the best almonds in the world, along with egg white, sugar, and salt, and that's it. Tender but chewy. Very different from those things that have become a fad among sweet-tooths in Paris and elsewhere: soft pastries filled with dyed goo.

The Adam chocolates were quite good too. But top-quality chocolates, which contain nothing but sugar and cacao, are fundamentally similar to each other in quality, since only a rare, few chocolatiers roast their beans and mill their chocolate from scratch. The French house of Valrhona supplies a great amount of the milled base for the world's luxurious chocolates, including Adam's. The chocolatiers personalize the final bonbons. The only person I know who makes his own chocolate entirely from scratch is Claudio Corallo, whom I met on the equatorial island of Principe, off Africa. He grows his own beans, from a rare Forestero variety of cacao that was planted on the island in 1822 by the Portuguese. That was before Forestero lost its high quality through pushed yield and became the international staple ingredient of chocolate. Corallo's beans, like no others, can be eaten raw—they're not bitter. His finished chocolate has a unique, earthy quality. I can't say it is far better tasting than Valrhona's but it is unique.

We came to La Halle, the food and fish market of Saint-Jean-de-Luz. The port has long been noted for the bringing in of sardines and tuna, but there was a vast array of many kinds of brilliant-eyed fish for sale. Beside it was La Buvette de la Halle, with a menu of fresh fish and numerous dishes written in Basque and French.

I was very tempted to stay for lunch. I've always been attracted by restaurants that are part of markets, drawing on the array of fresh things around them. I remembered our lunches at a market restaurant with Pennyslvania Dutch delights a long time ago in Philadelphia, and at the big market below the Liberty Bridge in Budapest. It was where the market workers ate well and cheaply: chicken soup, smoked goose, and an Eastern European noodle and cheese pudding for dessert that only my mother and my sister, her disciple at it, could do better.

Should we stay? Joanne reminded me that we had a reservation for lunch a few kilometers away, in-country, at Arcangues, and that the Auberge d'Achtal there was not a place we'd want to miss.

I hung fire. A meal in that market restaurant seemed precisely the kind of close-to-the-source thing I wanted for this book. I decided

I would make the trip back here from Paris, even just for lunch, and so we headed for Arcangues.

As usual, Joanne had the right idea.

L'Auberge d'Achtal

A sign bearing two escutcheons hangs among the vines on a wall marking the presence of the Auberge d'Achtal in Arcangues. One, the current owner, Jean François Bonefons, told me, is the coat of arms of the province of Labourd, one of seven Basque provinces of which three are in France and four in Spain. The second is the shield of the Arcangues family, whose castle is a few minutes away on foot, and at the same time the escutcheon of the village. Until 2003, when the Bonefons family, which opened the *auberge* in 1927, bought the property, the Marquis d'Arcangues had been the landlord of the place.

Serious and discerning eaters, but not tourists, come here from Spain and even farther away, just to spend an afternoon at the plain wooden tables inside or on the leafy terrace. The sound in the dining room served by one husky waitress is the sound I often find in a restaurant with good food in France. It starts out a bit loud and turns into a mellow purr, a paradigm of contentment. I compare it to the shrill cacophony of a room full of anxious expense accounters trying to snow each other at a restaurant of the moment in New York or London.

It was Guy d'Arcangues who first suggested that I make a detour to eat here, when I was on a reportage in the region. The marquis didn't need to do publicity about the place, which, quaintly perhaps, his family owned and leased to have a great place nearby to eat. Their nearly nine hundred years of nobility didn't separate them from the unpretentious, authentic food of the region. The contrary. I knew the Marquis Guy in Paris, because his wife and Claude de Leusse, a fashion reporter in my Fairchild office, had been in-house models for Coco Chanel at the same time. He was an accomplished novelist, son of a poet, and mayor of the town that bore his name. In Paris, he was what they called a *noctambule*, part of the night into morning community of wits and talents at the bar Chez Castel. In Arcangues, Guy was a very devoted mayor, as his forefathers had been. The town, while it keeps its Basque look, is more manicured than others in the region; the marquis had built a golf course that helped draw a spiffy population of secondary home owners, not insensitive, either, to being near a château that is a nineteenth-century luxurious successor to a twelfth-century castle. The Auberge remains the only restaurant in town, and the spiffy mingle with the other townies to eat food that has changed almost not at all—not since, on Guy's counsel, I'd first tasted the excellent *omelette aux cêpes*, a copious omelet with Portobello mushrooms picked in the mountains, to start out a meal with other local treats.

"We have not only been here for three generations," Bonefons said, "we've had three generations of customers coming here for the same food." Two cooks in their thirties, neither from the Basque Country, who had cooked elsewhere, follow the venerable recipes. They both told me after lunch that they got their satisfaction simply by keeping alive a tradition.

Monsieur Bonefons informed us that the *prix fixe* menu was exactly the same as it was in 1927, except for the price. These days you get the *omelette aux cêpes*, followed by *confit de canard*, with homemade *frites*, a salad, and a homemade *gâteau basque*, for twenty-eight euro.

I ate milk-fed roast baby lamb. It wasn't the season for baby lamb in France, but the Spaniards had baby lamb, and Monsieur Bonefons crosses the border to keep it on his menu. A whole shoulder of spring lamb, with its delicate flavor, fit into my plate. Joanne had a *confit de canard,* having begun with a savory vegetable soup while I had enjoyed a *pâté de grives* as a starter.

For dessert, I had the one thing the house didn't prepare itself: a *caillé de brébis*, sheep's milk not yet cheese, sweetened with honey. Joanne had the homemade vanilla ice cream speckled with vanilla bean.

We had seen an *omelette norvégienne* on the menu, and I saw it coming out, an impressive dish with billowing, gold-tipped meringue. What was an *omelette norvégienne*, known in English as baked Alaska, doing on the menu of a country inn in the Basque Country? It had gained fame as an impressive dessert of ice cream, pastry, and meringue at the fancy Delmonico's of New York in the nineteenth century. The name was a tribute to the American purchase of Alaska from the Russian Empire.

It had been a French dish before then, and, Monsieur Bonefons made clear: "It's been a dessert here since the beginning." Bonefons seemed a tad defensive, fearing, perhaps, having been taken for a yokel. "Lots of places in the region did it then," he said. As we saw it go by to another table, Joanne regretted a little the ice cream that was her dessert and I my near-cheese. You never see this dessert on menus these days. The last time we had it was when the island of Ibiza was a refuge for creative people instead of a crowded haunt of clubbers. An excellent, distinguished little restaurant near the water in Santa Eulalia called Sa Punta regularly served baked Alaska with a Spanish name that I forget. Basque or French, what went by us with the conspicuousness of a banner was a proud exemplar of the Bonefons tradition of great food at Arcangues.

We made up for our regrets by getting the family recipe for an *omelette norvégienne*, as he described it:

Omelette Norvégienne at l'Auberge d'Achtal

Prepare an ovenproof platter with four ladyfingers soaked in Grand Marnier.

Cover them with strawberry jam.

Add four scoops of ice cream, two of vanilla, two of strawberry, and sprinkle this with fresh strawberries.

Beat stiffly eight, yes, eight, egg whites, sugaring them before they're totally stiff.

Cover the ice cream preparation with the egg whites in the form of an igloo.

Add a few more strawberries to the top.

Bake it rapidly in a 500 degree Fahrenheit oven until the egg whites turn golden on top.

Remove the dish. Heat 5 oz. of Grand Marnier, and when it starts on fire pour it over the omelet.

Eat immediately.

This is for one person, Monsieur Bonefons says. But have at least two spoon bearers ready or maybe four. Everywhere in the *auberge,* the idea of portions is beyond generous, but nobody seemed to have been getting fat among the contented diners. . . .

Jean Laborde, the owner of the Buvette de la Halle in Saint-Jean-de-Luz, informed me, when, back in Paris, I phoned, that the place was closed as a restaurant until the summer crowd came, as of July. The *buvette* would then spread itself with tables on the wide sidewalk outside the Halle. The tempting menu I saw sitting permanently on an outside wall of the market was the summer menu. The rest of the year, the *buvette,* as its name means, is a snack bar for the market workers, who have their breakfast glasses of wine with things on sale in the market, sausages and such. Jean, who is there at five thirty in the morning to pour the *coups* of red or white, said he sometimes fries them an egg if they bring him one.

We got to talking. He was the third-generation Laborde renting the concession from the town, since 1937. I told him that I had come to Saint-Jean especially to eat a *ttorro,* such as I'd delighted in and written about in 1994, and had been disappointed.

He commiserated, adding that the *buvette* didn't ever serve a *ttoro*, because it was unsuited to a restaurant—a dish to be made in quantities for just a family and prepared fresh.

I heard someone talking in the background.

"My mother says she'll make you a *ttorro* when you're next in Saint–Jean."

"Thank her," I said, and then, with the reflex of a reporter for whom chutzpah is a necessary fault, I asked, "Does she really mean that?"

"She wouldn't say it if she weren't delighted to do so."

"How about next Saturday?" I asked. . . .

The TGV train from the Gare de Montparnasse took me from 7:10 A.M. to Saint–Jean–de–Luz before one o'clock, but not in time to get to the Adam pastry and chocolate shop before it closed for lunch. I had said that I'd bring dessert, an Adam *gâteau basque*. I was chagrined, but as it turned out I don't think we had room for dessert.

A group of Jean's friends were filling the little barroom when I arrived and Jean and his chef, Philippe Labarthe, were pouring Jurançon dry white wine from not far away and setting out a platter of smoked eel. Philippe Labarthe, who is the *buvette* cook in high season, brought the eel from his stand in the market not far away, where he also practices the craft of a *saurisseur*. A *saurisseur*, yet another specialist in the annals of French food, preserves fish by smoking and salting. If you thought that his virtues had been outmoded by the invention of refrigeration, you'd think again if you tasted Labarthe's smoked eel.

The eels are local, except when they're too thin, in which case Philippe brings in wild eels from Denmark. "I do them very, very slowly, unlike the industrial smokers," he told me. "They cook and are smoked at the same time on a beechwood fire, for hours."

The result is a mild, buttery delight. At his *saurisserie* he also smokes haddock, cod and cod's eggs.

Jean brought out a platter of ham and poured more Jurançon sec. "Basque ham," he informed me, "The race is called Kintoa. In 1981 there were only twenty-odd Kintoa hogs still alive. They were far less profitable to raise than other hogs, but incomparable. A handful of farmers in the Aldudes Valley decided to save the race from extinction. There are now eighty farmers producing Kintoa ham. Bayonne ham, in comparison, is banal, and it's produced across a whole swath of the Southwest."

Jean's ham had a smooth flavor that resembled the Spanish Jabuco *belota*, with a definite nuttiness. Jean couldn't tell me what the Kintoa ate. *Belota* ham, as I've noted, comes from little black pigs who live half wild and feed on acorns. Later the Internet confirmed my taste-buds. The Kintoa, while bigger, white-and black-faced animals, are fed corn and barley until they mature and then are let out to roam feeding off acorns and chestnuts.

"People see all our plastic chairs and tables on the sidewalk and think that this is some kind of ordinary place," Jean said, "but we concentrate on what things should precisely be."

We went over his summer menu.

"For the grilled tuna with *pipérade*, we use only rod-and-line caught red tuna, from fishermen who make short trips in and out of the port of Saint–Jean–de–Luz," he said. The industrial fishermen, he pointed out, who have threatened the survival of red tuna by over-fishing, bring in fish who injure each other fighting in the nets and die of suffocation, all of which degrades the flesh.

For his *pipérade,* made of fresh tomatoes, the pepper presence is a bit of *piment d'Espelette* and a quantity, equal to about a fifth of the recipe, of another pimento, the mellow *piment d'Anglade*, from another Basque village.

"Julia Child used green pepper," I said.

"The cookbooks are full of *pipérade* recipes using green pepper," he said. " Ridiculous."

Piment d'Anglade, piment d'Espelette, Piquillon, and Guernica pimento from Spain, which Philippe and Jean's mother, Marguérite, uses to stuff with a *brandade* of salted cod—I'd begun to learn just how much the Basques could be the nuance-devoted aficionados of pimento.

Jean confessed that the sardines he grills in summer come from the Mediterranean and not from the local fishermen. "It's the season when they go out for tuna here," he explained, "and it's much more profitable than fishing for sardines. Sometimes they bring me a few that they catch by chance."

The *gambas* grilled at La Buvette are wild, from Bilbao in Spain not far away, he said, "not the ones you see all over, farmed in dirty pools in Asia and fed the animal flours that caused the mad cow disease and that should have been incinerated."

The *buvette's* limited menu includes *axoa,* a common Basque dish of sautéed minced veal shoulder with *piment d'Espelette.* I'd eaten Sabine Aguirre's *axoa* in the past. At the *buvette,* Jean explained, the veal is milk-fed, the pride of a butcher renowned in the region, Pasquale Massonde, in the village of Souriade. . . .

Marguérite Laborde removed my promised *ttorro* from the stove in the *buvette's* little dining room and kitchen, where fish had just been poached in her sauce.

"Six kinds of fish," Madame Laborde declared, as she ladled out the redolent stew over boiled potatoes, to the dozen of us who stayed for lunch. Madame Laborde knows her fish. Her father was a fisherman when her mother tended the *buvette,* and her six brothers are all fishermen sailing out of the port of Saint–Jean–de–Luz.

Madame Laborde was categorical about her *ttorro.* "The fish go in always at the last minute," she said. "The kinds of fish can vary, since the dish began when the fisherman brought home the ones they'd caught in too small quantities to bring to market." In our bowls were monkfish, hake, conger eel, *roussette,* a pink-fleshed fish (which translates unflatteringly and unjustly as dogfish), *vive,* a fish rare to American markets called weaver, and *grondin*, or gurnet, a fish in the mullet family. Langoustines were added to the fish.

The sauce was thick, redolent, and spicy.

"A *ttorro* is a stew," Madame Laborde made clear, "and not a soup like they serve in restaurants. It is meant to be eaten at home, done fresh. The fishermen feed it to their families."

I asked for the recipe. She refused politely, but categorically.

"I intend to pass it on this winter to my son and daughter," she said.

"You'll have to be adopted to be included," Jean quipped.

I think I doped it out: a traditional broth made of fish bones and some flesh, later discarded, with onion, white wine, and probably two kinds of pimento, *Espelette* and *d'Anglade*, the former sharper and more earthy, the latter mellow while very present. Reduce the broth, poach the fish. . . .

We had a salad whose vinaigrette, Jean pointed out, called for three kinds of oil: a strong, *sabor intenso,* from his small olive oil producer in Spain: sunflower oil to reduce the intensity of the olive oil: and some filbert oil to add a touch of nuttiness, which Jean gets from a neighbor who lives outside town, where he grows his own filberts and makes his own oil.

Mamia was on his summer menu for finishing a meal. It was the Basque word for a *caillé de brebis,* the sheeps' milk curds, such as I'd enjoyed in Arcangues.

"Our *mamia*," Jean explained, "comes only from the race of sheep native to the Basque Country, *maneche tête rousse* and *tête noir.* They are free-range and eat only hay, not pellets or silage in winter. After August, the *maneche* sheep no longer give milk for three or four months. So we only have *mamia* in season. You may see it in stores all year round, from any kind of sheep cooped up and fed all kinds of industrial food, while they happen to give thirty to forty percent more milk than the *maneches.*"

We ate some *maneche* hard cheese that had aged several months. The Adam *gâteau basque* that I'd promised for this copious lunch would have been indeed redundant.

Jean summed up the *buvette* and its three generations as he walked with me to catch my train. "Open since 1937, no progress, no amelioration," he joked. I said that I hadn't sensed a need for amelioration.

He broke from French into excellent English. He revealed to me that he'd taken a doctorate in economics at Washington University in Saint Louis and his wife, incidentally, was a psychoanalyst. He'd had five academic job offers, he said, when he'd finished his studies, but back home it was time for his mother to pass on the *buvette* to the next generation.

"I've been attached to this place forty-seven years," he said, "since I was a year old. I earn my living well. I see all my friends at the *buvette* all winter, and I'm home at two in the afternoon. I spend a lot of time with my children. I have a great life."

13

THE SOUTHWEST TRINITY

Knowing Beans

Occitania, once the Roman Acquitania, is a name sometimes given to a brace of provinces covering roughly the southern half of France. Before you get to the mountains of the Basque Country to the west and to the Pyrenées Orientales eastward, it covers a lot of fertile plain, where agriculture has been the pattern of life since far back in the history of civilization. Nowadays farming has gone very much the way of industry here, as it has elsewhere in the world. You can drive for a long time through vast cornfields where sprinklers play continually, threatening, as the ecologists point out, the survival of the water tables. Corn on the cob has relatively recently begun to be appreciated as food for humans in France, but using a breed of maize for animal food is a long-established custom. It is essential to the French practice of force-feeding geese and ducks to produce *foie gras*, a common, rich presence in the stick-to-the ribs regional cuisine of the Southwest.

The farming has become more mechanized, but the style of food in this farmland has lived on: a diet that would fuel a hardworking peasant's day. Sausages, ham, and *confit de canard* are common fare. And with these, there is the prevalent presence of beans. Easily preserved, beans were a staple when highly calorific food was a positive thing rather than the opposite that it is today. They prevail in the local diet, not out of nostalgia, but because the sturdy forefathers also rendered them delicious, and no more so than in the dish called *cassoulet*, which was invented in the region.

In this part of the world, traditions indeed prevail in fugue with the advances of technology. Many people can still speak *la langue d'oc*, the dialect of Occitania, and the local cuisine is treated with endearment. They drink astringent wines for the digestion while they eat the rose-skinned garlic of Lautrec, with its great reputation among gourmets.

And they reverently cook *cassoulet*.

Given the French reputation for refined cuisine, it may be hard to believe that, in the annals of French soul food, they deify the bean. But there they are: beans taken to a claim of the sublime in *cassoulet*.

"The god of Occitanian cooking," is what Prosper Montagné, that legendary gourmet, dubbed *cassoulet*. "A god with three heads," he wrote. "Castelnaudary is the father, Carcassonne the son, and Toulouse the holy spirit." For today's devotees of this stew of beans and meat, Montagné's words are scripture. However, which meat, and equally important, which particular beans, are issues that continue to divide the faithful.

Driven by appetite and curiosity about their exalted passion, Joanne and I set forth to commune with the Trinity.

Carcassonne, Castelnaudary, and Toulouse are towns that lie on a straight line of about sixty miles long, in a sunny region in turmoil eight centuries ago during the repression of the Cathar heresy. In the fourteenth century, Castelnaudary was besieged again by the British during the Hundred Years' War. Legend has it that the Castelnaudarians, unable to leave their fortress for fresh food, blended all they had to eat and gave the world *cassoulet*. The fortress was nonetheless destroyed, the town sacked, and the people massacred. Not, it seems, before they were somehow able to perpetuate a recipe: local beans, potted duck, pork rind, potted pork loin, local sausage, garlic, and herbs, all cooked in a pyramid-shaped clay dish called a *cassole*.

Castelnaudary, once a market town for the grain on the nearby Lauragais plains, is a tad shabby now. The Church of Saint Michel's polychrome marble baroque altar and its Gothic and Renaissance north face are, we learned, pretty much the major aesthetic attractions of Castelnaudary. We headed to a sleepy hamlet, just three miles away. Alongside a rivulet lined with tall maples, we came to the largely thirteenth-century Abbaye de Saint-Papoul. It's a landmark of Gothic and Romanesque architecture with some rare capitals on the pillars inside that go back beyond the Romanesque. Pepin le Bref, a great ruler in French history, founded Saint-Papoul in 768. The quiet, resonant beauty of Saint-Papoul almost made us forget that we were hungry. We went back to Castelnaudary.

Castelnaudary boasts of being not only the founder but also the capital city of *cassoulet*. It is a claim that Jean Ramond, grand chancellor of the Universal Academy of Cassoulet, told me was tied to the dominant and, for him, baleful presence of the canners. Each day, they turn out ten to twenty tons of a tinned product they call *cassoulet*, prepared with additives, frozen duck legs, and cooked in vats that have no resemblance to the *cassoles,* the *sine qua non* recipient of orthodox *cassoulet* preparation. Why the *cassole*? Ramond pointed out that the inverted pyramid shape of the *cassole* promotes the slow percolation of the *cassoulet* sauce, and there are also devotees who claim that the earthenware pots bestow a flavor.

The academicians are restaurant owners, gourmets, regional wine-makers, cold cuts and preserved duck artisans, who have proselytized true *cassoulets* to aficionados and restaurateurs as far away as Japan. They form, in all, a select group of eighty, as estranged from the Grande Confrérie du Cassoulet, the brotherhood of *cassoulet* canners of Castelnaudary, as the Cathare Perfecti were from the pope of Rome.

The can opener is commonly believed to be the secret weapon of the innumerable restaurants of Castelnaudary that feature *cassoulet*. However, with Ramond as our source, we met a bona fide academician in town with a tiny, modest restaurant called Au Petit Gazouillis. "Gazouillis" means bird chirpings. What the noise of birds might have to do with a restaurant specializing in bean stew was a question to which Alain van Eesbeck did not venture an answer. Twenty years ago, having worked in restaurants in several parts of France, van Eesbeck, a Parisian with distant Dutch descendants, bought the place from a man who'd been cooking *cassoulet* there for at least as long. He never asked why the chirping, but he carefully preserved the traditional Castelnaudary recipe: beans, pork rind, potted pork, potted duck, the shank of a local ham, sausage from a local butcher, thyme, laurel leaf, and lots of garlic. The beans are soaked and boiled first, then put in with the rest in a *cassole* to cook slowly for at least two hours and cooked again when ordered.

I asked the crucial question: Which kind of beans? Ramond had educated me on this point. The canners had made a try at adding value to their reputation by planting beans and applying for their "*appellation contrôlée,*" the label the government gives to a local product of distinction. They tore up wheat fields in the Lauragais plain for their beans, but the government never gave the prestigious label, and the canners have gone on to use cheaper Argentine beans as well. "I've been told that the Lauragais beans are inferior to the Mazères beans south of here," I said to Van Eesbeck. (In Carcassonne I'd get the reasoning about this.) He shrugged. "These are Lauragais beans," he said, "I like them because they are less floury than the Mazères."

Joanne and I could not nitpick about the beans that came in our *cassole*. The *cassoulet* was rich in blended flavor, and nicely garlicky. I asked about the scant crust. In my copy of *Larousse Gastronomique*, it's said that the crust of a cooking *cassoulet* has to be pierced seven times before it is ready to eat.

"Folklore." Van Eesbeck shrugged again.

The Petit Gazouillis' *cassoulet* came, astonishingly, on a seventeen-euro menu with a starter and dessert. "I keep the price down," Van Eesbeck explained, by potting the duck and the pork myself." With a Corbières red Languedoc wine, astringent yet mellow, at eleven euro, the *cassoulet* went down well enough for me to order a dessert that I hadn't seen on a menu in decades: a *dame blanche*—ice cream, chocolate sauce, and whipped cream.

The walled old town of Carcassonne, classed as a world treasure by UNESCO, is as impressively medieval-looking as you might imagine, even though it's what Eugène Viollet-le-Duc imagined it should be, when he restored the ruins into which it had fallen by the mid-nineteenth century. This is the man who created what we see as the Cathedral of Notre Dame in Paris, again, out of ruins and his imagination. With exceptions when it came to sculpture, I think that he had a lovely imagination. The stained glass in the Saint Nazaire basilica is, in any case, authentic thirteenth century, and as important as you'll find, even in the Saint Chapelle in Paris. Particularly the Tree of Life window of the Holy Cross Chapel.

Downtown, Carcassonne's neo-classic Musée des Beaux Arts is one of those endearing, provincial French museums where nearly no one goes, filled with hand-me-downs from the Louvre, but also arresting stuff that testifies to the taste of unsung local aesthetes— patrons for whom art was their sublimation of life far from the glamour of Paris. We took in a Courbet landscape, a Chardin still life, an Ingres head and torso, as well as a rare lot of eighteenth-century Moustique faïence. A case housed one of Bonaparte's swords and also the knife that an Islamic fanatic used to assassinate General Kléber, the man Bonaparte left to mind the mess he'd made in Egypt, when he, himself, sneaked away to do a coup d'état in Paris. Since both are characters in *Chant d'Adieu*, a novel of mine published in France, I was moved to see that knife.

We met up with Ramond and André Jauriac, the academy's grand master and ambulant taster, with whom we headed to a genuine medieval castle in the suburbs, where Jean-Claude Rodriguez, the academy's originator, has his restaurant, Château Saint Martin. Rodriguez has worked in kitchens since he was thirteen. When he was offered the post of head chef at the luxurious Hôtel Negresco in Nice, Rodriguez, distantly Spanish, headed home to the region where he grew up. On a plane coming back from visiting a former fellow apprentice in Japan, he had this epiphany: He must preserve the culture into which he was born by defending the authenticity of *cassoulet* against the onslaught of the canners. He drew up a declaration that became the bylaws of the Academie Universelle du Cassoulet.

It was too late for partridge, the ingredient that, in season, distinguishes a Carcassonne *cassoulet* from all others. Rodriguez nonetheless produced an estimable stew of beans, pork rind, fresh pork loin, pig's cheek, pig's knuckle, sausage, garlic, thyme, bay leaf, parsley, onion, and garlic, with a presence of cloves. The cloves were a tribute to his mother's cooking—a spice that didn't come from her garden, but which Rodriguez maintained has its presence in the local culture, because the region was on the ancient spice route from the East. Did he break the crust seven times? Rodriguez concurred that that was folklore, even though breaking the crust allowed for bullion to rise and keep the beans at the top of the *cassole* from drying out.

As we finished the Mineverois regional wine, Ramond and Jauriac joined the voluble Rodriguez in a vigorous defense of the Mazères beans in his stew. Ramond is a twinkly-eyed, avuncular, retired arms merchant, whose career reached a high point when he supplied Saddam Hussein in his war against Iran. He has since followed a piece of Voltaire's advice and devoted himself to his garden. And to the cause of *cassoulet*. Jauriac is a sturdy man who was in the construction business in Paris. Beans, they pointed out, "feel at ease," as Rodriguez put it, in the light and gravelly soil of the plain at Mazères, south of Carcassonne. The Lauragais beans, they said, grew in clayish soil and were less delicate, thicker skinned.

Ramond allowed that the *lingots de Pamiers*, beans from near a town not far away, were also acceptable. I wrote down Pamiers, adding it to what would become a sizeable list of bean pedigrees.

Toulouse is worth the voyage, as Michelin says, *cassoulet* aside. The eighteenth-century Capitole is doubtless the most elegant town hall in the world. The rose brick churches, some of which Viollet-le-Duc shored up, are remarkable in their forms—structures lyric and audacious. In particular, the Saint Sernin basilica, one of the largest and loveliest Romanesque churches in the South of France. Les Jacobins, built after the heretics were put down militarily, has the air of a graceful fortress. It houses the gilded tomb of Saint Thomas Aquinas, while in the former Gothic convent that is now the Musée des Augustins, there is an exceptional collection of Gothic and Romanesque sculpture. The best Renaissance town house in Toulouse is the seat of the Foundation Bemberg—three floors of a collection put together by George Bemberg, heir to a German and Argentine fortune, novelist, playwright, and book connoisseur, who lived late into his nineties in Paris and New York. His Veronese paintings seemed curiously atypical, but who could quibble with Bemberg's rich eclecticism? Eighteenth-century furniture signed by the masters Jacob and Riesener, Canalettos, Guardis, Lucas Cranachs,

Matisses; Picasso, Degas, Modigliani, and Toulouse-Lautrec drawings. His roomful of thirty Bonnard paintings is the largest Bonnard
collection I know of other than the forty paintings, drawings, and
notebooks in the new Bonnard museum in Le Cannet.

From this food for the soul, we went on again to more soul food.
We chose to experience a Toulouse *cassoulet* chez Emile, in the Place
Saint Georges, where, in medieval times, people were publicly
drawn and quartered. The restaurant is regionally renowned for its
cassoulet.

Rodriguez had told us that mutton was the special characteristic
of *cassoulet* in Toulouse. The vineyards near Carcassonne harbored
partridge; sheep grazed on the pastures near Toulouse. Christophe
Fazan's *cassoulet*, however, was muttonless. What, principally, was
different about it from what we'd known was the crisply fried potted
duck that he put on top at the last minute. It was a nice touch. Over
another appropriately regional Languedoc wine, a La Clape, I cleared
my throat and asked about the beans. "From l'Ariège," Fazan replied.
The Occidental department of l'Ariège includes both the Lauragais
region and Mazères. Where in the Ariège? "It's all the same," Fazan
declared. "The only truly superior bean is the *tarbais*." He struck
a chord. I'd eaten *tarbais* beans from an area in Occitania, close to
Spain, prepared in Paris by Alain Dutournier, who'd been serving *cassoulet* at Le Trou Gascon—a name attached to his homeland, Gascony,
near Bordeaux—as far back as when Orson Welles came to chow
down. Dutournier praised the thin skin and the tender consistency
of the *tarbais* bean. Only the *pochos* that the Spaniards cooked with
clams were, he'd said, more delicate. *Tarbais* beans, he pointed out,
were planted in cornfields, where their vines rose high, wrapping
themselves around the corn stalks. "That made them," he said, "feel
at ease." I remembered that, according to Rodriguez, Mazères beans
felt at ease where they grew, too, but I didn't press the argument.
Fazan was forgoing *tarbais* beans in his *cassoulet* to be faithful to local

products, he explained, but the fact that the reputation of *tarbais* beans had driven a sack of them to the price of about $13 a pound might have influenced him as well.

A list grew in my mind:

I remembered having eaten the delicate *mojettes* that grew in the swampy Poitevin region near Poitiers, but when I'd mentioned them to Rodriguez, he'd scoffed. They were a variety of ordinary *flageolets*, the bean of choice with leg of lamb, but too mushy, he said, to survive in a *cassoulet*. The man who sells us fish in Paris swears by the flavor of the *cocos de Pampol*, from the Breton coast. Near Belgium, the *lingots du nord* have obtained the Label Rouge label of quality, while in Corsica, the Bastia beans that I've eaten in something like a *cassoulet* with *figatellu* sausage, are nationally renowned. In the Sud Ouest restaurant in back of a grocery store near the Arch of Triumph, I've also eaten a formidable *cassoulet* with big *challosses* beans, from the Occitanian Landes region beside the Atlantic. They resemble *soissons*, the lima look-alikes originally from near Compiègne, often used in *cassoulets*.

Finally, let me confess: When I went recently to a Paris store specializing in dried legumes, to get beans for my own *cassoulet*, I bought some big, plump . . . and reasonable . . . ones. Where were they from? "From Poland," the Armenian owner told me, "that's all we get now." They turned out delicious, although the skins were a tad thick.

Let Poland be Poland. And although McDonald's keep sprouting on the landscape, La Douce France hangs on by her teeth as a country of nuance, a key factor, all things said, of civilized intelligence. And, I no doubt, have a long way to go before I truly know beans.

Meanwhile, I have pondered over which of the trinity to favor with a recipe here. I was particularly fond of the *cassoulet* of Claude Rodriguez, with the authenticity that behooves the founder of the *cassoulet* academy. Rodriguez wrote the recipe for ten people. You can cut it down, but as is, it will be great for a party, and it's always better reheated.

Cassoulet at Le Château Saint Martin

To serve ten at a party, or ear still tastier, a second day as well.
Or even a third.

2 ¼ lb. of dried white beans

1 pig's shin

1 pig's knuckle

½ lb. of pork rind from fresh pork

1 ham bone

6 sausages (nonsweet Italian is good)

5 portions of the leg and dark meat of *confit de canard*

½ lb. of pork loin

1 head of garlic, diced

4 big onions, diced

a bouquet garni (parsley, celery, thyme, and bay leaf)

8 cloves

coarse salt

pepper

The night before, prepare a broth with the knuckle, shin,
and ham bone and the bouquet garni. Cook for two amd a half
hours on a slow flame. Degrease, salt lightly.

The night before, as well, soak the beans.

Next morning, dry the knuckle, shin, pork rind, and ham.
Filter the broth. Cut up the other meat.

Squeeze the bouquet garni to get out its juice. Fry the sausages and fry the confit gently. Remove.

Brown in the fat coming off the confit, the loin cut in cubes.
Remove.

Brown lightly the diced onion and the garlic.

In cold water, blanche the beans. Skim, cook for five to ten
minutes.

Moisten the beans with the original broth, add all the meat and the onion and garlic and the juice of the bouquet garni.

In an earthenware pot, put the meat at the bottom along with the sausage lightly cooked in the oven and cut in pieces. Cover with the beans.

Bake in the open pot for about two hours at a low temperature, adding broth from time to time if necessary.

14

ALSACE

Stew of all Stews, Pig-Out of all Pig-Outs

D riving through the pretty province of Alsace, in our age of malls and strips, is a rare pleasure. In winter, the vineyards, with their vines pruned down like distorted crosses, bring a touch of melancholy. But that thought gets erased village after village, with the look of an operetta taken from fairy tales. The village streets of mortar-and-timber houses that sometimes go back to the sixteenth century inevitably have at least one alluring country inn. This endearing countryside is all the same dwarfed by the treasures of high civilization in two major towns of the province: the town of Colmar, with its renowned Grünewald altarpiece, and Strasbourg, one of the most beautiful cities in all Europe, a fact that has not gone unnoticed by tourists.

The 1648 Treaty of Münster, which ended wars within the Holy Roman Empire, gave Alsace to France, but Alsace was a persistent *casus belli* between France and Germany until after World War II.

The population speaks a dialect of German as well as French, while it has always been drawn to the more glamorous association with France. Alsatian cuisine is a cousin of German Küche. The down-on-the-farm influence is strong in both cuisines, but Alsace is more like France in elaboration or refinement. There's nothing in the Alsatian repertoire on the order of lung soup, such as I was once presented in a Munich restaurant. A dish of sausage or a ham hock with sauerkraut is what it is in Germany; an Alsatian *choucroute* at its best is a salute to the wide-ranging artistry of hog butchering, while an Alsatian *coq au vin riesling* can be as fine as a *coq au vin* anywhere in France.

I didn't go back to Colmar. The cooking at La Maison des Têtes d'Or, a historic gem, had become very sophisticated since Joanne and I had enjoyed its *coq au riesling* with *Spätzle*, fresh noodles, a long time ago. Anyway, I knew Colmar well. It's a modest town with a picturesque "little Venice" on the Lauch River, worth the voyage if only for one thing: the sixteenth-century altarpiece attributed to Matthias Grünewald, in the thirteenth-century convent of Isenheim, now a museum. The painter's brilliant vision of mysticism enforced by powerful realism makes the altarpiece one of the most celebrated works of art in the world. The same museum also houses the renowned 1470 altarpiece by Martin Schongauer of the *Virgin among the Roses*. Schongauer was the most admired northern engraver before Dürer, and his paintings are rare.

My mission on this latest trip was to experience Alsace's two most noted specialities: a *Baeckeoffe* and a *choucroute garnie*. A *Baeckeoffe* is, I think, the best stew I've ever eaten. I ate it long ago in the pretty village of Kintzheim, at a restaurant called Auberge St-Martin, owned by a man named Frédéric Toussant. I'd been put on to Toussant by Marc Haeberlin, the chef who has been earning three stars from Michelin for decades at his family's L'Auberge de l'Ill at Illhaeusern. Joanne likes to refer to that inn as the restaurant with the most detailed attention to quality that she's known. And I can't remember any other place that would contradict her.

Since my *Baeckeoffe* epiphany, at the Auberge St-Martin, Toussant had made his place world-known, having anointed himself the Emperor of the *Flammenküche*. The *Flammenküche* is to Alsace what pizza is to Naples. It is a thin crust garnished with cream, Gruyère cheese, and bits of bacon, and baked, preferably in a wood-burning oven. Toussant was featuring his *Flammenküche* or *tarte flambée* when Joanne and I ate his *Baeckeoffe*. Until he retired a few years ago, after twenty-five years, he was sending his frozen tarts around the globe. Would his *Baeckeoffe*, this country dish originally baked overnight in the oven of a *boulanger*, still be what it was when he gave us the recipe, which we still have? I could go back and see, but I had also heard much about the *Baeckeoffe* at the big historic Kammerzell restaurant in Strasbourg and also about the *choucroute garnie* at a little Strasbourg *Winstube* called Le Saint Sepulcre. Along with the exemplary dishes, here was the opportunity to get a feel for a local tradition of conviviality—the two ways that Alsatian city people liked to dine out. The ancient Kammerzell has four hundred tables on four floors and, as I learned, if I didn't reserve long in advance, I couldn't book a table for a Sunday evening. The place, the night that I managed a table, was animated by groups of people, taking obvious pleasure not in doing a deconstruction of the chef's imagination but chowing down and being very vocal in their enjoyment of being together.

A *Winstube* could translate as "wine bar" but it doesn't connote the fashionableness that the term brings to mind in English. A *Stube* has an intimate, informal environment, and the term associates itself with good food, good wine, at a good price. Waiters in black suits and ties serve with grace at the Kammerzell. At the little *Winstube* Saint Sepulcre, with its checkered tables, the waiters are informal youngsters directed by the thirty-three-year-old Julien Ott, nephew of the owner.

I think that there is something in the Alsatian personality exemplified by these two distinct kinds of venues. The Alsatians are conservative; the region was a staunch supporter of Charles de Gaulle. They're appreciative of formality, but also very down-to-earth and of relaxed gregariousness. Their recent ancestors lived simply off the land, in a region very fertile for farming. The Kammerzell has the expansive mood of a German beer hall, but the waiters in black suits, the lower volume of discourse, and the aesthetic presentation of the fare create a difference. The *Winstube* has the other northern characteristic of coziness, with perhaps the subtext of a shelter. When the Mediterraneans are already sunning themselves at their sidewalk cafés, the Strasbourger is often still snug in his *Stube*. The word for the corresponding intimate, congenial mood in German is *gemütlich*. The Dutch say *gezellig*.

Alsace developed in the nineteenth century as a center of brewing, of the now nearly extinct textile industry, and of potash mining: all of which made the place particularly prosperous. Recently, there is talk of even reopening the region's petroleum wells. The native population is still generally better heeled than elsewhere in France, very bourgeois but without denying peasant attachments. All of this may explain the opulent portions of the dishes served in Alsatian restaurants—a trait not distant from Germany either.

It was serendipitous that the places recommended to me for experiencing two deeply traditional Alsatian dishes were both in Strasbourg. The idea of spending a couple of days taking in the splendor of Strasbourg was greatly appealing.

If pink sandstone could turn into lace and reach toward the sky, it would be what happened when a Romanesque church, begun in 1015, became the intricately elegant, soaring Cathedral of Strasbourg as of 1284, in the hands of the master architect Erwin de Steinbach. Goethe, who studied in Strasbourg when he was twenty-one, and climbed the 328 steps of the steeple, called this masterpiece of High

Gothic the "sublimely towering, wide-spreading tree of God." Time has smudged the pink stone, but the sculpture on the portals is of a quality to compare with any in the world. The early-twentieth-century copies among the rest are exceptionally close to the originals that are to be seen in the Musée de l'Oeuvre Notre-Dame, next door. The stained-glass windows that go back to 1250 were being restored when I was there this time. Scenes from the New Testament adorning a wing of the nave had been wiped with fine brushes, delicately vacuumed and sprayed with demineralized water and sodium sulphate. The cultural authorities had pondered long over preserving the glass before coming up with this recipe. Most of the windows had yet to undergo this patient restoration. A fire in 1298 gave the *vitraux* their first experience with pollution, added to over the centuries. In the sixteenth century, there was already an effort at cleaning up the glass, while in the nineteenth century the work was done cavalierly by our standards with little bits of glass being replaced in a few places. Even in their current condition, the windows are extraordinary.

If you want to see stained glass close to your face, a rare possibility, a museum on the Cathedral Square has a room full of brilliant examples taken from nearby churches. These are only a glimpse of the extraordinary treasure in the Musée de l'Oeuvre Notre-Dame, which contains, I believe, the finest medieval and Renaissance sculpture outside of Italy—along with ivory, gold, and silver works going back to the eleventh century, and fragments of Jewish tombs that date before 1439, when Jews were expulsed from the city.

Next door, in the grand and vast eighteenth-century palace that belonged to the Cardinals of Rohan, there is an impressive floor full of furniture such as Louis XIV used on an official visit, as did Marie Antoinette, sojourning on her way from Austria to her ill-fated marriage with Louis XVI. Upstairs there is a small but exemplary collection of Northern, Spanish, French, and Italian painting—with works by Raphael, El Greco, Tintoretto, Canaletto, Botticelli. . . .

I could go on longer about all there is to delight the eye in Strasbourg. The old town, of which the cathedral is a beacon, is an oasis of charm, an island between branches of the Ill. Anyone who comes to Paris should get on the train that takes you to Strasbourg in a little more than three hours.

My *Baeckeoffe* venue, a few minutes from the cathedral, was served in the most prominent building in Old Alsace, a classified monument, but, as I said, in no way a quiet museum.

Twenty-five years earlier, Guy-Pierre Baumann, the son of Alsatian farmers who enjoyed a successful career owning Paris restaurants for fifty years, bought the place, renovated it, added what had been bedrooms to his dining rooms, revived a local lodestone of conviviality and perpetuated the cooking such as he'd known at home: "linked," as he put it, "to the soil, the climate, and the culture and lightened for our time."

A wealthy cheese merchant built the half-timber Kammerzell with Renaissance wooden sculpture in 1427. It was later owned by jewelers and drapers until it became a restaurant in the ninteenth century. Baumann, who just turned seventy-one, sold the place two years earlier. He had earned his retirement after founding eleven restaurants in Paris, including five *brasseries* that bore his name, and I expected he might be out on some golf course when I arrived for lunch. He was at the edge of the dining room, checking it and his reservations, looking very reserved, almost surprisingly timid, as his eye roamed over every detail. Baumann's deal when he sold was to stay on at the place for a couple of years to help keep things as they were, a charge that he seems to be taking very seriously.

We spoke while I waited for my *Baeckeoffe*.

"My father wanted me to be a doctor, a lawyer, or a priest," Baumann said, "but my mother knew that I was always looking admiringly into her pots since I was eight or nine." After hotel school in Strasbourg, he traveled the customary route from scullion to chef, moving, from the age of fifteen, through such prestigious kitchens as those of Maxim's, the Paris Ritz, Lasserre, and the National Assembly. His attachments to vernacular cooking passed successfully through the changes in French cuisine.

"Twenty years ago," he said, "things were going to people's heads in the kitchen. Now things are returning to the more simple and modest. I'm one of the people who learned to cook from their mothers. They cooked with products that were natural and had their own taste."

The *Baeckeoffe* that came out had its own taste, and a delicious one. Beef, lamb, pork, and a pig's knuckle, each distinctive, united in a thickish sauce, brightened by a wine marinade, but roundly oniony and unctuous from the gelatine in the pig's knuckle.

Baumann had gone off to see to his diners. I went back to the kitchen to see the chef, Hubert Lepine, a native of Tahiti, who had worked in Baumann's restaurants in Paris, and, now forty-four, had been chef at the Kammerzell for twelve years. Lepine explained his *Baeckeoffe*.

"It's neck of lamb, beef chuck, pork loin, and a pig's knuckle, potatoes, and onion," he said, marinated for twenty-four hours in white wine, cooked all night at very low temperature, 85 degrees centigrade [185 Fahrenheit], in an earthenware pot, ideally sealed with flour."

Could I have a detailed recipe?

"You know," Lepine said, "Monsieur Baumann makes an excellent *Baeckeoffe*, which he doesn't do anymore. It's somehow better than I ever can. He doesn't add anything else. He has some kind of secret. His juice is thicker. Maybe it has something to do with the potatoes."

"I do the *Baeckeoffe* that I learned from my mother-in-law," Baumann told me afterward. "*Baeckeoffe* is not a dish of the Upper Rhine, where I'm from. Our typical dish is fried carp. My wife is from the Lower Rhine, where her mother made an excellent *Baeckeoffe*."

I asked him if my American readers could add their tributes to his mother-in-law. The recipe, please?

He was uncomfortable. "I think that a *Baeckeoffe* is hard to achieve for someone who doesn't have the habit," he said. "It's difficult to execute. I don't recommend their trying."

I didn't press him for the secret. Back home, I had a long-yellowed fax from Frédéric Toussant, with the recipe for the *Baeckeoffe* that Joanne and I had eaten at his restaurant in Kintzheim. Lepine's *Baeckeoffe* was delicious. Monsieur Baumann's, even if he didn't add anything, was conceivably even better, but in my memory the Emperor of the *Flammenküche* merited all the same a second crown for his *Baeckeoffe*.

I changed the subject, explaining that I had also come to town to eat a *choucroute* at the *Winstube* Saint Sepulcre, where they boast of a dish with seven kinds of meat.

"We do ten," he told me. "Or eight if you prefer." I looked around where everyone was indeed eating a *choucroute,* but with a fish garnishing.

"I invented fish *choucroute* in 1970," Baumann informed me. "It became very popular. I serve fifteen thousand fish *choucroutes* a month. All in all, I use up fifty tons of *choucroute* in a year."

Fish was not what I was after. But ten kinds of *garnitures*? The full Monty. Philip Danforth Armour, the nineteenth-century Chicago meatpacker known as "the pork baron," once said he used "all the pig but the squeal." In that spirit, a *choucroute* with ten garnishings would well be the acme of what Alsatian butchers or farmers can accomplish with the preserved meat of the hog. I managed a table for dinner that night.

The fish *choucroute* intrigued me, nonetheless. No farmer in Alsace, so far from the sea, would think of it, but Baumann was a man whose horizons went beyond the Upper Rhine. I ordered enough *choucroute aux trois poissons* with dinner to taste it. A garnishing of poached salmon, halibut, and smoked haddock came out over a mound of cooked sauerkraut set in a *beurre blanc*. I ate it and could have eaten it all, were it not for my forthcoming destiny with ten kinds of *charcuterie*. The *beurre blanc* was unctuous and rich; the *choucroute*'s acidity was a nice contrast. The salmon and halibut were mild, setting off the smokiness of the haddock.

I cleared my palate with some 2009 pinot noir rosé by a bottler called Hering in the town of Barr. Earlier I had a small glass of Hering's 2009 Gewürztraminer *vendange tardive*, a white whose grapes are picked late, when they're flecked with "noble rot," making them sweeter, but less so than the Eiswein harvested after the first frost of winter. Alsatians are wont to begin a meal with a glass of sweet wine, which goes well with a bit of *foie gras*, very much a regional speciality. Alsatian wines are of the same varietals as the Rhine whites of Germany, and can be just as good. These two were.

The full Monty arrived. The *choucroute* was delicate. Not greasy, as it can be, when the cook goes heavy on lard cooked with it. The kraut was neither too acid nor bland. I made my way through the *garnitures*. Kassler, i.e., corned pork chop, smoked bacon, corned bacon, a frankfurter, a knackwurst, a slice of garlic salami, some ham hock, black pudding, a liver dumpling, and a Montbéliard smoked sausage. I fared forward. The black pudding disappeared, the knackwurst soon after, the Kassler, luckily, was too dry to eat much of, the bacon . . . I gave up, but not without regret.

Baumann doesn't do his own cuts of meat for the *choucroute*. No restaurant does. They go to their favorite *charcutier* for that. But I wanted to hear about his *choucroute*, of which he prepares those fifty tons a year in a place specially devoted to that, outside town.

When I got back to Paris, I phoned him up. He explained, as I knew, that *choucroute* changed flavor with the seasons. "I never use the *choucroute nouvelle*, harvested at the end of August," he said, "it's too bland." I agreed. *Choucroute nouvelle* in *brasseries* is a promotional thing like Beaujolais nouveau, the abortedly vinified wine that true Beaujolais lovers won't touch.

"You harvest the cabbage up until early winter, shred it, pack it with just salt in what used to be wooden barrels and are now cement containers. It lasts until the next harvest. When you're ready to cook, you wash the *choucroute* in lukewarm water and squeeze it in your hand—not too tightly, so it's not too dry, and the number of times you wash it depends on how far along it has come in acidity, during the year it sits in the vats.

"*Choucroute* is traditionally cooked with lard," he said, "to give it a mellow flavor, but for me that's the past. For the fish *choucroute* we don't use any fat. For a traditional *choucroute*, we use duck fat. It's more delicate, and healthier."

Science, I pointed out, confirms that duck fat is indeed healthier, along with goose fat. It is high in monounsaturated fatty acids, good for HDL, bad for the villainous LDL in the blood.

"You sauté your onions before they turn color in the duck fat," he said, "and add them to the *choucroute*. Allow about three hundred grams of it per person. . . ."

At that point the memory gave out in my digital recorder. I had to call back later. Not to take up too much of Baumann's time, I phoned a woman in his office to get a complete recipe from him when he had a moment to spare. The word came back from Christiane Dollinger: The *choucroute* the Kammerzell people prepare in their place outside town is flavored with a special, natural "infusion." Monsieur Baumann informed her, in any case, that his exact recipe for cooking *choucroute* is "jealously kept."

So be it. Weeks after my visit, Hubert Lepine sent me the exact recipe for the *Baeckeoffe* as served at the Kammerzell. I've compared it below to the one at the Auberge St-Martin, dear to my memory. I thought it would be a fool's errand to press Guy-Pierre Baumann to edit Lepine's recipe with his secret, personal touches. As for knowing what a *choucroute garnie* at the Kammerzell in Strasbourg tastes like, you'll have to make the trip next time you're in France. It would not be a fool's journey.

French homemakers, in any case, don't cook their own *choucroute*. Neither do many restaurants these days. A *choucroute* dinner at home is a convenience dish; you pick it up at a *charcuterie*, the cabbage and the *garnitures* as well. Reheating does no harm. In fact, it is harder to find fresh sauerkraut in France than cooked *choucroute*. If the reverse is true where you are, I've included the quite delicious recipe for *choucroute* of the *Winstube* Saint Sepulcre, near the end of this chapter. The garnishing will depend on what you have at hand.

Before lunching at the Saint Sepulcre, I stopped in at the shop, directly across the street, of Georges Bruck, a family business that has been making *foie gras* since 1852. I hadn't been foolish enough to eat a dish of Baumann's *foie gras* before tackling, for the cause, the solid fare ahead. Baumann's *foie gras* was the duck variety. Alsace was traditionally renowned for goose *foie gras* rather than duck *foie gras*, for which the Southwest otherwise gets the laurels in France. Nowadays, Baumann told me, people even in Alsace preferred the stronger-tasting duck variety, which the lady in the Georges Bruck shop, who sold much more duck than goose, would call "gamier." Geese were more trouble than ducks to raise and force-feed, Baumann added, and the flesh of the fatted goose was tougher than that of duck when preserved in fat, in a *confit,* and less commercial.

I bought some of Georges Bruck's jarred goose *foie gras* to compare, when I got back to Paris, with the duck equivalent from the Southwest a friend had given Joanne and me that was in our refrigerator. We'd open the two versions with friends and take a vote on preferences.

The Saint Sepulcre, with its checkered tables and old-time façade is an anachronism on the rue des Orfèvres, a street named for gold- and silversmiths, an association that suits the current sleek, expensive shops on that little lane. Julien Ott, nephew of the owner, who runs the place, said that no one could tell him exactly how long it had existed. Some customers told him that Mozart had eaten there in 1778, when he played in Strasbourg, on a then recently invented instrument called the pianoforte, on his way back to Salzburg, from performing in Paris. It was likely that Mozart would have taken his meals in Strasbourg at a little *Winstube*. He wrote that his several concerts in the city had earned him no more than three Louis d'or, but he claimed that, before his sparse audiences, he had "gained honor and fame."

Four years ago, Christian Ott, a clothing manufacturer, saved the Saint Sepulcre from being replaced by a jewelry shop, and set up his then twenty-nine-year-old nephew Julien to run it.

I think that a customer who buys a restaurant bestows a far greater accolade than does a critic who praises a chef. You could even call it evidence of an ultimate, privileged attachment to an endearing stop-off in life's journey. In some sense it's a way of stopping time, which is what we do in grander works of historical preservation.

Dominique Le Meur's father with Cartet and Gilbert Meslin, at Les Vapeurs in Trouville, were such customers who became patrons. At L'Ami Louis in Paris, when old Antoine was in financial trouble, the late Thierry de la Brosse stepped forward and bought the place together with Alain Ducasse. I'm reminded of the anecdote that Hugh O'Neill, Lord Rathcaven, whom I knew while writing for *Town & Country*, had passed on to me about Wilton's, a restaurant of which he was fond.

I never lived in London, and went to Wilton's for lunch only once, with the writer Julie Kavanagh, when we were led to an obscure table. I looked around and asked one of those prim, white-aproned ladies who served how old you had to be to get a good table there. Wilton's, founded in 1742 and renowned in particular for seafood, was preserved as in amber, and the faithful customers were like members of a good old club. Hugh's story was one he had learned that had taken place during the Blitz:

A V-2 exploded nearby, causing the dining rooms to shake, and the owner, on the edge of his nerves, said that was it, he was selling. A customer looked up from his dish of gulls' eggs. "Put it on the bill," he said. That didn't happen, but he had, it's said, not spoken in vain. Wilton's, less stuffy, lives on.

Saint Sepulcre, or Heilich Graab in Alsatian dialect, as it also reads on the façade outside, is the term for the tomb of Christ. No one, Julien Ott told me, could say why exactly this estaminet bore that holy name. Reproductions of Christ's tomb were done in church buildings in the Middle Ages. I saw the vestiges of one that had been excavated near the fourteenth-century buildings of the order of the Hospitaliers de Saint Jean de Jérusalem, the religious knights whose history goes back to the Crusades. The polychrome vestiges are now housed in the Musée de l'Oeuvre Notre-Dame. Maybe those relics had to do with the *Winstube*'s name. The going explanation, Ott said, had to do with the coffin-like appearance of the place's long *Stammtisch*, the table where in Alsatian, German, and Austrian restaurants, regulars eat together, as in a club.

The Saint Selpulcre's *Stammtisch* was in any case the round table, so to speak, of the town's worthies, wits, artists, and intellectuals, for generations. Before Christian Ott owned it, Charles Lauck and later his son Robert had become legendary as the figures who fit the role, frequent in French restaurants, of eccentric owners. As the newspaper story from 1972 on the back of the current menu of the place points out, the Laucks would close promptly at one o'clock while they ate their lunch, along with whoever happened to be there before they locked the door. Charles Lauck refused to serve coffee at the *Winstube*, directing those who asked for it to an Italian restaurant. . . .

My *choucroute garnie* came out. I enumerated smoked bacon, cured bacon, knackwurst, Kassler, garlic salami, Montbéliard sausage, and a liver dumpling.

A glasss of dry Kritt Gewürzraminer 2009 from the house of Greffer in Andau helped me to do service to the dish. It was flinty and pleasant. I ate enough to judge it well worth trying to eat more, somehow, but Ott had mentioned another house speciality, rhubarb pie with a meringue topping and homemade whipped cream on the side. A typical Alsatian pie, he said, made with a *pâte brisée*.

I confess: I ate it. I ate it all. Maybe my system had somehow adapted itself, in two days, to the generosity and richness of Alsatian food. But I happened to get my first gout attack in years when I returned to Paris. I have no regrets.

Sébastian Terugret, the day's chef, came out while I was finishing a tender dab of meringue, to ask how things were going. I complimented him. Terugret was normally the second in command in Emile Mayer's kitchen, but the head chef Mayer was off because his wife had given birth. Terugret was pleased to give me the house recipe for *choucroute*. As with duck fat at the Kammerzell, the *choucroute* at the Saint Sepulcre has a personalized ingredient. In reheating, you splash chicken broth over the kraut. So:

Choucroute at the Winstube Saint Sepulcre

For six people

(can be reheated for a second meal, if fewer people)

5 lb. of raw sauerkraut

2 oz. of lard

3 big onions

about 10 juniper berries

¾ of a bottle of white wine, preferably Riesling

1 ½ lb. smoked bacon in one piece

1 ½ lb. cured bacon in one piece

Mince the onions and fry them in the lard before they turn color in the lard.

Put the onions in the bottom of a casserole or preferably an earthenware pot. Salt lightly; add the kraut with the juniper berries mixed in and cover with the wine. Add the meat. Cover with the wine.

Either bake the dish in the earthenware pot for two and a half hours or cook it on the stove for an hour and a half. In the oven, uncover shortly before the dish is finished, to brown some tips of the kraut.

Slice the meat when it is cold. Add to these garnishings whatever cured pork products you like and have at hand.

Before serving: Add chicken broth diluted with a little water to cover the kraut when reheating. Do not add more wine. Briefly heat all your cured pork products in water brought a boil.

Serve with separately boiled potatoes.

Frédéric Toussant's Memorable Baeckeoffe

This is the recipe he wrote by hand and sent me. I have changed the metric equivalents to American measure. The dish was delicious when we ate it at the Auberge St-Martin, with the potatoes well proportioned to the meat in our plates. We took the plunge, though, and cut the prescribed potato content of four kilos for the whole dish to a bit more than four pounds, when we prepared it at home. You need just enough potatoes, sliced to about an eighth of an inch thick, to form alternate layers with the meat, until you run out of meat. Guy-Pierre Baumann's mother-in-law might have quarreled about the veal neck rather than stronger-flavored chuck, but the veal does suit the white wine better than beef does. The veal tail is not what you find at the Kammerzell, and Lepine uses Riesling for the wine, rather than the frutier Sylvaner, and in a smaller amout. All things said, my memory salutes Marc Haeberlin's recommendation, but the versions are not far apart.

Serves six people
    2 and a half bottles of Sylvaner wine
    8¾ lb. of potatoes Bf15 (or Idaho in America)
    1¼ lb. of veal neck
    1¼ lb. of pork shoulder
    1¼ lb. of lamb shoulder
    3 raw pigs' feet
    a veal tail (optional)
    a *mirepoix* (the French culinary term for combined minced vegetables) made up of:
    two carrots
    the white of a leek
    two onions
    a bay leaf, a clove, and a pinch of thyme
    salt and pepper

Mince the vegetables and add the bay leaf, clove, and thyme to them.

Cut the meat into stew-size pieces, and marinade it overnight with the *mirepoix* in the wine.

Salt and pepper to taste.

Next day: Blanch the veal's tail and the pigs' feet, each foot cut in four parts.

Cut the potatoes in slices.

In a long earthenware pot, alternate layers of the meat and the potatoes, putting *mirepoix* on each layer. Put the pigs' feet and the veal neck on top, with the veal tail in the middle.

Pour on enough of the wine marinade to cover the ingredients.

Seal the lid of the pot with a flour paste.

Bake for an hour in a very hot oven, or for two and a quarter hours in a medium oven.

In classic cuisine, a *mirepoix* is lightly sauteed in butter before adding to the rest of the dish. This is not mentioned in the recipe, but it would add a little something else to the flavor. Some Alsatians add a few grains of juniper berries, as in making *choucroute*. If you're tempted by that faintly piney flavor imparted to the stew, go ahead.

Baeckeoffe at the Kammerzell

For six people
  1 lb. 9 oz. pork loin
  1 lb. 9 oz. lamb shoulder
  1 lb. 9 oz. beef chuck
  3 chopped onions
  2 chopped whites of leeks

3 chopped carrots

5 lb. 5 oz. of potatoes

marinade: ⁴/₅ of a .75 liter bottle of Riesling

2 cloves

a bouquet garni

salt and pepper

Cut all the meat in pieces of about 3 oz.

Salt and pepper the meat and the chopped vegetables to taste, and marinate it all with the meat for twelve hours

Wipe the meat dry and place the sliced potatoes at the bottom of the *Baeckeoffe* clay pot, cover that with a layer of the chopped vegetables, then of the meat. Add a layer of potatoes.

Add the marinade to cover the ingredients halfway.

Seal the pot with a flour and water paste.

Cook for three hours at 320 degrees Fahrenheit. (This need not be an overnight cooking.)

When I returned to Paris, Joanne and I opened our two Mason jars of *foie gras*, with their traditional rubber-closed lids, and put pieces without spreading them on lightly toasted slices of Poilâne bread, a customary way of eating *foie gras*. It's usually served either on country bread or *brioche*. Unexplainably, the Georges Bruck brochure that came with the jar said that putting *foie gras* on bread is a no-no: You eat it with a fork and for some reason not with a knife. It was easier for us to serve our friends *foie gras* canapés that you could hold in your hand while drinking champagne, and I can't imagine what a change in flavor a knife might have made, although I'll go along with the principle that serving something very delicate like caviar with a metal utensil slightly harms the taste of caviar—not that I've had that much to do with the matter. My caviar-gorging days go back to when a kilo tin was a hundred dollars cash, acccording to the waiters' discreet, parallel, private room service, at your hotel in Soviet-era Moscow. Such were a journalist's shady perks, in an otherwise dismal place. In our kitchen drawer, Joanne and I do not have regulation mother-of-pearl caviar spoons. As for the two *foies gras:*

We were six. The duck *foie gras* came from a maker near Cahors, Michel Catusse, in Montdoumerc, a town dating to the tenth century, population 386. Both it and the goose version from Strasbourg were *foie gras entier, mi-cuit,* cooked lightly, with no alcohol flavoring added to the natural taste, in Mason jars. *Foie gras entier* is cut from a whole lobe of liver and is neither a paste nor a composition of *foie gras* pieces. Aficionados of the delicacy might have argued that both competitors would have been better if cut from a fresh terrine. I can't attest to that, but it wouldn't have likely changed their relative qualities. Drinking champagne lets the *foie gras'* own flavor prevail, rather than enhancing it with sweet wine. There was no contest. Blindly, everyone chose the goose version. It was nuanced, smoother tasting, with an appealing, lightly nutty aftertaste. The duck was stronger tasting, yes, "gamier." Far less elegant.

Guy-Pierre Baumann, the man who created, successfully, eleven restaurants, learned that people prefer the stronger taste. The goose variety is more expensive, but the French pay well for their gourmandise, given, for example, the amount of very high-priced oysters consumed in France. Goose *foie gras* is definitely subtler than the duck variety, and goose *foie gras* is often hard to find in stores these days. Is it a stretch to deduct that we are living in unsubtle times?

Postscriptum: A considerable quantity of duck and less goose *foie gras* processed in France comes in raw from Hungary and Israel, where it is produced on a more mass scale. It's cheaper, grainier, and, yes, less delicate than the artisanal French thing. The law does not require that the foreign source be disclosed on a label, but French producers using domestic livers often make a point of telling you that.

15

THE FATTED STEER OF BAZAS

Is This the Best Steak I'll Ever Eat?

I know a few friends who do the Michelin pilgrimage. They travel through France, eating at least one meal a day at a three-star restaurant, enriching their lives by knowing the unique achievements of some rightly celebrated chefs. I understand their devotion. My own idea of the most privileged eating is also to experience something extraordinary that you could not have eaten any other place. They stick in your mind, these tiny discoveries about not just a personal achievement but a piece of the world; they're not so momentous as Brillat-Savarin's hype about the astronomical joy to the human race of a newly invented dish, but they stay with you all the same. I remember, for example, a variety of beautifully formed and delicious sea snails that they serve in the sherry producers' booths at the Horse Fair of Jerez, in Andalusia, such as I've never seen or eaten before or since. They were a burst of bright sea flavor mated with the sherry. I remember Maine lobsters that made a rapid trip from flapping around on the deck of a little boat to a few minutes in the pot, and the grassy, delicate, fresh February olive oil pressed from green olives in Lucca, eaten on *farro,* a starter that was a porridge the Roman legions ate. And my hat is off to whoever the G.I. was who endowed the beer garden in the Englische Garten in Munich with the recipe for the best spare ribs I've ever eaten.

These treats have always been the bonuses of my travels, but this time I had coaxed Joanne along on a deliberate trip, 345 miles south of Paris, to eat some meat that we'd heard a lot about. Would this be the best steak we would ever taste? Bazas, France, population five thousand, twenty miles or so south of Bordeaux, claimed to be the home of some of the tastiest beef in the world. To borrow that accolade that Michelin bestows on restaurants to guide the gastronomically inclined, would it be worth *le voyage?* Well, Bazas, I'd read, has been an interesting place for twenty-five centuries, and fatted beef has been an element of pride in its particular culture since, as best records show, 1286.

The appointed time was the weekend of the feast of the *boeuf gras,* the fatted *bazadais* steer, of a breed that exists nearly nowhere else. It begins on the Thursday before Mardi Gras. Once, several French villages would parade fatted cattle on a day before Lent, but that's a custom all but gone, and Bazas's story is far more special. About four million cattle, mostly all cows, are raised for beef in France, of which there are some twenty-six breeds, including a handful of predominant ones, charolais, *blonde d'Aquitaine, limousin, Salers,* and Aubrac in particular, The *bazadais,* an unexpected bounty of the Moors' eighth-century invasion, is a rare breed revived from near extinction by a number of not-very-money-oriented farmers in the 1980's. It now amounts to a herd of just about fifteen hundred in the whole Gironde department, which encompasses the history-rich region of Aquitaine. Some sixty cattlemen in the Gironde raise *le boeuf bazadais,* mainly for veal and the meat of cows, eventually that of *vaches reformées*—a euphemism for old cows whose last stop in the food chain is becoming stews, steaks, and chops. Once a year, however, some 150 specially raised, coddled, and fatted *bazadais* steers come to market as *le boeuf gras*, and sleepy Bazas transforms itself into a state of heightened carnivorousness, ending with a competition for the prize steers and a feast that brings more than a quarter of the number of townspeople together under the same roof. From two weeks before Mardi Gras to the first day of Lent, while the treasure lasts and the only time that it is available, the townspeople descend on the four butchers who sell the *boeuf gras*, for steaks at twenty-odd dollars a pound. None of it gets exported outside Bazas. It's here or nowhere. No one in town would, I believe, swear by any other beef. They live year to year for it.

Before we got into the parading, singing, dancing, and feasting that the *boeuf gras* excites in the people in Bazas, we drove out to see some happily gluttonous steers unaware that their numbers were about to be up. At the wheel was Bernadette Darcos, who works for the association that promotes the raising of the breed, called Excellence Bazadaise.

We drove through the flat landscape of meadows dotted by a few vineyards—the Graves properties of Bordeaux are nearby and some people make humbler table wine near Bazas. Mademoiselle Darcos explained why, by her estimate, ninety-five percent of the beef in France comes from cows, not steers. A cow gives milk and calves for veal and when it's no longer good at that, it's "reformed," as they say, for the table. At the first two of these money-earning stages, the government provides subsidies as well. A steer has only itself to give and it eats its way toward its destiny at an increasingly high cost. A fatted, long-lived *bazadais* steer is even more ridiculously uneconomic, but a tradition is a tradition. Mademoiselle Darcos, a pert woman whom you don't imagine hanging around barnyards, told us that British and Australian cattlemen use the *bazadais* steers to improve the local breeds, by increasing the amount of quality meat on their torsos—without doing the *boeuf gras* routine. She explained the beast's history.

"There are several theories about the origins of *la race bazadaise*, she said. "The most plausible one is that the Moors of the eighth century, coming up from Spain to conquer, brought an Iberian race with them to feed off, and the Iberians were crossed here with a local lean race called Marini."

Until the 1950s the *bazadais* cattle were beasts of burden and earned their keep first of all by pulling plows and wagons in the fields and in the logging camps of the nearby Landes forests. They were fattened and slaughtered at the age of seven or so, when they were no longer good at pulling plows and wagons.

Seven bulging gray steers were munching feed at halters out at the farm of Philippe Bedubourge, who makes his living off the hundred-odd cows he raises for veal. *Le boeuf gras*, for him, he said, was "the cherry on the cake." I asked Philippe what was so great about a mouthful of fattened *bazadais* beef. "It's not fatty, but marbled. It's delightfully tender without being flabby. Its grain is tighter and finer than with the meat of other breeds. And it has an incomparable taste." Like what? "*Noisette*," he said. Filberts. During our four days in Bazas, I would ask several people very familiar with that taste—breeders, butchers, eaters—and filberts was the word. As for my uninitiated self, I would perceive nothing nutty there.

Following the mandatory criteria for doing *boeuf gras*, Bedubourge keeps his steers with their mother cows from the age of two to six months. They are then on free range all year round until the age of three and a half. For six months before slaughtering, they then feed, haltered, on hay, linseed cakes, and corn silage. The rules for a properly fatted steer say that the corn that Philippe feeds his steers at the rate of forty-four pounds a day each, can't account for more than half their diets, otherwise they develop "the bad kind of fat" under their hides.

Industrially raised cattle, kept immobile in feedlots, have a lifespan of not much more than two years. French law, at the same time, prohibits the hormones and antibiotics that cattle get with their feed in the States, to make them mature fast. For Bedubourge there's no comparison between the taste of beef from feedlot cattle and that of a steer that lives mostly free and to a mature age. He conceded that his *boeuf gras* steers would produce even fuller-tasting meat if he let them graze at least a year longer, but the economics of it are against him.

Afterward we drove on to the farm belonging to Nathalie Marlot, president of the Confrérie des Bazadais du Boeuf, a fraternity of *bazadais* beef lovers. Her eighty-year-old partner on the farm, Henri Manseau, brought up old times: "The steers competing for the prize this year," he said, "are worth nothing compared to what they were when they were at least six years old and often seven." By worth he meant flavor. Beef gains much more flavor, he pointed out, as it gets into that age range. I remembered that in Prosper Montagné's *Larousse Gastronomique*, the age of a steer for any suitable beef, and not just *boeuf gras*, is five years.

In Manseau's time, the seven-year-old-or-so steers were fattened on rye and *regains*. *Regains?* It was a word I'd never heard of in my acquaintance with foods and fodders. A *regain,* he explained, is the resprouted hay of a second cutting, when there are more leaves and fewer stems, and when the stems are tenderer than with the first cutting. "The steers loved it. And it made them drink more, so they got still fatter."

Manseau has been raising *bazadais* beef since the fifties, when they were still the local ancestors of tractors, but he raises only *bazadais* cows for veal now. No cherries on the cake. During his lifetime the breed totally lost favor among the farmers, who went on to pursuing crops or to raising other breeds, when the tractors came in and other breeds were more profitable.

"The *bazadais* is not a great milk producer," Mademoiselle Darcos added, "and a lot of farmers chose to rear cows for milk instead. It meant receiving a monthly subsidy check. . . ."

Before the parade of the candidates that would end in the contest for the best fat steers, we acquainted ourselves with the town. The cathedral square edges the ruins of the town's fortifications that go back to a fortress of the Gauls of the seventh century BC, and even further to the Romans' *opidum*. The town was called Cosio by the Romans until the third century AD. Afterward it got it name, a deformation of Vasates, after the community of Gauls so named. Some of their stone caskets are in the UNESCO-registered cathedral, which dates to the mid-fourteenth century. A cathedral in a town this size is a rarity, but Bazas contained a relic that made it an important site for pilgrims. The legend behind the relic, implausible as it seems, recounts that a local woman, already a Christian, was in Judea at the time when John the Baptist was beheaded, and she came back with a vial of his blood. After 1798, a hotheaded revolutionary threw the vial in the latrine of the neighboring bishop's palace. The revolutionaries did perhaps worse, destroying the bishopric, and the Protestants, during the bloody civil war of the sixteenth century, had vandalized the cathedral as well. Those Huguenots, persecuted as they were, did not fail to do evil in return, but a payment of ten thousand ducats to the Protestants who took the town saved the medieval sculpture on the portals of the cathedral from being destroyed, a few centuries before the revolutionaries did their mischief. The main entrance is coiffed by a surviving, extraordinary Judgment Day, where Jesus, his saints in heaven, and devils and poor sinners in hell are depicted with a verve that might even have given the Protestants further pause in their destructive intentions.

Beyond the ruined walls, a steep hill leads to the valley of the Beuve River, just a stream actually, which eventually flows into the Ciron, which brings humidity to the prized vineyards of Sauternes, not far away. The path alongside the river is where generations of children have learned to walk and then ride bikes, while residents of the old folks' home that was once a grain mill take their constitutional strolls.

Past the cathedral square, in the narrow, cobbled streets of Bazas, there are a few handsome houses that go back to the thirteenth century, which have escaped becoming the palimpsests of stucco and stone that most old houses in town now are. During one of their renovations, Mademoiselle Darcos told us, the owner punched open a wall and found a big crock full of thirteenth-century pieces of gold.

Down these streets, the contestants for the best *boeufs gras,* wearing garlands of paper roses around their necks and roses pinned to their tails, were led by their owners, drawn by tractors like Miss Somethings on floats, to the town square. They were accompanied by a fife and drum corps, along with very young children in nineteenth-century costumes, as agile as their elders as they all strode on perilously high stilts. Out of eleven contestants, the judges chose the prize winners in three categories: sheer bulk, the amount of meat they'd yield; quality, the amount of best cuts of meat that they'd yield; and their conformity to the appearance of the breed. The last involved a kind of beauty contest for these gray behemoths with sloe eyes that reminded me of young elephants.

While the judges pondered, other officials who'd been grilling meat on charcoal fires went about with platters loaded with chunks of it for the assembled crowd. The meat was delicious, tender, and rich tasting, but that gesture was nothing compared to the banquet that night.

Some twelve hundred people had come together for the feast of the *boeuf gras.* From back in a big kitchen used for such events, behind a stage, came the smell of broth and later of meat being grilled on charcoal fires outside. We were gathered in a big building at the edge of town, called La Salle Polyvalante, which meant that—whenever a lot of townspeople weren't together in that hall for whatever excuse for each other's company, and the name suggested there were many such—kids played basketball here. Tonight, we were all dining at yards of tables beyond the hoops. And we were fed with admirable efficiency by a small troop of volunteer women, with a meal that ran through *boeuf gras consommé*, *boeuf gras pot au feu*, *entrecôte* or rib steak of *boeuf gras* served with *pommes forestières*—potatoes sautéed with Portobello mushrooms—cheese, salad, and a local puff pastry. The *pièces de résistance* were those thick slices of the *entrecôte,* garnished with just minced fresh shallots. The *entrecôte bordelaise*, a speciality of the region, often grilled over vine branches, traditionally comes with a cooked sauce of shallots, wine, and marrow, but the elders of Bazas who organized the feast did not see fit to change the taste of their unique meat with a sauce. The shallots were enough to sharpen the flavor.

We drank nonfamous but quite drinkable young red from the nearby Graves vineyards. Graves has just a few great reds, as well as the renowned sweet Sauternes of the area, of which a small owner was distributing bottles at various tables. Deputies, worthies of industry, doctors, lawyers, a journalist, and a butcher were ceremoniously inducted into the Confrérie des Bazadais du Boeuf by Madame Marlot and her associates. A man on stage sang brilliantly in lyrics of the *langue d'oc* tongue.

Soon everyone was singing along, waving their napkins over their heads, swaying together holding onto each other. They got up and danced a *pasodoble* to an accordion and a lindy from Bill Haley days to the music of a small band of middle-aged rockers. Young and old, well-off and humble. Twelve hundred souls. That small brigade of women miraculously served us all so briskly that everything was hot in your plate—and they came back with freshly grilled seconds of the steaks before we sealed our stomachs with the Sauternes. That nicely crusted rib steak was incredibly tender and full-mouthed in flavor. Filberts?

Next day, we took Bernadette Darcos to lunch for some more of that meat. We had fillets with a homemade *foie gras* topping, a version of the old-fashioned *tournedos rossini*. A fillet is usually a bland cut of meat, but this one's flavor came through superbly. Our rustic restaurant was part of a farm. It was a member of the *fermes-auberges,* the group of small farmers helped by the government to create restaurants on their properties, with menus composed substantially of products grown on the farm.

So how did the *boeuf gras bazadais* compare with our memories of great steaks past? The comparison is conditioned by the fact that French butchers cut their beef differently than we do in the United States. The rib steak is roughly the same. The t-bone has not existed in France, except in recent rare cases, although it happens to be the cut of the *bistecca Fiorentina* in Italy. In America, our prize steaks are sirloins, and the French do have a similar cut called *l'aloyau.* We decided to bring a hunk of *boeuf gras bazadais* home to Paris, for us both to compare with what we'd known of the hallowed American steak, a sirloin.

Nathalie Marlot cautioned us. "Beware, there is an association of growers that produce what they call Le Boeuf de Bazas, which is only a regional attribution, and it can include meat from the *bazadais, blonde d'Aquitaine,* or *limousin* breeds. Buying a piece of beef in the town of Bazas is no guarantee of getting *le boeuf bazadais,* and *le boeuf gras* is rare to find." "Four butchers," I said.

She raised an eyebrow as if to say it might be rarer than that, and with that she drove us to her own butcher, Michel Laffon.

"Michel will never sell some unenlightened person who asks for Le Boeuf de Bazas an inferior piece of meat," she said. But Michel, although he had a stock of genuine *boeuf bazadais gras*, was out of the cut *aloyau*, French cousin to sirloin.

Que faire? We took our chances at the butcher shop on the cathedral square of René Aureglia. I can't remember who was the chauvinist in town who'd cautioned me that Aureglia was not a native of Bazas and the reliability of the pedigree of his meat was to be considered in that light. But one look at the size of the slabs of meat in his shop told us that they were not from normal-size beasts, and, in conversation, Aureglia showed great knowledge and respect for *la race bazadaise.*

He was a Niçois who had worked all through France before buying this butcher shop in his ex-wife's hometown, five years ago. He'd dealt with the esteemed *charolais* and *limousin* breeds, as well as with the more rustic beef of l'Aubrac. Of the lot, he said, the *limousin* came close but no cigar to the *bazadais*, for full flavor. We took home a kilo of genuine *boeuf gras bazadais*. It had only been aged two weeks he said; a week more would have been better. René was a devotee of aged beef. He had aged a roast beef of *boeuf gras*, he told us, for forty-five days before eating it and it was superb.

In Paris, Joanne and I enjoyed the grilled *aloyau*. Next day, we went to Le Languedoc, one of the last of the neighborhood simple bistros, in town, run by the Dubois family since 1974. No chauvinists, and intent on value for the money, they serve rib steaks that come to the Rungis market, of the Bavarian Simmenthaler breed. Simmenthaler beef is widely praised and rightly so. We compared it with the main dish of our Bazas feast. And next day, we ate steak that was sirloin in a Parisian Argentine restaurant of great repute.

The Bavarian rib steak was less tender than the *boeuf gras côte de boeuf* that we'd eaten at the Bazas feast, the flavor more intense but less subtle. The Argentine beef was faintly acid and it was the same shape but smaller than the American sirloins we'd known. It reminded me a little of the baby beef t-bones that the Florentines fancy. As for the *gras aloyau* that we grilled at home—was it better than, say, Peter Lugar's, which has made Brooklyn a Mecca to carnivores for several generations?

I remember the gargantuan portions in America, but to be totally honest, I don't remember much about the rest of the meat's personality. It was very good, but odds are I'll forget the precise flavor of all these steaks. All things said, in the roll call of things that are important in life, meat is no more than meat. But I tell you what I will remember: Twelve hundred people sharing a time-honored feast together: dignitaries, honchos of various stripes, artisans, and sundry ordinary folk, eating and singing together and, with the excuse of this maybe unreasonable tradition, confirming the bond that made them a community. UNESCO would have, no doubt, been impressed. Two opposing politicians in the harsh political climate of France, the Socialist candidate for parliament and Sarkozy's man, were chowing down together. Snow was falling heavily outside, and far worse was hitting the fan all over the planet. Was it worth the voyage to be there at that repast?

I'd recommend it.

16

LE MASSIF CENTRAL

Hearty Fare in the Heartland

The Massif Central is a big knot of mountains at the navel of France. It is the place the French think of first of all when "La France Profonde"—that expression that evokes collective nostalgia—comes to mind. France, despite its industrial pockets, was a nation overwhelmingly populated by small, independent farmers into the twentieth century, and the Massif Central, and in particular its regions of l'Auvergne and l'Aveyron, were the heart of hearts of that sylvan culture. Given that former makeup of the population, French city people will often tell you about their particular country roots, the way many Americans trace their families back past Ellis Island. Like Rousseau, perhaps, the nostalgia tends to romanticize country life and its virtues. But in the Massif Central, once below the flat land near the city of Clermont Ferrand and past round, former volcanoes, you're among jagged mountains with a few breathtaking, narrow 00000river valleys, where extensive cultivation is not possible, and austerity was the rule. The principle cash product of a farm here is cheese from herds of cows. Nowadays, roads that climb up mountain can reach the *burons,* the little stone huts where the farmers, having driven their cattle up there, would spend months away from their families, milking their cows and making and maturing a volume of big cheeses that would pay for what a few rabbits, a yearly pig for ham and sausage, chickens, and the kitchen garden didn't provide. That way of life still existed half a century ago.

The vernacular architecture, both in l'Auvergne and l'Aveyron, is beautifully chaste: well-proportioned houses of stone with sharply peaked, snow-shedding hip roofs tiled with schist. Even the walls are charily assembled, with more spacing between stones filled with mortar than you see elsewhere in France. Frugality is a leitmotif here. Dutch burghers, who seek second homes in the Massif Central for the exotic experience of high-altitude life, are surprised to learn that the ground floors of those farm dwellings were inhabited by cows, whose presence helped warm the rest of the house during the mountains' harsh winters.

More superbly, medieval castles and tenth-to-twelfth-century churches embellish the landscape wherever you turn. The churches with their Romanesque compact architecture often have striking "comb" belfries, walls of stone with bells interspaced.

The most cherished site of the region is the medieval village of Conques, with its abbey, built on the pilgrim's road to Saint James of Compostelle. It contains some of the best Romanesque architecture in the world.

Antique dealers cherish the rustic furniture that got passed on for generations down here—the bread-making chest, the armoires and long tables sometimes with hollows in them where the woman of the house poured soup, saving her crockery for special meals. When you visit some of the local hotels, decorated in the strangest ideas of elegance and with tiny bedrooms, you see that sophistication is not a tradition passed on, in what has been this hardscrabble place.

Yet, if the farm couldn't create the wealth that an environment of refined decoration implies, it kept people fed. And more than just fed. Frugality meant primitiveness but not destitution. Food was a pleasure at hand and esteemed bounty. From those country products, natural and simple, a tradition of loving cuisine developed, and it still exists. And as if it were the Good Lord's reward to *La France Profonde*'s culture of piety and frugality, that country cuisine is delicious. I have rarely eaten anything luxurious that was more more-ish than a bowl of *soupe à l'ail*, garlic soup, as the family dish is perpetuated at the hotel Le Bel Horizon at Vic-sur-Cère, in the Le Cantal department of Auvergne.

Le Bel Horizon

Le Bel Horizon looks like the kind of hotel I mentioned above. The beauty part in the name comes from the panorama of mountains through the windows of the dining room. I won't suggest you stay there, but nowhere I know serves such delicious, authentic regional food. There are two menus, one that shows the sophistication of Eric Bouyssou, the cook who came home from learning his craft in distinguished places elsewhere to take up his father's role as chef and hotel keeper. The other is the menu of the food that the father, André, took with him from Badaillac, his native village in the mountains, population 120. André's father was born in the nearby hamlet of Loubiac, where he saw his first automobile pass on a gravel road, with wooden wheels.

Vic was a spa town proud of its water as a cure for a variety of diseases until the mid-twentieth century, when water cures went out of favor. For the children of the neighboring farms, working in the Vic hotels, now nearly all closed down, was a chance for a new way of employment, less rigorous and better paying. André Bouyssou, a descendant of generations of farmers, whose aunt ran the little bistro in Badaillac, was one of those children. He was born there seventy-four years before the time that we recently spoke, when his son Eric prepared us a delicious meal.

Before the autoroute came this far into Auvergne, Joanne and I and the kids used to stop at Vic for lunch, and afterward take the winding mountain roads further into Auvergne as part of a day-long trip from Paris. We were back again in Vic, especially for the *terroir* dishes that Eric perpetuates, having begun his career in the kitchen of the Tour d'Argent and cooked in various city establishments in France and in Canada.

"You have to leave to come back to appreciate what you have," he said.

The Auvergnat menu varies with the season, and it runs through a variety of dishes that includes stuffed cabbage, potted sausage with compote of cabbage, stuffed veal from a small organic farmer in the neighboring hamlet of La Prade, and more.

Eric was preparing a big festive meal of his bourgeois cooking, so the soul-food menu was a bit restrained when we came, but the delight of a few simple things were in our memory: first of all the garlic soup, *pounti,* a dish like no other you'd find anywhere, and *truffade,* a superior version of hashed browns.

We drank a bottle of Saint Pourcain 2008, an inexpensive wine from the Alliers part of Auvergne. Auvergne is not an important wine region. Saint Pourcain has had the right to call itself an A.O.C., a wine with a noteworthy pedigree, only since 2009. Not long ago, the Louis Latour Burgundy people began doing chardonnay whites in the region, encouraged by a climate that accommodated them, but the original Auvergne wines tend to be modestly pleasing, as was the case with our Saint Pourcain of the domaine Nebout. It had a very appealing, clear ruby color, and after breathing, its clean, acid thinness gave way to some pleasant berrylikes notes. At only twelve degrees alcohol, it left no aggressive disturbances on the palate. Years ago, before my time, simple wines drank well at eight degrees alcohol, which made them hard to store for long. Nowadays they're even pumping up Bordeaux to fourteen degrees, for the current generation of *nouveau* wine drinkers. My one favorite wine in the Massif Central, not on the Bouyssous' list, is a Marcillac, from a small crop with a gentle microclimate in the northwest of the Aveyron. It seldom gets talked about, is produced almost entirely from a grape locally called *mansois*, officially the *fer servadou*. It has a round, while astringent, grapey but not jammy taste, and is inexpensive. As best I know, it has not been planted outside of France.

I order the *pounti to* start my lunch and Joanne a bowl of the *soupe à l'ail*—which came with a copper pot full of more soup. I was not ashamed to ask for a second spoon. Eric told me that the garlic for his soup was from the Auvergnat village of Billom, which enjoyed a great reputation among gourmets. "I use," he added, "local products every chance I can." By the taste of the soup that principle wasn't a touch of arbitrary chauvinism. Later on, I called Jean Jallat, grand master of the brotherhood of Les Grands Goussiers de l'ail d'Auvergne in Billom, a society devoted to honoring the local garlic. What was so special about Billom garlic, I asked. I knew that there were three kinds of French garlic, designated by the color of their skins—white, violet, and rose—and they are ranked, in that order of increasing quality, for the richness of their flavor. The guy who sells me garlic in the market charges nearly twice the price for rose garlic over violet and wouldn't touch the white stuff. The most prestigious widely known French garlic is rose-skinned garlic from Lautrec.

Jallat claimed that Billom garlic, also rose, was better. It was, he explained, a winter-planted garlic with a subtler, grassier flavor, which a blind testing had once proved. And it stored better than other garlic; it kept its flavor without deteriorating.

I didn't have the wherewithal at hand for a blind testing, although we do eat Lautrec garlic at home. I kept dipping, nonetheless, into Joanne's soup and it was a very rewarding breach of etiquette.

The *pounti,* André explained, was once the Auvergnat peasant's main Sunday dish, instead of the appetizer or side dish it is today. It was made of whatever leftover meat there was from the week, usually roast pork, chopped chard, a bit of bacon, milk, eggs, yeast, onion, parsley, and prunes, all baked together in a loaf. Strange combination? It's been around for centuries down here. My plate of it was excellent. I had a roast sausage next and Joanne a steak of beef from the local breed of cattle, Salers. These are the cows you see on the mountainsides, long-horned, lean, with red hides. Their milk goes into the hard cheese, Salers, a cheese that bears the regional name of Cantal when milk from more productive cows is used. Some of the cheese is still made up in those *burons.* Joanne's steak had the lean, faintly gamey quality that makes some Paris bistros feature the beef of *Salers* cows that have become meat after no longer giving much milk.

Both of us ate some *truffade* with our meat. A *truffade* is truffle-less. The word in the local *patois* for a tuber vegetable—potatoes and truffles included—is *la truffe.* Our *truffade,* one of the most common dishes in Auvergnat cuisine, was made of potatoes, some bacon, and *tome fraîche,* which is generic Cantal cheese, or its *Salers* or Laguiole subregional varieties, white and unripe, all cooked together in a frying pan and stirred.

We passed on desserts, after this hearty food. I felt compelled all the same to taste a few Auvergnat cheeses: some ripened *Salers,* and a *bleu d'Auvergne,* which resembles Roquefort, but is made of cow's rather than sheep's milk. That gives it a fattier taste.

The blue mold, André pointed out, used to be made employing moldy bread, but now the cheese is injected with penicillin cultures. A third cheese was a Saint Nectaire from the area closer to the city of Clermont Ferrand, semihard, with spicy, almost smoky notes.

Before we pushed on, after that ample meal, we cajoled André into a recipe for his garlic soup. Here it is. Try, indeed, to use rose-colored garlic. And from my experience avoid the garlic from China, Argentina, or Mexico that gets sold all over, despite its metallic taste.

Soupe à l'ail at Le Bel Horizon

For four people
  4 cloves of chopped rose garlic
  4 qt. of chicken broth
  3 tbs. of butter
  3 tbs. of flour
  8 slices of bread moistened with olive oil
  3½ oz. of grated cheese, ideally Cantal
  ¼ qt. of crème fraîche
  2 thin slices of *ventreche*, French cured pork similar to
  pancetta

Make a *roux blanc* of the butter and flour. Add the broth and the garlic and boil for ten minutes.
Strain and add the cream.
Present the soup in a tureen, covering the bread that has been browned with the cheese topping for ten minutes in the oven.
The slices of ventreche are optional.

Joanne and I intended to be back in the Massif Central on July 14, Bastille Day, to repeat one of the most memorable picnics we'd known. It was in the village of Calvinet. The day ended at the *salle des fêtes,* the village hall for events, when people danced the old-fashioned *bourrée* to an accordion, a flute, and a *cornemuse*, a version of a bagpipe. Old hat folklore if you like, but both young and old were doing the thing they do. Before that, there was the simplest of delicious feasts.

The aroma of grilling local sausage filled the air around the meadow where the crowd gathered, while a handful of men with long wooden pestles pounded the contents of big, charcoal-fueled cast iron portable stoves. What they were pounding, to eat with our sausage, was called *aligot*. It was quite delicious, and *sui generis*. The bellies of their stoves were full of a combination of potatoes, cream, and *tome fraîche*. They pounded their potatoes, butter, and cream to a purée of a consistency they knew was neither too thin nor thick; then they added the chopped cheese, and the pounding soon became a circular motion, until their pestles drew up long strands. That was the *aligot* they heaped on our plates of sausage. No longer potato purée, but something with the consistency of taffy. It melted nicely in your mouth. The cheese hadn't garnished the potato purée. They'd mated and become something new like nothing else.

Delicious.

So I called the town office of the village of Calvinet, to be sure that that feast would be on next July 14. It wouldn't. I combed the Web to find out where else it might happen. It seemed that communal *aligot* feasts were quite common. My best source was a catering company that handled such events. Thing was, there'd been a big change: The powers that be had ruled that the cast iron stoves were unsanitary. Likewise, I was assured, was peeling potatoes al fresco. Nowadays, the *aligot* for these feasts arrived made with industrial potato flakes and were reheated by gas-fired stoves. So there things stood. We hankered nonetheless for the real thing, even if we had to forget the open-air stoves that gave a faint touch of smoke, like a spice, to the dish, such as with *socca,* the thin chickpea pancakes that are a beloved street food in Nice, when grilled on portable charcoal stoves. I called up André Bouyssou of the Bel Horizon and asked where we could eat a genuine *aligot* again.

"You know we do *truffade* with our potatoes and cheese, and not *aligot*."

"It was delicious." I placated him, waiting for his insider's tip.

"*Aligot* is an Aveyron dish and we're Auvergnats."

"We had it in Calvinet, and that's in Auvergne."

He didn't challenge my veracity; it was totally plausible that the delights of *aligot* would have crossed borders and been readopted.

"In fact," he said, "there's a woman who does *aligot* the right way, and she's made quite a reputation at it. She's in Maisonneuve, and her hotel is called le Moulin des Templiers."

I took down the lady's name and the number.

"She's on a stream that gives into the Truyère River," he said, and with a conciliatory note: "In Auvergne—but very close to the Aveyron border." There we headed.

The best road from Vic to the hamlet of Maisonneuve swings up through the town of Saint Flour, rather than your crossing the mountains in constant hairpin turns that wear you out. Saint Flour has a lovely old town and a museum that is so typical of the little gems of civilization you can discover wherever you go in France.

Alfred Douët, born into a banking family in town, spent his life riding horses and attending the Paris auction house la Salle Drouot. He restored a medieval castle outside town and made it his home, and then he bought and restored the town's Maison Consulaire, with its rare Renaissance façade, and endowed it with treasure, in particular a collection of exceptional ceramics that dates to the thirteenth century and includes a rare original of the legendary fifteenth-century ceramist Bernard Palissy. Douët died in 1952 at the age of seventy-seven, leaving the place as a fascinating public museum.

Le Moulin des Templiers

The Moulin des Templiers sits twenty-two miles due south of Saint Flour. The name suggests a historical monument, but the place is the simplest of hotels, run by a very hospitable woman named Sabine Gascuel, daughter of the man who bought an old building burnt by the Germans in the last war. Her mother ran a café there, while she, having gone to hotel school, returned to cook and care for the place for the past nearly thirty years. The site is where the Templiers, those noted Crusaders, had a flour mill, some relics of which were under the road to the hotel. Pilgrims on their way to Saint James of Compostelle in Spain once passed through the area as well.

We ate Sabine Gascuel's *aligot,* with steaks from the local Aubrac herds. It was quite good, the steak less exceptional, the local ham, in a salad starter with local blue cheese, a bit hard, the cheese cold. The compensation for the flaws was that it was all inexpensive. In the morning, I ate a *farinette*, a peasant dish somewhere between an omelet and a pancake, tasty and special enough for us to pass on the recipe below. The *aligot*? We took that recipe, too—but serendipity would have it that, as good as it was, we'd come upon better, even though *aligot* from scratch had become rare in this region where it was created.

Sabine Gascuel's Farinette, at Le Moulin des Templiers

For two people
1 egg
1 ¾ oz. flour
1 ¾ oz. sugar
a dash of milk

Beat together and fry like an omelet.

We drove Southwest into L'Aveyron, onto the miles of high plateau where Aubrac cows were grazing, until we came to the Lot

River, and we followed the Gorges du Lot, where the river cuts through high granite and forest, less dramatically than at the Gorges de la Truyère River to the East, but beautiful all the same. A long time ago we followed the Lot from the time it trickled out of the ground until it emptied into the Garonne, and the gorges are just part of a spectacular panorama that takes you past ancient stone and schist villages and towns such as Entraygues, where the Lot meets the Truyère, that other principal waterway of the region. From Entraygues we drove just two and a half miles to spend the night at a *ferme-auberge* that we remembered as the most appealing one we'd known. It belonged to a couple who restored a place that had been a farm since a Roman official owned it in Gallo-Roman times. La Méjanasserre is a group of houses in the local vernacular style, with a view on the valley below and the mountain across that will take your breath away. Véronique and Frédéric Forveille came here to revive the vineyard, thirty-one years ago.

He had grown up on his parents' apple and pear orchard in the Loire Valley. His roots were from near Rodez not far from La Méjanasserre. She was from Dunkirk, in the North, and had met him when she'd come down to visit her sister, who'd been in a community that bought an abandoned village and restored it.

The vineyard proved long in becoming profitable, and in the face of that, they joined the *fermes-auberges* group at a time when eighty percent of the products the farmers served in their *auberges* had to come from the very farm itself. "I was doing the vineyard, raising pigs and fowl, cultivating potatoes and vegetables. But it's unrealistic to think you could do all that well and serve food," Frédéric said.

Since then, the rules of the group require a "substantial" part of the food to come from the farm's own products, while the rest can be provided by similar, accredited farmers. The Forveilles post the names of the nearby farmers on whom they depend, and they make their own bread in an old outdoor oven, from stone-ground organic wheat milled nearby. They buy organic vegetables where they find them in the region. Their garden provides herbs and fruit, a few vegetables and flowers, some of them edible.

Véronique's soup of nettles and comfrey—an herb like the borage she puts in her salad—wasn't, we regretted, on the menu the night we were there, but the dinner was replete, hearty, and with delightful discoveries. From fresh sausage preserved in oil, made on the farm, served along with the farm's potted pork and fowl *rillettes*—that typical French shredded *pâté*—we went on to fritters of *bette cabbage*, and from there, with sautéed potatoes, came the *pièce de résistance*, local free-range duck. On alternative evenings, Frédéric roasts either ducks or young pigs on a spit in a big fireplace in the dining room, slowly, for three hours. Next came an assortment of regional cheeses, *bleu*, Cantal, Saint Nectaire, and *cabicou*, little local goat cheeses— this to prepare us for the finale of raspberry mousse with a strip of coconut cake and strawberry pie with whipped cream.

After all that, the word *digéstif* seemed a plausible alibi for the *marc*, which Frédéric came around with. His *marc* is a distillation of the pomace of the cabernet franc and cabernet sauvignon portions of the wine that he assembles, along with the *mansois* varietal, the signature grape of Marcillac. It was good brandy, and the wine with the dinner from his vineyard was quite drinkable, very tannic but it mellowed in the glass as you drank.

We slept in one of the handful of bedrooms Véronique had furnished from continually shopping among the region's *brocanteurs*. Her collection of charming old things spoke of the culture of the region: old country beds and chests, attractive nineteenth-century pottery, mirrors, and prints.

After breakfasting on *fouace,* a more rustic, regional version of *brioche*, with fresh fig and quince jams from the farm's garden, we headed along the Lot to the old town of Estaing, where a medieval castle sits close to the river. It was the family seat of—among other illustrated figures—Count Charles-Hector d'Estaing, the admiral who sent his fleet to help the Americans during our revolution against Britain. Not a car was moving. Strolling in Estaing, you could, at moments, feel that you'd stepped well back in time.

Below the eleventh-century castle, there's a little hotel and restaurant called Les Armes d'Estaing, whose terrace, with tables, faces the town's thirteenth-century arched stone bridge. The luncheon menu included something light, which we were ready for: a mixed salad and version of the *croque monsieur*, the open melted cheese sandwich common to France. This riff on it was melted Cantal cheese, local ham, and a layer of a few sautéed potatoes. We went for it, along with a glass of red Estaing wine, which proved surprisingly floral and pleasant. That was all we needed, but . . . they did do *aligot*. We couldn't resist, and after assurances from Pascale Catusse, the woman who served and who owned the place, that it was *aligot* from scratch, we ordered a little bowl of it. It was the best we'd eaten.

Pascale's forty-one-year-old husband, Rémi, told us afterward that he'd been cooking *aligot* along with everything else for the past twenty-one years. He was of the fourth direct generation that owned the place, while the *auberge* had been handed down between cousins since the French Revolution. His cooking couldn't be called regional—his menu was more imaginative, while not excessively so, yet still based on local products.

"My husband," Pascale interjected, "has been awarded the certificate of a *maître restaurateur*." The distinction, she explained, was given by the regional prefect, France's equivalent of a governor. "For you to earn it, ninety-eight percent of the food you cook has to come from fresh products," she said. "We rely on everything that is raised locally. Aubrac beef, veal from the village of Ségala. . . ."

We talked *aligot*. We told Rémi that we'd passed through the town of Laguiole where the headquarters of the Cooperative Fromagière Jeune Montagne was doing a land-office business with travelers who'd stopped by. They were chiefly buying Laguiole cheese in degrees of aging. Laguiole is a subcategory of Cantal cheese, made from the milk of Aubrac brown-skinned herds, just as Salers is made from the red, long-horned Salers cows that graze in those mountains. They were also buying *aligot* kits and frozen *aligot*. It was there that we learned from a poster that three bishops of the region had met where their borders touched on a day in the Middle Ages, and had shared a meal. One brought cheese from Aubrac cows, like the Laguiole cheese of today, another cream, and the third bread. It's said that they cooked it all together, and from the Latin word *aliquad*, meaning "something," a dish called *aligot* was born. Later the monks of Aubrac served it to stick to the ribs of pilgrims crossing the mountains on their way to Saint James of Compostelle. The poster said that potatoes replaced the bread after the war France lost to Prussia in 1870. What that war had achieved to improve *aligot*, no one in the cooperative, which processes the milk of the local dairymen into Laguiole cheese, could tell us.

A film shown in one room taught us that the famous cook Michel Bras was one of the promoters of the *aligot* kits, cheese and cream in one envelope, dehydrated potato flakes in the other—you add a quantity of water and you too can make *aligot*, like pancakes from a mix. Tempted as I am, I shouldn't use the word perpetrate to criticize Bras's endorsement; he was, after all, giving the local small farmers his much-needed help in surviving. We had eaten *aligot* and other things we've forgotten at Bras's restaurant when it was a little place in the town of Laguiole, where he'd already earned his admiration from Michelin. Later, we'd stayed at his big white hotel on the top of a nearby mountain, which we couldn't help but think of as some ocean liner stranded up there like Noah's Ark on Mount Ararat. There was an unenclosed bathtub in our bedroom, an edgy thing in hotel design at the time. Since which the rooms, I'm told, have been redesigned less edgily. Bras is the son of a blacksmith whose

mother used to cook for the locals and did good business on the days
when cattlemen came to the fairs in Laguiole. He credits his mother
for his appreciation of food, while his *shtick,* if you will, or his forte, if
you prefer, is inventing dishes using local plants that have existed on
these mountains since before man, and which no one apparently had
thought of eating until he came along. His mother, now well into her
eighties, had continued to do the *aligot* in his restaurant, which has had
three Michelin stars for decades. She used to do it for the customers,
later just for the help, until she retired from the task recently.

I told Rémi that the *aligot* we'd eaten on his terrace was, as best
we could remember, better than hers.

"*Aligot,*" he said, "is easy to make. I don't understand why people
buy the kits to do it at home. But ninety percent of the restaurants
in the area use the kits. It comes out cheaper. You can't fight with
the kits regarding the price."

I told him that at the cooperative, a sign proclaimed that it sold 74
tons of *aligot* in kits and 231 tons of frozen *aligot* a year and that it had a
team that could cater *aligot* for 100, 500, or as much as 4,000 people.

He gave me his recipe, done for two people at a time. I don't think
it would be easy to find the equivalent of *tome fraîche,* the freshly made
hard cheese of Auvergne, in the States. On the chance that, combing
the Web, you might, I pass this on:

Rémi Catusse's Aligot at the Armes d'Estaing

For two people
    4½ oz. of potatos
    2½ oz. of tome *fraîche*
    a clove of garlic
    a dollop of crème fraîche
    salt and pepper

Cook your potatoes with the skins on. Peel.

Add salt and pepper to taste.

Heat the cream with the peeled clove of garlic.

Add the cream to the potatoes, enough for a soft but not runny purée. The amount you need will depend on the nature of the potatoes at hand.

On a heat high enough to melt the cheese but not high enough to cook it, add the cheese chopped well.

Using a circular motion, moving from the edge of your pot, which is the hottest part, raise the contents in the air until you can create very long strands. Keep it up until all the contents are no longer purée but very elastic.

Serve.

The cheese should be added and the whipping operation done just before the dish is to be served.

Rémi's *aligot* contains garlic. It is often done without garlic. We found that the hint of garlic created by the one clove enriched the flavor without overpowering the dish.

He was curious about our keen interest in food.

"We're doing a book," I said, "about the place of food in the ways of life in France."

"You should speak to Marinette."

"Marinette?"

"She's been cooking up in Le Fel about eight kilometers from here for more than twenty years, and people come to her restaurant from all over the place to eat the food their grandmothers and mothers used to make. She's retired now, but you should talk to her."

We drove up a mountain to the hamlet of Le Fel, a tiny group of little houses overlooking vineyards. Population, 171. An old sign on an outbuilding said Restaurant Chez Marinette and we rang the bell of the house next door.

It turned out that Marinette had not retired after all.

"She's resting," said the young girl who came to the door. But soon she herself appeared, and we sat down and talked.

Marinette Mousset started to cook at the age of fifty, when her niece, who had gone to hotel school and did the snacks at the café they ran, got married and left the business. Marinette, now seventy-seven, who had never married and had learned to cook from her mother, took the place over and began cooking more than snacks. "I just like it," she said, and soon enough people who liked what she did began flocking up the mountain.

What do you cook? we asked.

"My speciality is a dish from around here. It goes back for ages: *chevreau à l'oseille*." It was kid in a sorrel sauce.

And?

"*Poule farcie au pot. Choux farci.* Roast chickens from the young couple near here that raises them, served with sautéed *cêpes* mushrooms. Roast local duck. . . .

We'd heard enough. A table?

Today? Impossible.

"There's just the two of us working here, and we're all taken up."

Tomorrow wouldn't do for us. We had important things to accomplish in Paris. We got her phone number and told her we'd come back up the mountain soon. Which we did.

L'Auberge du Fel

Once again luck brought us a delicious discovery. We hadn't noticed that up the narrow road, where cars never seemed to pass in Le Fel, there was an inn. It was owned, we learned, by a couple called Elisabeth and Jean-François Albespy. His family had been running l'Auberge du Fel, first as a café, ever since his great-grandparents created the inn. They had gone up to Paris at the turn of the twentieth century and come back home, when the First World War meant that the army requisitioned the horses they used in their water, coal, and people transporting business.

The Auberge, like many country inns, had very simple rooms. Just ten of them. What set it apart was a great cook.

Elisabeth had been a nurse. "I learned cooking what my mother-in-law cooked here before me." she explained, after we'd arrived to stay at the Auberge on our second trip to Le Fel.

She too was doing a Sunday lunch next day, such as the one we'd reserved to eat chez Marinette. We would miss her version of *chevreau à l'oseille*, indeed a local speciality, while enjoying Marinette's, but dinner the night before, cooked by Elisabeth, was superb.

I became aquainted with *farçou*, our starter that came with a slice of local raw cured ham. I remembered the *pounti* we'd eaten at Le Bel Horizon in Auvergne. The *farçou*, equally native to Auvergne and to l'Aveyron, where we were now, was a relative of a *pounti*.

Elisabeth rattled off her recipe, which she never measured: lots of *bette*, spinach, celery, leeks, onions, garlic, and parsley, in relative quantities she judged to be about equal, the onion and garlic considerably less so, added to both cured and smoked bacon in a ratio of about three to one, the vegetables to the meat, all chopped well together, bound together with egg, some rye and some wheat flour, and fried, not deeply, using a sparing amount of olive oil, in patties shaped by a soup spoon. She dried the patties on a paper towel afterward. A *pounti,* she pointed out, was made of the same basic ingredients, plus prunes. The batter and the prunes are placed in alternate layers in a terrine, and the dish gets baked in a double boiler at a low temperature until a crust forms on top.

It was a toss-up for Joanne and me between the great flavor of Elisabeth's *farçou* and of Eric Bouyssou's *pounti* at Le Bel Horizon. What came next was incomparable. A classic *lapin à la moutarde* done her way, with a rabbit from a neighbor's hutch. "It's the product above all that counts in a dish," she likes to repeat, and on the outside wall of the Auberge, Elisabeth has posted the list of the local farms from which her products come. Joanne and I had eaten *lapin à la moutarde* before, and were never terribly fond of what a common mustard sauce did to improve the blandness of the rabbit. Elisabeth, with her recipe printed below, produced a delicately savory, unctuous dish, served with new potatoes in their skins stuffed with minced mushrooms, *a duxelle*.

We drank the wine that Marinette's nephew Laurent Mousset produced, down the road, on a fourteen-acre vineyard, a red made of *mansois* and cabernet franc and cabernet sauvignon grapes. It was deep red and very tannic—the tannic quality, beyond a presence of astringency, had a pronounced dark taste, not disagreeable but assertive. It was an honest wine with strong personality and, in sum, it was pleasant, with no defects to put up with.

Elisabeth makes her own ice cream. In a separate wing of her kitchen, to be sure, in accordance with the sanitary protocol required. I had coffee ice cream with a bit of chocolate *fondant*. Joanne had another sampling of the regional cheeses.

It was an excellent dinner. Lunch next day chez Marinette was one of the most pleasing that we'd ever experienced.

Restaurant chez Marinette

The weathered signs that say "Restaurant chez Marinette, Cabicou, Vin du Fel" on a little stone outbuilding, a quintessential picture of local architecture, won't encourage you to believe how exceptional our meal was, in a modest, former café next door. A grandfather's clock, an old armoire, and long tables in three rooms with wooden floors are the setting for the lunches that Marinette prepares, three times a week.

Marinette was on the phone when we walked by her kitchen. She was calling around among the neighbors to borrow a few bunches of parsley. The grandfather's clock struck noon. Early lunch, but we had a train to catch again. The place was already full, though, with people who must have been waiting for this event all week. The room had that telltale purr of contentment that transfigures the environment of some restaurants.

On Sunday chez Marinette, you get a choice of the main course between two things; the rest keeps coming out, a programmed concert of delights. From starters of asparagus in vinaigrette, from a nearby garden, along with *foie gras* garnished with poached pears and fig compote, as well as Marinette's homemade rabbit *pâté*, we went on to the delicate *chevreau à l'oseille* for me and roast local duck for Joanne, lean and savory, with a bowl of hashed potatoes for both of us. Marinette had got her parsley. The garnishing on the potatoes was the evidence.

Once again, after salad, we sampled an array of cow and goat local cheeses, along with sheep's milk Rocquefort, which is also an Aveyron cheese. Dessert was Marinette's oversized puff-paste *choux*, stuffed with fresh whipped cream and served with a big bowl of local strawberries.

We drank more of Marinette's nephew's wine. Wine, food, and coffee, sixty-five euro for two. The tables were filled with groups of friends and families. There had been travelers at l'Auberge, as you'd expect at an inn. Chez Marinette was filled with locals, a fact that their country accents gave away as they conversed.

From what we could hear, no one mentioned the wonderful food. They weren't there to talk about or judge the food. They were wearing Sunday clothes, having probably been to the church in the next hamlet. The food was a part of an ephemeral wonderful Sunday in the country, an element giving its own glow to the whole gestalt, but not the nucleus of what that moment meant. Someone might someday write memories of such Sunday lunches, just as Proust brought meals in Combray back to life, and maybe even the asparagus will have its cherished place in lost time, like Proust's. But this moment chez Marinette that lasted much of just an afternoon had its own unexamined grace. A special meal was a frame for these people's enactment of bonding, as it has been all through the history of our civilization, both religious and lay.

Chevreau à l'Oseille chez Marinette

For two people
   about 4 large pieces of kid (or spring lamb)
   2 cups of puréed fresh sorrel
   a tbs. of flour
   enough bouillon to cover
   salt and pepper
   ½ cup of crème fraîche
   butter or oil

Brown the meat in butter or oil, sprinkling with the flour.
   Cook the combined ingredients except for the cream for thirty minutes in the bouillon.
   Add the cream after the dish has slightly cooled.

Elisabeth's Lapin à la moutarde at l'Auberge du Fel

   a rabbit
   3 large onions, chopped or blended to a paste
   a clove or two of garlic, chopped
   5 to 6 tomatoes, peeled and crushed
   white wine, about a cup
   a scant handful of finely chopped tarragon

4 tbs. of traditional mustard, *moutarde à l'ancienne*, the kind
with seeds and white wine, available on the Net (ordinary
mustard will not be good.)
a little less than that of crème fraîche

Brown the rabbit cut in pieces in olive oil. Throw away the
grease.

Sauté the onions in the same deep pot till transparent. Add
the garlic, deglaze with the wine.

Boil off the alcohol from your liquid.

Add the peeled tomatoes and the tarragon.

Let it cook until the meat is tender.

Remove the sauce and reduce it. Add the mustard and cream
once removed from the stove.

17

SAINTE-TERRE, WORLD CAPITAL

Population 1,700

World capital of the lamprey, the roadside sign proclaimed. The lamprey is a yard-long-or-so near vertebrate three inches thick, whose species has been swimming around the world, unchanged, for half a billion years. It spends its mature life in the ocean, where it feeds only on the fluids in the flesh of fish on which it fixes itself, with a mouth like a suction cup lined with rows of sharp teeth. A salmon or a shark is equally its prey. The lamprey swims up the Gironde and Dorgogne rivers to breed and then die. It pursues that goal in a few rivers all over the world, but Sainte-Terre and the neighboring Bordeaux region are nearly the last places on earth where these beasts are caught upstream on their fateful mission, and then transformed lovingly into a culinary delicacy that goes back, in various recipes, at least to Roman times.

The British used to fancy cooking lampreys caught in the Thames, and somewhere in the United Kingdom they might still do so, but the lamprey has, for them, a disturbing history. King Henry I, the first Plantagenet, died of ptomaine poisoning after eating a dish of potted lampreys in 1135, at his hunting lodge in Normandy. In the eighteenth century in London the same fate struck the poet Alexander Pope, virtuoso of the alexandrine meter. In Portugal, some lampreys are still caught in a few rivers and prepared with rice. My editor, Jessica Case, tells me that there are lamprey eaters in Alaska. The Internet says that there are lamprey fanciers in Oregon as well. Joanne and I have excellent memories of salmon grilled on sea salt and little oysters in Oregon, but we missed out on the lampreys.

"Lamproie à la bordelaise" is in any case soul food in the Bordeaux region, perpetuated in a few restaurants in the city of Bordeaux, but more widely consumed, as preserved in either metal or glass, by enough of a tradition-oriented population to keep the tradition going. Lore holds it that the dish improves with age once jugged, but there are homemakers who prepare and eat it fresh, which was my intention on this trip. Thierry Marx, one of France's celebrity chefs, born in Paris, with roots in Poland, prepares the dish in his famous restaurant at Pauillac, while doing a riff on it by grilling the lamprey and lacquering it in a chocolate sauce, recalling Japanese-prepared eel.

For the real McCoy, some three thousand lamprey fanciers, not only French, descend on Sainte-Terre, this village thirty-odd miles east of the city of Bordeaux, at the end of April. They spend Easter weekend dancing, eating, and observing a ceremony to celebrate the virtues of *la lamproie à la bordelaise.*

I came down from Paris a fortnight earlier to cook the dish, alongside a dozen men and women who'd signed up with the town government to be initiated into the *sui generis* procedure. We were neophyte amateurs, as well as one guy with nostalgia for the dish he'd known growing up, and a couple of sub-chefs of the region.

Once again, I had gone off alone on a food adventure. Joanne's decision had been unremitting: "I'm not enticed by eating, let alone cooking, a prehistoric bloodsucker."

The TGV fast train takes you from Paris to Libourne in a bit more than three hours, and Sainte-Terre is only ten miles away through the flat vineyards of Saint Emilion with their stunted, pruned-down vines. The region is called Le Pays Libournais. A *pays* is a subdivision in French geography, based on the change in the lay of the land rather than political history. Afterward the map breaks down into towns, villages, and *lieux-dits,* little "named places." The village of Sainte-Terre is surrounded by a number of rural *lieux-dits* all counted in the population of no more than 1,700.

Prehistoric bloodsuckers aside, the plethora of things of interest in this sparsely inhabited region is great proof that anywhere at all you go in France, off the beaten tourist trails, you'll enrich your life with what you find. Le Pays Libournais has twelve little museums of local culture, a megalith, a dolmen, and a menhir of prehistoric times, a Gallo-Roman site with beautiful ceramic designs, five medieval forts and towns, six medieval castles, Renaissance vestiges, four windmills, five gardens of horticultural repute, and a grotto. You can learn about each at the very welcoming tourist office of Sainte-Terre.

The architectual jewel of the *pays* is the medieval town of Saint Emilion, surrounded by ramparts and with remarkable churches and cloisters. UNESCO classified Saint Emilion's outlying vineyards as world treasures in 1999, the first time wine country earned the accolade. Saint Emilion had been snubbed in the 1855 Classification of Bordeaux wines from Médoc and Sauternes, but just a hundred years later, the government gave the region its own honor roll. Two of the wines in this region, where the merlot grape gets preference in assembly with the cabernets, are classed First Growth A, and, in the wine world, they hold their heads up among the greatest Médocs. They're Château Ausone and Château Cheval Blanc. Legend has it that in 1935, Clarence Dillon, the noted American financier, was intent on buying Cheval Blanc, when he got lost in a fog on his way to the château and wound up at Château Haut Brion in Médoc. He fell in love with Haut Brion, a first growth, and soon bought it. Cheval Blanc belongs, as I write, to two other tycoons, Bernard Arnault, of Louis Vuitton fame, and Albert Frère, a magnate on the European financial scene.

The Pays Libournais also includes the region of Pomerol, no stepchild in the family of fine Bordeaux wines. Its Château Petrus is often more expensive than all other Bordeaux.

Anyone touring the area should, I think, pick up his car before-hand in the city of Bordeaux, another UNESCO treasure, the world's most exceptional example of an eighteenth-century city, including nearly 350 historic monuments classified by the French government. Before leaving town, park and stroll through the city center from the Place Gambetta to the Garonne River, past the Grand-Théâtre, the city hall, the townhouses built for the wealthy wine merchants and sea traders.

Sainte-Terre, compared to all this splendor, owes its renown among the initiated entirely to the creature that Joanne accurately described. Sainte-Terre is a sleepy place on the Dordogne River before it flows toward the province of that name, dear to Dutch and British retirees. It has neither a hotel nor restaurant, and just one café. The name Sainte-Terre, "holy earth," seems peculiar in that modest context, but it has a history. In the twelfth century, veterans returning from the First Crusade decided to have built a church at the highest point in the village (an elevation that compares with the bumps on flat landscape the Russians sometimes call hills). On top of the mound, these crusaders spread earth that they had piously brought from Palestine. The church was then built, a modest example of the chaste Romanesque style of the region, which in Gothic times acquired decorative sculpture around its central portal, and which saw other changes in the eighteenth and nineteenth centuries. This church honors Saint Alexis, the fifth-century Roman Christian, who, like Saint Francis centuries later, abandoned his birthright of riches to become a beggar. I couldn't find out why this relatively obscure saint in the canons of both the Eastern and Roman Catholic faiths gave his name to the little church of Sainte-Terre. Nearby there are a few handsome, squarish stone townhouses that speak, with their vernacular elegance, of earlier wealth: when the Dordogne was a waterway for commerce, sending wine downriver and bringing in all sorts of goods in exchange.

There is also a sandy beach bordering the Dordogne River, where swimmers come in warm weather and where there were once *ginguettes,* those nineteenth-century cafés and dance halls, such as those that used to be near Paris on the Seine and the Marne. They say that people traveled the thirty-odd miles from Bordeaux in those carless days, for a night out at the *ginguettes* of Sainte-Terre.

I went down near that beach to talk to a fisherman, one of the very few in France who fish for lampreys.

The Gironde River, its estuary, and the Dordogne are where nowadays lamprey fishermen ply their craft—those still at it. In earlier times lampreys were fished for on the Loire and Adour rivers, where they are sometimes still caught. Sainte-Terre, with its energetic promotion efforts and a river that the creatures, for some reason, favor more than others, has held on to the title of World Capital of the Lamprey for decades.

Gérard Durand lives on the banks of the Dordogne, in a stone whitewashed house with a wooden porch, resembling the one a few yards away, which his father built and where he was born. The Durand family has been fishing for lampreys as far back as he can remember. At sixty-three, he's been at it for forty years. His thirty-five-year-old son, Mickaël, has followed him in the calling for a decade.

"We're five lamprey fishermen in Sainte-Terre: my son and me, two nephews, and a friend," Durand explained. "I count fifty-four people fishing for lampreys in the whole region. These days the demand isn't big enough to make it a profitable pursuit. Luckily, the Portuguese fancy lampreys and come here to buy. Otherwise it's some housewives in the markets or the canneries."

Gérard, his wife, Mado, and Mickaël spent fifteen thousand euro to create Mickaël's own little cannery in an outbuilding, observing EU standards of sanitation. Mickaël takes their *lamproie à la bordelaise* to outdoor markets in the area when he's not fishing. The season allows for Lamprey fishing runs from December 1 to May 15, when the lampreys swim as much as 150 miles upriver from the Atlantic. The rest of the year, the Durands fish for other species, in particular the European shad, but when I was there, there was a five-year prohibition on shad fishing because of depletion. Since 2000, on the other hand, the number of lampreys arriving had increased greatly for some reason, surpassing demand. There is a theory that a drop in the population of eels in the sea, who eat lamprey larvae, has caused the increase in lampreys. The world's eel population has been reduced by the appetite that gourmets, particularly in Spain, have for baby eels. The current lamprey harvest in France is about 140 tons a year.

The lamprey fishers set forth, one to a boat these days—having more aboard wouldn't be profitable—with a regulation-size net of 130 meters long and two-and-a-half meters deep. They are allowed to use as well 150 *bourgnes,* traps made traditionally of wicker, now often in plastic, in which the lampreys enter to rest and can't get out. Since the lampreys stop feeding the moment they decide—no one knows how—to leave the ocean and breed in a river and die, there is no point in trying to catch them with bait. Fluids sucked out of fish is their only diet, in any case, once they cease to be larvae living in the mud and feeding on microscopic algae and river protozoa.

In high season, Durand goes out with the tide at noon, returns at six, and leaves again at midnight, when the lampreys are most active, and he is on the water until morning. Thirty-six lampreys would be a good catch, after trolling for a half mile. Once a week he harvests the lampreys trapped in his *bourgnes*.

Durand likes his craft. It's a daily challenge and comes with the self-assurance of identifying with a way of life attached to the place he was born.

Mado explained that the recipe of the lampreys that the Durands put in cans corresponded to the classic formula. "It's better once canned," Gérard pointed out.

"Some people put in unsugared chocolate, some people put in prunes. Any old thing." She sniffed. "We cook lampreys and leeks with a bit of sugar and thyme and bay leaf. In a sauce, of course, made of Bordeaux wine and the blood of the lamprey."

It would be the same recipe at the class tomorrow morning, she said. In the meantime, Mado kindly gave me a book called *Le Livre de la lamproie* by Jean-Etienne Surlève-Bazeille, a biologist and university professor of the region. It contained, she assured me, everything I might want to know about lampreys. And more than that, Joanne might say.

In Professor Surlève-Bazeille's book there is a photograph of lamprey larvae fossils found in Chengjiang, China, in outcrops of stone 530 million years old. The lamprey is classed among vertebrates, although its spinal column is not bone but cartilage. It has a brain and a cranium. A hole in its head acts somehow like a nose detecting the presence of larvae of its own species. It is that capability to sense the presence of larvae from far away that draws the lampreys to nest in the same rivers, not necessarily the ones they were born in.

Once upriver, the male secretes a pheromone that draws the female to where the male has created a nest, moving stones into place with its mouth. They couple when the male latches onto the female, squeezes out her eggs, which it then fertilizes, while the female stirs the stream to make mud stick protectively to its eggs. The lampreys that hatch live for as long as eight years burrowed in the mud, eating the microscopic plant life. Then they grow up and swim out to sea where they live off the fish that they latch on to and suck the fluids until, somehow they get the call to find a river to breed in and die. And then for some reason, they stop eating and hurry to their destiny. In 1830, lampreys headed up the Saint Lawrence River and soon wound up in the Great Lakes, where they stayed, no longer returning to salt water, finding plenty of fish to feed on and fresh water in which to breed. They became a scourge for the lake trout fishermen and are still considered pests, decimating the native lake fish population. American authorities combat them nowadays by trapping the males and sterilizing them with injections.

The lamprey's nervous system has been a subject of scientific interest that goes back to the work of none other than Sigmund Freud. Freud was twenty-one years old, an ill-paid researcher at the Institute of Physiology in Vienna, when he began work on a paper published in 1877 on the nervous system of the lamprey. The lamprey's neuron structure, while that of a vertebrate, was a conveniently small subject to examine. Freud challenged the going belief that a mammal's nervous system was composed of a syncytium, of several neurons bound together in the same cytoplasm. His observations proved the unicist theory of linked independent cells. Sixty years later, the electronic microscope proved him right. Four years later, young Freud received his medical degree and, influenced by Charcot and Breuer, he turned his inquisitiveness toward more world-shattering cogitation about the mind.

Currently, the lamprey's nervous system is involved in studies that may lead to breakthroughs in bionics, the direct control of prostheses by the brain, among the handicapped and spinally injured. There are also studies at work regarding the medical applications that might be possible regarding the anticoagulants the lamprey's saliva secretes when bleeding a fish.

My lamprey cooking session, at the row of stoves and sinks in a building in the Jardin de la Lamproie, began at nine in the morning, so that the dish could cook until after lunch, about six hours. The *jardin* is indeed a garden that contains some lovely plants and trees, the town office promoting lampreys, and the cooking school used three days a year for making *lamproie à la bordelaise*. We were in the *lieu-dit* of Lavagnac, where there were just a few houses and the *jardin*. I read that Christian Sanchez, the retired fisherman interviewed by Professor Surlève-Bazeille, had also proclaimed the greater virtues of canned *lamproie à la bordelaise* compared with a fresh batch. "My lampreys that were in the can for five years," he declared, "were far tastier than the ones I'd cooked the day before." Lunch, while our pots simmered, was going to be the canned version of the dish; I'd have the opportunity of knowing both types.

A fisherman brought in the lampreys, flapping in buckets. From there he dipped each creature three seconds into boiled water, which stopped the commotion. We were allotted our lampreys. Some of us had signed up to cook two. We suspended them from hooks above our stoves and, with a knife, scraped them clean of the silt that clung to their speckled skins. Not fish, they had no scales. We dipped them in cold water, hung them up again, placed a bowl containing a bottle of Bordeaux wine, a Bordeaux Supérieur, Côtes de Castillon from nearby under them and made deep incisions into the lampreys every few inches so that the blood flowed into the bowls.

Meanwhile we cut the white of eight leeks into slices about an inch and a half long. We cut the lampreys into slices about two inches long, poked out the entrails in each slice with a knife, and set the slices aside, having added a fresh bay leaf and a pinch of fresh thyme along with two lumps of white sugar to the liquid. We brought the liquid to a boil. We flamed it with a match to get rid of the alcohol. We added the lampreys and leeks to the liquid, and set our stoves to simmer. And that was that. The morning's lamprey butchery convinced me that I was not cut out to work in a slaughterhouse. But these creatures had come here to end their lives, hadn't they? Although nothing in their sensory equipment might have foretold that they'd end up chopped, in a pot. From a gustatory point of view, the denizens of Sainte-Terre staunchly believed that they had not lost their little lives in vain. Well. . . .

We enjoyed a copious lunch while our lampreys simmered. *Soupe de poisson* got us started before we went on to *lamproie à la bordelaise,* as canned by la Conserverie d'Aquitaine. From there we had some local *confit de canard* with sautéed potatoes and fresh green beans. The *brie* that followed was ripe, and went well with the Côtes de Castillon 2007 we were drinking, a *Bordeaux supérieur,* that was well balanced, with body, although not very loquacious. Dessert was a wicked strawberry tart of *pâte brisée,* custard and homemade whipped cream.

We lingered like a jury over the lampreys, before the *confit* came out. The garnishing was only garlic toast, such as the tradition specifies. The sauce was unctuous, a savory and subtly blended flavor of wine, leeks, a touch of herbs, and, yes, blood. Blood and red wine sauces, known as *civets,* are common in French traditional cuisine, often done with game. The Norman dish *canard à la rouannaise* was interpreted into a house speciality for the tourists who frequent the luxurious Tour d'Argent restaurant in Paris. The duck is smothered, so as not to lose any blood in slaughtering; the blood is collected for the sauce and the duck served with the carcass pressed of its juices. This extension into epicuranism begins with an axiom like something moral in the culture: Everything edible is to be eaten, and even exalted. I remember a lunch Joanne and I had on the banks of the Lot River, in the portion of l'Auvergne called la Rouergue. For starters, before serving us river fish, a favor not allowed to be on a restaurant menu, the owner of the local inn urged me to try a *sanguette,* a local pancake of shallots, bread, and chicken blood. It tasted better than it sounds.

The lamprey in my plate? The slices had turned gray, but were still intact inside the skin. The flesh of the lamprey is fragile and can get lost in the sauce if the dish is stirred while cooking, which we'd been warned against in our session. The taste is often described as also "delicate."

I took up a forkful of gray lamprey meat. I still tasted the sauce, but the meat had no taste at all. Was my palate indelicate? I recalled what the veteran lamprey fisherman Christian Sanchez had told Professor Surlève-Bazeille—that in *lamproie à la bordelaise* the sauce was essentially it:

"The flesh is insipid, insipid, without odor, with no true taste. . . . You need to add the necessary ingredients. . . . The paradox of the lamprey, it's that it's insipid and delicious at the same time. It is thus that it became a special dish . . . almost mystical."

Beside me at lunch, Christian Lafargue, fellow chef for the day, hadn't made touch with the mystery, nor had his companion of forty-five years, Josephine Brussac, opposite us. Having driven here for the event from their village near Bordeaux, they were disappointed.

"I came here thinking that I might rediscover the taste I had in childhood," he said. She said that the dish in our plates lacked the flavor of the lampreys that they put up in jars together at home. "I don't get the same taste of the lamprey and the wine," she said. "I don't get a certain fish taste."

Lafargue explained that he was born in the city of Bordeaux, but his grandparents lived near here, and, as a child, he'd visit them on vacations. They'd followed, he said, a family recipe for lampreys handed down for generations, of which his sister was the last vestal. It's seven, seven, and seven," he said. "Seven kilos of leeks, seven kilos of lampreys, seven liters of Bordeaux wine, fresh thyme, and bay leaf, two handfuls of sugar. Nothing else."

That didn't sound very different from what we'd cooked that morning, the quantities aside.

"It's also in the way it's done," he said. "You cook the dish for three hours on the stove, and then you put it all together and cook it for about as long in a corner of the fireplace."

Christian and Josephine promised me a DVD detailing their own preparation of *lamproie à la bordelaise* at home, without resorting to a fireplace.

After lunch, the dishes we'd prepared were simmering. My sauce had turned quite thick and black. It was time to put the dish into glass jars to take home. No one had told me to bring a jar. I had none, but after tasting my dish, I didn't think it was likely to be something that I could convince Joanne to share with me. The sauce was quite good, the meat—well, I could not identify a taste. The dish was, I esteemed, a successful rendition of the genre. I gave my dish to the woman across the table from me, who had cooked two lampreys, and she was delighted to take home a third.

After I got home, Christian Lafargue's DVD arrived as promised. Step by step, his preparation resembled pretty much what we'd done in Sainte-Terre. The lampreys were bled cut up, into a pot of wine, rather than hung above to bleed. Seven, seven, and seven, as noted above, were observed, and Christian and Josephine finished the process by jarring in glass that great quantity of soul food.

I didn't show Joanne the DVD. I didn't detail my experience, and found it unnecessary to mention the option that I'd had of taking her some *lamproie à la bordelaise*.

She asked me how things went, and I told her, as they used to urge you in the Levi's ads, that I had entered the legend.

She seemed to appreciate that this was not, all things told, a waste of time. With that, we enjoyed a roast farm chicken for dinner.

18

NICE AND MARSEILLE

"Poor but not Stupid"

Nice: The quintessential, legendary Riviera starts east of town, on the way to Italy, on the sometimes breathtaking, jagged coastline that Hitchcock filmed so well in *To Catch a Thief.* The city of Nice is different from all that awesome nature. You have to get Nice right. Once I read a story in a travel magazine about a beachside vacation in Nice. The beach at Nice, having been found cleaner than most on the coast, is nonetheless composed of gravel, and a busy highway runs alongside it, where Queen Victoria once rode on her donkey while her faithful Mr. Brown walked after her.

Nice has a richly evocative past. The city began as a settlement by the Phoenicians, half a millennium before Christ, and was, in the nineteenth century, the winter resort of royals and those noble Russians fleeing the ice back home and rushing to the roulette tables. Touchstones to a fascinating past are still here in the fascinating architecture. Old Nice with its tall pastel-colored buildings hovering over narrow streets is picturesque although sometimes risky at night. Mary Blame, an old friend, who wrote an illuminating book on the Riviera, moved out of her apartment there some time ago, because of criminality. The Cours Saleya, which runs between Old Nice and the sea and ends at an ochre house where Matisse lived and painted, is touristy today, recalling the Place du Tertre in Paris. Matisse, ailing, moved out of Old Nice to be cared for with hotel service in the Excelsior Hôtel Régina, uphill. The Régina is a splendid and vast example of Belle Époque exuberance.

Travelers would be advised to take a short drive and then stroll, up there where there's a small Matisse museum. The Régina, where Queen Victoria also stayed, is just one of the extraordinary villas and hotels in the reaches of Cimiez and Mont Boron—mostly condominiums as well as the Régina these days. Here and in more scattered locations downtown, Sébastien Biasini, an architect worthy of greater renown, built palaces that glorified the sensuously driven wealth of the late nineteenth century. His accomplishments can still be seen not only in Nice but also all along the coast as far as Italy.

For the rest, you have a bustling, modern metropolis, with some good museums and a culture that's both feisty and colorful. The fishing was never very good in the Bay of Angels and the mountains behind are too rocky for cash-crop farming. The titans of society who enjoyed themselves here never gave more to the economy than jobs for servants. The native Niçois are by and large a relatively poor people, attached to their heritage as if to a rich inheritance.

In a plebiscite of 1860, in the time of Napoléon III, the citizens of the city overwhelmingly voted to return to being French, after Nice belonged for a period to the house of Savoy. This sign of allegiance said, the Niçois have always seemed to me more attached to the ways of their city than to the nation. Don't suggest to them that they have "Italian roots," although their names often make you think that. They'll remind you that they were there before Italy, as such, existed. They speak their own language, *Niçard*—as well as richly accented French—and despite a few inroads of contemporary French cuisine, eating in Nice is more easily a matter of making touch with the vital perpetuation of distinctively Nice traditions. The choice of restaurants for that is large.

When Somerset Maugham wrote that the Riviera was "a sunny place for shady people," he didn't have Nice particularly in mind. (His villa was in Cap Ferrat, the summer place, when I knew it, of Lynn Wyatt, a charming Texan socialite who would have the steaks for her barbecues flown in from home.) Graham Greene, on the other hand, wrote a pamphlet called "J'Accuse, the Dark Side of Nice," and from what I know he was on target. I met the mayor whom he attacked for sinister corruption that harmed one of Greene's friends, when I was writing a travel article on the city. That was a while before the mayor went on the lam to Uruguay. His name was Jacques Médecin. He was mayor of Nice for nearly thirty years, almost as long as his father had held the post before him. When Médecin was busy elsewhere, civic affairs were handled by an unelected adjunct known as Max le Glacier, "Max the Ice Cream Man," who was otherwise distinguished by owning the only two-store soft ice cream stand in town.

In his dealings with the Mob and others, Médecin gave and took a lot. I confess to what he gave me. Médecin was an aficionado of Nice cooking, which is like being a Yankee fan in New York. More than that, he loved to cook himself. The cookbook he wrote that he bestowed on me proved that.

Stockfish, the dried or salted cod stew that dates to the days when Scandinavian fishermen came here to exchange their preserved fish for salt; *daube à la niçoise*—the dish that Virginia Woolf's heroine spent *To the Lighthouse* dotingly preparing—batter-fried zucchini flowers, *bette* gnocchi, and more—some 305 dishes are lovingly explained in Médecin's book. Other principles aside, Médecin was strict about aberrations in Nice cooking. He chided me when I mentioned that some people put orange peel in a *daube* and others olives.

We never got to have a meal together, but I have cooked his *daube à la niçoise*, learned from his mother. This little contribution to the history of a culture might not have pardoned His Honor's sins, but, pace Virginia Woolf, it's the most authoritative recipe for the dish that I know.

Jacques Médecin's Doba à la Nissarda

For six people

    2 lb. 10 oz stewing beef

    2 onions

    4 carrots

    4 cloves of garlic

    6 large tomatoes

    a bouquet garni of:

    1 celery branch

    1 bunch of parsley

    1 bay leaf and 2 sprigs of thyme

    1 lb. 2 oz. of dried Portobello mushrooms

    1 glass of red wine

    1 glass of marc (grappa will do)

    a couple of tablespoonfuls or less of lard

    salt and pepper

    optional: grated parmesan and lemon, to be put on the table for sprinkling, but not in the cooking, which would ruin the meat for later use in raviolis.

    cayenne pepper

Soak the mushrooms in water.

Cut the meat in cubes of about 1 ½ in.

With part of the lard, sauté the onions, cut in quarters, the carrots in rounds, the whole cloves of garlic.

Brown the meat in a separate frying pan with the remaining lard, on a high flame, getting a crust that will help keep the meat from falling apart in the cooking. Place the meat in the thick-bottomed pot that the dish will cook in. Let it simmer there about ten minutes.

Crush the tomatoes, peeled and seeded, and throw them in the pot with the meat. Add the bouquet garni of the celery, parsley, herbs, and vegetables, the glass of red wine and the glass of marc and throw on enough boiling water to cover the dish.

Bring to a boil. Then bring to a low temperature and simmer for three hours.

Add the mushrooms, having dried them off. Season, adding a pinch of cayenne pepper if you feel the need.

Cook on a very low fire for another hour. Degrease on serving, leaving a little fat all the same.

I have great memories of eating in Nice restaurants. The legendary one that still exists in the old town is called La Merenda, run by a modest couple when I first knew it. It is a hole in the wall with a few tables, for which they didn't see the need to encourage crowds. No phone, no reservations. *Habitués* showed up ahead of time at noon to say that they wanted a table later for lunch. A former chef at the classy Hôtel Negresco, who bought the place a decade ago, perpetuates the no-reservation setup. Thing is, La Merenda, which also perpetuates hearty, very authentic Nice dishes, is now an internationally touted tourist destination and the charm of the couple's idiosyncrasy has given way to a standing chapter in restaurant sadomasochism. I have no reason at all to believe that the *daube,* the *stockfish,* and the rest have gone down in quality at the Merenda. But Nice cooking is hearty, and, done honestly, it is not hard to accomplish well. Instead of turning up as a traveling hopeful at the doorstep of La Merenda and holding my breath, I chose on this last trip to have dinner at a restaurant run by a nephew of the original couple. André Alziari, his wife, Anne-Marie; and his son, Michel, did not disappoint me.

An ancient shop in the old town bears the name Alziari, made famous over generations for the quality of its olive oil. André's father sold the family's business. André started a hardware company, which did poorly, so thirteen years earlier, he and Anne-Marie, who'd been his wife for forty years when we met, decided to create a restaurant, taking over a place that had been closed for years, beside the well-known restaurant L'Escalinada, in business for half a century. Neither André nor Anne-Marie had any training in cooking—she was an accountant—but Anne-Marie—who'd loved the "conviviality" of receiving at home—got to work in the kitchen doing "what my mother, my grandmother, and my great grandmother cooked."

L'Escalinada has a big list of local dishes posted outside near its big terrace, which fills up with both tourists and locals. La Table d'Alziari is smaller, and the Alziaris keep the menu small but always fresh and equally Niçois, even if L'Escalinada's recipe for breaded sheep testicles is never the *plat du jour* at La Table Alziari. "Not exactly the pinnacle of our regional gastronomy," André noted. "When people ask me what is our *plat du jour*," he added, "I tell them that everything is the *plat du jour*. We start every day's menu every morning from scratch when Anne-Marie comes in." Michel, thirty-eight, who studied engineering but was turned off by his taste of corporate life, assists in the cooking.

The Alziaris' one amendment of traditional fare is their lamb rather than beef *daube*. They make a beef *daube* just to stuff ravioli, which, so stuffed, is normally a Nice second-day dish.

"With Nice cooking, imagination had to replace resources," André said. "Poor but not stupid, we had to rely on what was at hand, vegetables from small gardens, olive oil, tomatoes. . . ."

Nice cuisine is repeatedly a matter of what he calls "recuperation": the *daube* that becomes ravioli, next day, the stuffing that stretches out the meal—stuffed fresh sardines, stuffed breast of veal, stuffed vegetables. . . . That stuffing of breadcrumbs, cured pork, greens, and herbs, deftly accomplished, becomes an embellishment beyond being a stretcher.

I sampled the excellent stuffed fresh sardines. Zucchini flowers were in season, and I started lunch with some. The batter was thin and crisp, rendering the dish more delicate than the flowers at La Merenda that I remembered. From there I ate a local version of a dish called larks without heads. *Alouettes sans têtes*, never fear, is not about endangered species reminiscent of *ortolans*. It's made of scallops of beef rolled around stuffing and cooked in a wine sauce much like that of a *daube*. With it I had *panisses*, as local a dish as you can find. They come from a specialist, the nearby shop, Barale, with a venerable tradition of doing *panisses*. They're like French fries composed of chickpea flour rather than potatoes. The same ancient house of Barale does *socca,* chickpea *crêpes.*

Dessert was a choice of traditional French dishes, *crème caramel,* apple tart. . . . I passed. Dessert was not a frequent element in Nice cooking, André explained. It was a luxury. The one Nice dessert the Alziaris tried to serve in the restaurant was a sweet pie with a top and bottom crust, filled with *bette*. "It was too fragile," André said. "If you baked that dish in the morning it was good at lunch, but the *bette* made the dough soggy by dinner time."

I finished lunch with what lingered of my wine, a white Bellet, called Collet Bovis Cuve Prestige 2007. You may never have heard of it nor of Bellet, either. I hadn't drunk a Bellet since I was last down here years ago. There are just twelve vineyards that produce that wine, and all twelve are in the city limits of Nice, on the hills to the southeast. The white is done entirely with a grape called *le rolle*, which gets combined with other varietals in wines in Provence. It was a very distinguished white, memorably so. It had the honey-ish, raisiny presence of late-harvested sweet whites but was clean and dry and rounded at the same time, with a long finish. The wine was a great finale to a great lunch. And like all the rest, a wonderful presence, an authentic part of where it was.

Alouettes sans têtes at La Table d'Alziari

For four people
  8 scallops of beef chuck, about less than ¼ lb. each,
  pounded thin
  a bottle of red wine
  a handful of dried Portobello mushrooms
  a bouquet garni
  2 cloves of garlic
  2 medium-size onions
  I tablespoon flour
  salt and pepper
Stuffing:
  ½ lb. of chopped, lean salt pork or unsmoked bacon

Stuff scallops with the chopped pork, roll and tie them and brown them quickly in olive oil, in a heavy-bottomed pot, sprinkling them with the flour.

Add the bouquet garni, the garlic, and onions to the pan.

Boil off the alcohol in the wine. Add enough to cover the meat in the pot. Salt and pepper to taste and let it all cook for an hour and a half, while you:

Soak the dried mushrooms, and then drain them.

Add enough of the rest of the wine to keep the dark sauce thick. Cook the dish another quarter of an hour.

Add the mushrooms before serving after removing the onions and the bouquet garni.

NB: The Alziaris' stuffing for this dish is purely meat, with no feculents. Jacques Médecin's family version, *li couaïete* (quails), puts two minced hard-boiled eggs in the stuffing. Varieties of the dish exist throughout the South of France.

Chez Fonfon

Grit and character are two words that fit Marseille, a boisterous sprawl of a sun-drenched city, whose folklore is full of colorfully savage mobsters and an endearing community of the poor, who make up a large part of the population. The city has known a growing North African population, but some common folk here with roots can claim a version of nobility by tracing themselves back to the Phoenicians, who later settled in Nice. And what cinema buff has not been a sucker for the sweet melodrama of Marcel Pagnol's proletarian Marius stories?

In recent years, a vibrant art community has settled in restored parts of old Marseille, people reminiscent of those who've taken over former slums in New York. They're attuned to expressing a raw reality and to cheaper living than in, say, Saint-Germain-des-Prés of Paris, where tourists shop for labels in what used to be a haven for intelligentsia and bohemians. Marseille was named Cultural Capital of Europe for 2013.

Travelers can pick their way across the jumbled face of the city to a number of good museums, a handful of architectural gems, and a few forlorn but still lovely seaside villas hemmed in among the rest on the Corniche, the strip of coastline that runs along the southern shore. There I headed, to commune with another presence in the spirit of the city, the restaurant chez Fonfon. It had become world famous among food lovers since I was last there years ago, when Fonfon himself, Alphonse Mounier, a loud and warm-spirited fellow worthy of the fiction and film of Marcel Pagnol, was at the stove. His speciality, as it is perpetuated by his grandnephew, is *bouillabaisse*. If ever a dish could identify a place, *bouillabaisse* means Marseille.

Chez Fonfon is in a place called Le Vallon des Auffes. A *vallon* is a little valley; *auffes* was the fibrous grass with which the people who lived there earned their living making fishing nets. When I first came here, the *vallon* was a cramped piece of flat land around a tiny inlet of the sea. Little pastel houses with terraces, with very small pleasure boats docked outside, surrounded the inlet, while highrise tenements loomed behind, on the hills of the city. The highway of the Corniche was overhead, blocking a view of the ruined Château d'If, once a prison, on a tiny barren island just across the water. That was where Alexandre Dumas locked up the future Count of Monte Cristo.

The tiny *vallon*, with the tumultuous city hovering behind it, still looks very much the same, like no place else. Its contrasts are a paradigm of the relentlessness of civic growth and the pathetic loss of unique, rural character that comes with it. The *vallon* is endearing in its survival.

The *bouillabaisse*, now perpetuated by the thirty-eight-year-old Alexandre Pinna, though it seemed less rustic, more urbane than his granduncle Fonfon's, is still quite authentic.

"Poor but not stupid." André Alziari's characterization of Niçois cooking suits the history of *la bouillabaisse* in Marseille. It was the dish that fishermen of the Marseille area or their wives prepared from the fish they couldn't sell. They were fish that swam among the rocks not distant from shore, feeding on algae that gave them a bright taste of iodine. But they were small, or not enough of a catch to make a sale. Nowadays, when rockfish have become rare, they're prized despite their homeliness and bonyness. *Bouillabaisse*, the spicy, garlicky, tomatoy dish that they compose, has become a gourmet attraction, and far from cheap.

The last time I was chez Fonfon, a group of amateur fishermen pulled up at the pier at the head of the restaurant with fish for Fonfon to prepare for them. They told me they'd fished up more plastic bottles than fish, and things have not gotten better in the bay off Marseille. Even back then, you could see trailer trucks with Breton identification parked near the Old Port, bringing fish from more bountiful waters. Alexandre still sends out boats to get rockfish, and manages to get what he needs to feed his diners. His chef, Denis Blanc, who's been at the stove there since 1997, a year after Alexandre took over the place, will still prepare the fish you've caught.

Pinna's waitress set before me a basket of hard toasted bits of bread and two bowls, one of *l'aioli* and the other of *la rouille*. The latter is a mayonnaise fortified with lots of garlic, red pepper—both mild and sharp—and saffron. The former is a kind of mayonnaise gorged with garlic. There are two schools of *aioli*. The one is an emulsion made up of only pounded garlic and olive oil; the other uses egg yolk as in usual mayonnaise. The white *aioli* in my bowl led me to believe that this was the hardcore stuff, just garlic and olive oil given a creamy reincarnation. Denis Blanc later informed me that it contained egg yolk—but he rightfully didn't spare the garlic either. It was delicious on the croutons, as I waited to be served. The *rouille* was tamer.

I began lunch with a sample of a *bourride*, the other fish stew that is quintessentially of the region, which went with the *aioli*. A *bourride* is a *fumet*, concentrated and clarified fish stock, to which *aioli* is gener-ously added, with white-flesh fish poached in it. I'd eaten *bourride* at Fonfon before, and this sample convinced me that between the two Marseillais dishes, *la bourride* was subtler, with a more choice variety of fish, while richly garlicky. Denis Blanc would tell me that my *bourride* was prepared with *chapon, galinette, loup, turbot, vive,* and *lotte,* an assortment that—if you could get it all where you are—would be scorpion, red mullet, turbot, monkfish, and weaver. I had ordered the signature *bouillabaisse,* however, and didn't have reason to regret it.

My waitress brought out the *bouillon,* in which fish had been boiled for stock, for a long time, along with tomato, tomato paste, saffron, red pepper, and garlic. With all that, it was clearer and less assertive than I remembered it. Tamer. When the fish in which it was poached came out, I added great spoonsful of *rouille,* as is the *modus operandi,* and it turned out right enough for many helpings. The fish were conger eel, weaver, turbot, and red mullet. No lack of bones, but well worth the trouble of dealing with them. My wine was a white Cassis, from the region of the town by that name eighteen miles away. The Cassis vineyards are perhaps the oldest in France, a fact that added to the interest of my Domaine de Clairmont, 2009. It was dry with no unpleasant quirks, but short. A delightful bouquet of flowers you got when you first raised your glass was soon gone—it was a "fugitive bouquet," as the French call it.

All in all, my lunch did not give my fond memory a lie.

Bouillabaisse chez Fonfon

Denis Blanc does a video of Fonfon's *bouillabaisse* at its website. Follow if you will, in French; you'll get the methodology but not all the proportions, which I've tried to get from him since, without success, knowing in the end that he doesn't measure and what else he'd give me he'd have to make up. Moreover, some of the fish he served me are different from the ones in the video. *Bouillabaisse* is not a refined dish. It was made of what the fishermen had at hand, so there is no orthodox *bouillabaisse.* But Fonfon's two-stage method is worth observing to create an excellent dish, as refined as it need be:

You start with fish meant just to provide the *bouillon.* He uses 5: 1 conger eel and 4 scorpion fish. He heats enough olive oil to spread across the pot, adds 2 diced onions and diced cloves of garlic—say 3?—and lets them turn blond. "Sweats" the fish there for 5 to 10 minutes, adds 3 crushed tomatoes and 7 oz. of tomato paste. Fennel seeds. Cayenne pepper. Salt.

Splash white wine over it all, cook for 5 to 10 minutes for the alcohol to boil off. Splash *fumet de poission*, already prepared, over it all and cook for 15 minutes more. Add *fumet* to cover well.

After 1½ hours more on the stove on a medium flame, you will have cooked the *bouillon*. Take out the fish, strain them over the pot in a sieve, crushing the fish, which you don't use. The *bouillon* is now relatively clear. Add saffron. I'd say a scant handful.

Now you add the fish you will eat.

First cook sliced potatoes in the *bouillon* for 10 minutes. Add the fish in two stages. Blanc says he allows 1½ lbs. in all per person. A lot. The fish that cooks the quickest goes into the lightly boiling *bouillon* for ten minutes after the potatoes; the others then get 5 minutes more of cooking.

As for the fish, my advice is to get yourself a combination of dark- and white-flesh fish. Truth to tell, this is a robust dish in which the taste of the *bouillon* dominates, and, as I say, he himself varies what types of fish he uses.

Key: Serve croutons and a little bowl of *rouille* with the dish. *Rouille* is the classic stuff to add generously to your *bouillabaisse* to give it more zip. If you can make your own mayonnaise, a *rouille* is just one more step. All making your own mayonnaise takes is patience, as you mete out oil in drops on an egg yolk and a spoonful of mustard, while beating, until you've got the consistency of mayonnaise that you seek. For *rouille*, you then add garlic, saffron, mild and sharp pimento to your taste. Forget about store-bought mayonnaise.

The taxis were on strike in Marseille, and I made my way back from the Vallon des Auffes to the Saint Charles rail station, changing from a bus to the *métro* at Le Vieux Port, where rows of stands with their fish from wherever were the subject of a crowded business. I saw once again the row of geometric buildings across the port, their faces rendered less stark by receded, planted terraces. They had replaced ruins that the Nazis had created after dynamiting much of the old quarter, to prevent the labyrinthine backstreets of that time from being a sanctuary for resistants. I remembered that those buildings, classified as historical monuments now, were the accomplishments of the most noted French architect of the post–Le Corbusier era, Fernand Pouillon. Using stone and other materials that challenged the poverty of cement, he achieved, within the genre of reductive modernism, harmonious buildings of exceptional quality in both construction and comfort. His work in France, Algeria, and Iran was always of great value compared to the cost.

I don't know how many people know that Pouillon was also a masterful cook, as I learned at his table.

Architecture was not my usual journalistic interest at the time, but my friend, Jean-Louis Faure, a brilliantly original sculptor, had a brother Jean-Paul, who knew everybody. Jean-Paul was a cinema agent whose accomplishments ranged from having been a hero of the Resistance to an early love affair with Françoise Sagan.

"Fernand, back from exile, is living alone in a house in the countryside near Fountainebleau," Jean-Paul told his brother. "How would you and Gerry like to go out and have dinner with him?"

A famous architect back from exile living alone in the sticks? I hadn't been living long enough in France to know Pouillon's story. Jean-Louis explained: At the height of his success, and with a devotion to creating urbanism of quality in a time that France was scarring itself with shameful, high-rise chicken coops, Pouillon had teamed up with developers and invested in their company, which the law at the time forbade architects from doing. His associates proved shady, got involved in a financial scheme that Jean-Paul described as *"la cascade"*—a sort of Ponzi scheme. Pouillon had spent a year in prison, after which he went on to do major projects in Algiers. Thin as a rail in his elegantly cut clothes, Pouillon was in ill health when I met him, but he would live to have President Pompidou grant him amnesty and François Mitterrand elevate him to an officer in the Légion d'Honneur, before he died in his château in the South of France.

The master cooked himself and served dinner himself. With our Bollinger champagne, we ate thick slices of roasted black truffles on toasted *brioche*. Next came the biggest wild sea bass I'd ever seen, served with a hollandaise sauce. The *bar* was delicious, yet more than enough for us to do justice to. I think Pouillon, who had very elegant manners, had adopted a graceful habit of the Arabs while living and working in Algeria. It is Arab custom for a host to serve his guests far more food than they are expected to be able to eat. I remember ordering a *couscous mechoui* at La Maison Arabe in Marrakech for my photographer and myself, and being presented with half a roast young lamb.

With the bass we drank Montrachet, that acme of white Burgundy, and went on to a Richebourg, a red that belonged to the revered vineyard that produces Romanée Conti, and which was just a notch less wonderful. We drank it with a *chaud-froid* of pheasant. It was the first and only time in my life I ate a *chaud-froid*, a classic in the lore of French cuisine. I don't think that there are many people today who can recall eating one. It had been a pillar of luxurious classic cooking into the early twentieth century and a dish complicated to make. Archaeologists found a possible origin of the recipe in a jar with food remains in Pompeii labeled *calidus-frigidus*. The dish exists in French recipe books that go back to the eighteenth century. It has been attributed to the culinary connoisseurship of the marshall of Luxembourg, who had a dish served him that had gone cold, when he came back to a feast he had to hurry away from, summoned to a meeting with King Louis XV. The favorite *chaud-froid* of the epicures of the Belle Époque was a *chaud-froid de bécasse,* of woodcock, which, like *ortolans,* is now classed as an endangered species. The *chaud-froid* is a fricassee of a fowl that is browned, sautéed,and simmered, with a variety of herbs, with slices of black truffles as the ultimately appropriate garnish. The fricassee is cooled; the sauce, with added gelatin, is congealed around it. Hence hot-cold, *chaud-froid.*

Sitting almost reclined, Pouillon ate only little bits of the banquet he'd prepared. I think it took a lot of his ailing strength to have done the meal, affecting afterward an appetite that befit conviviality toward his guests. The conversation turned to Charles de Gaulle, whose popularity was in great decline; he was being maligned by both the Left and the Right. Not long afterward, the general would resign as president of France, when a referendum he drew up was voted down by the population. He wanted to make mandatory the practice of workers' owning shares in companies and having presences in their administrations. It was de Gaulle's "third way" between Socialism and capitalism, and the nation, with shrill opinions on both sides, would have nothing of it.

De Gaulle's courage and probity, not his politics, was what the talk was about over dinner. Jean-Paul, as a youth, had served him clandestinely in occupied France, and had been tortured for it. Jean-Paul and Jean-Louis' father had been close to the general in London, when he wasn't flying secret missions to France, and once gave heart to the population by ordering a plane from Britain to strafe a parade of German soldiers on the Champs Elysées; another landed him in the Struthof concentration camp, where he nearly died. Both father and son were spared execution, thanks to the intervention of Jean-Louis'suncle and namesake, an important member of the Collaborationist government, whom the general spared punishment after the liberation.

I wondered how the general would have reacted to our little feast. He was a frugal man, but I think there was something in Pouillon's careful achievement and the superior quality of everything that was on his wavelength. Remembering everything about that dinner, the word integrity comes to mind. "*La classe,*" the French say. The food, too, was classy in its honest refinement.

In a few days, I repaid Pouillon's hospitality by inviting him to lunch in Paris. The venue I chose was chez Garin. Garin was considered by many serious eaters to be the best cook in town, doing interpretations of cooking reminiscent of the *haute cuisine* of yesteryear. Garin officiated personally at the "piano," as chefs called their stoves, behind a glassed-in kitchen at the end of his restaurant in Saint-Germain-des-Prés, for all to witness his skill. Richard Olnay, the great food writer and cook, was a close friend of Garin's, and he'd praised the master's extravaganzas, such as lobster soufflé with calf's liver and truffles, and partridge consommé with partridge *quenelles.* Olnay himself was capable of whipping up such productions as stuffed calf's ears poached, breaded, and fried, but both he, who wrote two books on simple French cooking, and Garin had a simple side. I wondered what Pouillon would go for, chez Garin. Sly perhaps, he chose not to pit the accomplishments at our dinner against Garin's culinary prowess. Pouillon opted for the simplest of menus, and I followed his lead.

We ordered flat oysters, the now relatively scarce, tan breed from Brittany.

From that plain luxury we went on to some nonfancy but excellent *boeuf bourguignon.* As we sipped champagne while the oysters were being shucked, I saw Garin pouring more *gros rouge*, the cheap North African wine that was a staple of common French tables in those days, into a pot of his *bourguignon.* Was Garin cheating? Not at all. Olnay's own *boeuf bourguignon* recipe calls for "a robust, deeply colored young red wine." A would-be purist might expect *boeuf bourguignon* to contain Burgundy wine. But good Burgundy, which is always expensive, would be a waste in a pot, and ordinary Burgundy is faint-hearted. To this day, I drink red Moroccan wine with *couscous,* and its naturally bold but rounded presence suits well that dish, with its spicy sauce and beef sausages.

We allowed Garin to pursue some dandyism, if you will, with an airy Grand Marnier *soufflé* for dessert. Our waiter had his own idea of elegance. He would turn the platter of oysters each time we took one, to have one in front of each of us, and between courses, he ripped the napkins off our laps to replace them with new ones. Chez Garin, with the simplest of décor and the most mannerist of serving styles, was a distinctive establishment. Distinguished in its way. Garin closed his place before he could earn a third Michelin star, and it became a banal Chinese restaurant. So it goes, as Kurt Vonnegut liked to put it, about more dire aspects of life. . . .

These memories of Pouillon and Médecin, Frenchmen to the bone, bring home a message. Fernand Pouillon once reached a pinnacle in his career as an architect. Jacques Médecin ran a major city for nearly thirty years. I imagine each home from a hard day at the office, starting to cook. Not as an eccentric hobby, but doing something that they turned to as part of who they were, with pleasure drawn on remembrance. Those images elucidate how firmly *la cuisine* has been rooted in the French way of living, with love and respect for it, and why the renown of *la cuisine française* has spread to the world for centuries.

19

L'INVITATION AU VOYAGE

F orgive me, devotees of Charles Baudelaire, for borrowing the title of that fine poem, in which he dreamed of the exotic land whence his mistress came. He did art, and I'm a chronicler here. But the title fits my message. Joanne and I could keep on going to every cranny in France where special, alluring food is part of the fabric of life, but I fear that our book of discovery involving people and their accomplishments might veer off into an encyclopedia. Doing a food dictionary or encyclopedia is far from a worthless bit of anthropology. No one, though, could do it with more erudition and charm than did Alexandre Dumas and, more recently, the late Waverley Root in his several books. I had the privilege of sharing meals with Waverley, when and after he was the Paris man for *The Washington Post* and anointed to the Légion d'Honneur. He knew well and loved his stuff, having raised food himself on a farm in Vermont. I'll leave his accomplishments unamended.

So, reader, it's your turn for the rest. Get on a train, rent a car. Wherever you go in France, if food fits into your own conception of

312

the warp and weave of significant culture, you might find yourself blissfully lost for a long time in France.

"You left out the Ariège," Joanne chastised. "Remember the delicious *azinat* in Mirepoix?" An *azinat*, in the Ariège, among the Pyrenees, is like a *garbure* in many other places in the French countryside. They are cabbage and meat dishes, similar but with differences, recalling, to the aware, such distinctions as between Madame Point's *ratatouille* and a *sydney. Azinat, garbure, fouace, pounti, truffade, farçu.* . . . who needs a chef's inventions, when there's all that nuanced exotica to discover? We could indeed go on. To the dire detriment of my waistline. (Joanne is far more in control about eating.)

We're home now. Let our trips end, then, with your invitation. Otherwise we might spend a lifetime at this.

"Should you have brought up the scatology?" she asked. What would a shrink make of those scatological names that the French give certain traditional French foods? Something to do with the trauma of early toilet training in France? Why are certain light pastries called *pets de nonnes*, excuse me, nuns' farts? Why do the Niçois call their green *gnocchi* goose turds? Why is a delicious little goat's cheese similarly called? Chalk it all up to the earthiness that is the *Doppelgänger* of French elegance? Like Pantagruel and La Princesse de Clèves.

We'll leave all that there.

So how do we dine at home, someone may finally ask.

Simply, although we spend time going from here to there to get the best produce. Joanne makes excellent *hachis parmentier,* and *navarin d'agneau,* for a couple of examples of her hand, but mostly we eat grilled fish, roast chicken, and less meat, of the best quality we know. I can be cajoled into making *blinis* in a day's exercise, to serve with wild salmon. Our sensibilities are on the wavelength of the heartiness of James Beard, rather than the fussiness of Julia Child, as fine and exigent a person as she was.

As I wrote earlier, we would get our fowl from a farmer who came down once a week to a market stall in Paris, until he got tired getting up before sunlight to make the trip. We get decent farm chickens since from our butcher a street away, but we cross the Seine to a neighborhood where we used to live to get fish from a pleasant couple. Ghislaine and Antoine are Normans by birth, with a house in Normandy by the sea, and belong to a group of four fishmongers who get their fish directly and immediately from *la criée*, the auction where the boats come into the port of Dieppe. It's the best fish we know of in Paris, and no more expensive than elsewhere.

Our bread person is in either of two organic food markets on different days, a bus trip from us in each case, but nothing compares with her *pain intégral*, the whole-est of whole wheat bread.

And so on. We eat simply indeed, while Joanne stores her energy for Thanksgiving. Thanksgiving is our food rite. We have about eighteen friends and our daughter and son to dinner—French friends and fellow Americans. Since our farmer stopped fattening a turkey for months to have one big enough for us, our butcher—though he laments that it keeps him awake at night wondering if he could find one in time—has assumed the task. The day before Thanksgiving, our mammoth bird, by French standards, sits in our proud butcher's window, decorated with two little American flags. People who have never seen a turkey that big stop and take photos with their cell phones.

Joanne's Thanksgiving menu is classic, and she does it all herself from scratch: turkey with stuffing, cranberry sauce (of small, wild *airelles*), candied sweets, etc. . . . Someone brings pumpkin and apple pies.

I'm just a first-generation American, and Joanne's roots in Eastern Europe resemble mine. Our Thanksgiving takes account of those lost ties: Before we sit down at the one table, Joanne puts out her *piroshki* done from scratch, with her own dough, and incomparable chopped liver with black radish slices. Great with vodka as well as champagne.

We're all good friends. It would sound corny to say that we all love each other. But there is, in the ritual dinner, a kind of act of love.

I recall now what I once overheard when we were in a celebrated New York restaurant. A woman at another table was exclaiming over her food: "It's better than sex!" Poor girl—where was she coming from? But this comparison of sensual delights is not bizarre. I can't remember who the astute writer was who used the term "mouth brothel" for the grand gourmet restaurants of our time. If a meal in a mouth brothel is like sex, a truly great dining experience is something far more rich and profound, like love. It reminds us of where we are in time and place as we partake of a particular bounty that sustains us, affirms our being, brings us together, while it gives us pleasure. Religious people give thanks for those moments by saying grace. With whatever else, I'm thankful that those portions of living are still out there, for us to know and understand.

Lust in Dante's list of the Seven Deadly Sins is number one . . . and gluttony comes right next. Fare forward, friends, aware as best you can be of what is what, and wary of encountering number seven. Pride. Whose corollary is called hype.

Happy trails.